THE CHANCELLOR

ALSO BY KATI MARTON

True Believer: Stalin's Last American Spy

Paris: A Love Story

Enemies of the People: My Family's Journey to America

The Great Escape: Nine Jews Who Fled Hitler and Changed the World

Hidden Power: Presidential Marriages That Shaped Our History

*A Death in Jerusalem: The Assassination by a Jewish
Extremist of the First Arab-Israeli Peacemaker*

Wallenberg: Missing Hero

*The Polk Conspiracy: Murder and Cover-Up in the
Case of CBS News Correspondent George Polk*

An American Woman—A Novel

THE
CHANCELLOR

The Remarkable Odyssey of
Angela Merkel

Kati Marton

**WILLIAM
COLLINS**

William Collins
An imprint of HarperCollins*Publishers*
1 London Bridge Street
London SE1 9GF

WilliamCollinsBooks.com

HarperCollins*Publishers*
1st Floor, Watermarque Building, Ringsend Road
Dublin 4, Ireland

First published in Great Britain in 2021 by William Collins
First published in the United States by Simon & Schuster in 2021

1

Copyright © Kati Marton 2021

Kati Marton asserts the moral right to be identified
as the author of this work in accordance with the
Copyright, Designs and Patents Act 1988

Interior design by Ruth Lee-Mui

A catalogue record for this book is
available from the British Library

ISBN 978-0-00-849945-7 (hardback)
ISBN 978-0-00-849946-4 (trade paperback)

Set in Bulmer MT Std
Printed and bound in the UK using 100%
renewable electricity at CPI Group (UK) Ltd

MIX
Paper from
responsible sources
FSC
www.fsc.org
FSC™ C007454

This book is produced from independently certified FSC™ paper
to ensure responsible forest management.

For more information visit: www.harpercollins.co.uk/green

For my daughter,

Elizabeth Jennings,

and for Ilona Fitzpatrick Jennings,

and the next generation

Contents

CONTENTS

Prologue

THE PASTOR'S DAUGHTER

She arrives quietly. No wailing sirens, flashing lights, or phalanx of aides announces Angela Merkel's entrance into the plain brick chapel in Potsdam, just outside Berlin. Her slightly hunched walk is purposeful. iPhone cameras light up as she passes pews, and she—this woman who hates cameras pointed at her—smiles indulgently. These are her people. Though the church is near the capital, this is a different tribe from Berlin's sophisticates with whom Merkel spends the majority of her working days. Her father had been pastor in a similarly plain parish church, and on this damp fall evening, the simple house of worship provides temporary refuge from the turbulence of her fourth and final term. Stolen days in her home province of Brandenburg—with rambles in the nearby woods—are becoming increasingly rare. She is too busy saving the world.

Tonight, as Merkel arrives at the Oberlinkirche, surrounded by people who could pass for family, the sixty-three-year-old chancellor of the Federal Republic of Germany briefly allows herself to drop her guard. She wears her uniform: jewel-colored jacket (dark green tonight) and black pants. Black flats planted firmly, Merkel settles into a straight-backed armchair in front of the altar, her fingertips touching lightly—a prayerful gesture now so familiar to Germans that there is an emoji for it. "Every morning of my childhood, the church bells tolled, as they did again at six in the evening. I miss that," she tells her hushed audience, which appreciates this rare personal glimpse of their supremely private leader. For just a moment, the chancellor's smile—not a politician's facsimile—erases the deep grooves carved into her features. In recent years, the world of Germany's first woman chancellor has been roiled by social and political unrest. Battered by the rising tide of worldwide populism, Merkel is vilified by right-wing extremists, now present in the German parliament (Bundestag) for the first time since World War II. The shock of an American populist in the White House heaping praise on Vladimir Putin, Merkel's nemesis in Moscow, is still fresh.

"On the first day of school," Merkel continues, offering a window into the complexity of growing up a pastor's child in atheist East Germany, "students were required to stand up and state their parents' profession." She recalled classmates advising her, "Just say 'driver,'" *driver* being a more proletarian-friendly profession than pastor—and, in German, the two words sound nearly identical.

"Pastor," she answered the teacher.

Merkel does not need to explain to this audience how dangerous candor could be in East Germany. Even children had to attempt to pass unnoticed by the all-seeing state. The Stasi's penetration of society was deeper and wider than that of its predecessor, the Gestapo. The Ministry for State Security had 173,000 employees, including informants, compared with 7,000 in the Third Reich. There was one informer for every 63 people. "Of course, this childhood shaped my life," she says, perhaps inadvertently providing the key to who she is, how she has maintained power for an astonishing decade and a half, and why she remains a figure of mystery even in her own country and certainly to the world.

Drawing the conversation back to the present, Pastor Matthias

Fichtmuller asks if the chancellor reads the books that are written about her. "Yes, but I don't recognize myself in them!" The parish joins her laughter. "I have made very sure that there are boundaries, so certain areas of my life are not open to the public," she says. Anything beyond her official role, Merkel has made plain, is none of the world's business. Such secrecy is now an article of faith within the chancellor's entourage. There have been no leaks, no tell-all memoirs written by even former staff or confidants during Merkel's sixteen years as chancellor. Her exceptionally loyal aides are fiercely protective of the woman whom most of them have served for a decade and a half. "You guys still all here?" US president Barack Obama marvelled, seeing Merkel's team during a 2016 trip to Berlin, virtually unchanged since he took office in 2008.

After several decades, Germans are not tired of her image, her voice, her looming persona—because Merkel does not loom. Despite knowing little about their chancellor's private life, other than that she comes across as leading a life not so different from their own, Germans thrice reelected her, each time by a comfortable margin. Once in a great while, they might see her dressed up for the Wagner Festival in Bayreuth, Germany, but they are equally likely to see her doing her own grocery shopping. She imbibed the lesson of predecessors such as Helmut Kohl—who paraded his wife and offspring as the perfect German family, until his wife died by suicide and his sons grew estranged—or the Cold War hero Willy Brandt, who was later revealed to be a depressive sex addict.

At times, Merkel's insistence on privacy verges on paranoia. She keeps no journal, does not use email, and texts only briefly and when necessary. An associate's revelation of a seemingly trivial detail of her private life can terminate the relationship. One political ally was never allowed back into Merkel's confidence after releasing a four-word email that read: "Thanks for the suggestion, AM."

In their attempts to pierce the enigma that is Angela Merkel, observers are sometimes reduced to absurd strategies. Take, for example, this analysis from *Die Zeit*, a respected German weekly: "While Merkel is standing talking in the ZDF [German state television] with a few others, she is turning the upper button of her jacket with her hand. Not back and forth, but in a circle, in a steady rhythm. When the chancellor is under a lot of pressure, she fiddles with her thumbnail using her index finger. Circles, on the other hand, mean silent concentration." During press conferences in foreign capitals, "the degree of her impatience with her host is evident from the frequency with which she glances at his stack of papers."

Some visual clues seem better grounded: her cocked head and wide-eyed look of disbelief when, during her first encounter with President Donald Trump, he commented, "We have something in common, Angela. We were both wiretapped [by Obama]"; her epic eye-rolls when asked at a press conference if she "trusted" the flamboyant Italian prime minister Silvio Berlusconi, or the same while Russia's Vladimir Putin mansplained to her; or her eyes, soft with emotion, even shedding a tear or two, as she said good-bye to President Obama in 2016.

However useful for her own political longevity, the extraordinary self-discipline that leads journalists to read into her every eye-roll and nervous tic is also something of a shame, because to understand the present era, we *need* to understand Angela Merkel. At a moment of global political and social rupture, no leader on the world stage has protected the post–World War II liberal democratic order as fiercely she did, confronting aggressive authoritarians from Putin to Trump. She transformed Germany into the leader of Europe—not just an economic leader but a moral one too—and into an immigrant nation by accepting one million Middle Eastern refugees.

How was this triple outsider—an East German, a scientist, and a woman of that rare European country to never have a queen—able to achieve all this? How did a politician with rhetoric as plain as her appearance gain such power and longevity in this digital age, with our ever-shrinking attention span? Intelligence and hard work are part of the explanation, of course. In a country where grandparents still recall torchlight parades and crowds that roared a demagogue's name in unison, Merkel's bland speaking style has also often been an advantage. When the head of the World Trade Organization, Pascal Lamy, once pleaded with Merkel for "a bit more poetry" in her speeches, Merkel shot back, "I'm not a poet." Her calm, analytical approach, developed during her years studying physics, allowed her to take a remarkably long-term view of governing. "I think things through starting at the end—from the desired outcome, and work backward. . . . What matters is what will be achieved in two years, not what we read in the papers tomorrow," she has said. Nor did she engage in the politics of insinuation or character assassination—or taken the bait of those who do. "She just doesn't play their games. She knows good and well when Putin or Trump are lying to her," former German president Joachim Gauck observed. Mostly she ignored their fabrications and pressed on with her own agenda.

To achieve what Angela Merkel achieved, and for as long as she was at the pinnacle of power, she had to be both fierce and determined—without those qualities being apparent.

On many sensitive issues, Merkel succeeded by working *sideways,* indirectly and without calling attention to herself. The fact that she was a divorced Protestant from the East living with her male lover when she rose to lead the center-right, Christian, culturally conservative, and mostly male Christian Democratic Union (CDU) of Germany is testament to her skill at keeping the spotlight off her persona. With a very light touch, she transformed Germany into a far more liberal society. After appointing Guido Westerwelle, the country's first openly gay foreign minister in 2009, she publicly praised his husband and their love story—yet without explicitly declaring her support for marriage equality. When Germany did vote on marriage equality eight years later, Merkel advised her conservative party to vote its conscience rather than toe the party line against marriage equality.

Thus, without speeches or policy statements from the chancellor, marriage equality became the law of the land.

She used the same subtle tactics to expand opportunities for women. When the head of the far-right Alternative for Germany Party, acronymed AfD, observed the women assembled around Merkel and growled, "Are there no men left in the CDU Party?" the chancellor's close advisor Eva Christiansen whispered to her boss, "We've won!" Merkel merely smiled her enigmatic smile. She has repeatedly demonstrated how much a leader can get done *quietly*, without boasting of her achievements.

Part of her political genius comes in recognizing good ideas wherever they originate. "She's fulfilled her rival parties' programs on energy, on child care, on marriage equality and women's rights," said Michael Naumann, the former Social Democratic Party (SPD) culture minister. This also serves as a clever way of neutralizing potential opponents. "Angela is very skilled at appropriating any issue as soon as it gains traction," said Gauck, a still-handsome octogenarian who bears an uncanny resemblance to the late American actor James Garner. "That's why rival political parties are scared of entering into a governing coalition with her." Nor did fear of her appropriations prevent Merkel from forming coalitions with rival parties necessary to keep the CDU in power for sixteen years—though at times, as we shall see, it made the process painstaking.

Another key to her political longevity is Merkel's insatiable curiosity. In her sixties, she still thrives on the new and the interesting. People, facts, history, problems to solve, disputes to untangle all still excite her. But apart from a love of challenge, what *drives* Angela Merkel? *"Macht, macht, macht"* ("power, power, power"), her mentor, Helmut Kohl, said once. Merkel learned by observing powerful men, and Kohl, Germany's chancellor from 1990 to 1998, is one of many male politicians who paid with their political lives for underestimating the woman he once called his *Mädchen* (girl). With very few women role models—the eighteenth-century Russian empress Catherine the Great and the French chemist Marie Curie among them—and no network to support her, Merkel had to invent herself as a politician. "Asserting authority is something you must learn as a woman. Without power, you cannot achieve much," Merkel has said. But the power she's cultivated is a very specific type.

Hubris, Merkel's behavior suggests, is a male weakness. A woman in power has more urgent business to attend to than her ego. Sometimes, however, Merkel's muting her ego caused her to miss opportunities to connect with people on a more personal level. In 2009, with the Polish prime minister Donald Tusk by her side, the chancellor addressed a large group in Hamburg; not once did Merkel mention that she was born in the city or that her grandfather had been born in Poland. Most politicians would have seized such an opportunity to relate to their audience. In her final years in office, this instinct of hers to depersonalize her leadership was challenged by the rise of charismatic leaders worldwide.

It is not that Angela Merkel lacks a robust ego. If she did, she would not have pursued a career in politics. When asked once who her role model in life was, Merkel answered, "Myself, as often as possible." She has redefined how a woman in power looks, sounds, and acts. And yet the enigma of Angela Merkel only deepens upon closer examination. She has been the most powerful woman on the world stage—yet she hesitates to call herself a feminist. A supremely successful politician, she prefers the company of musicians, singers, actors, and writers. In an age of garrulous strongmen, she is quiet.

She is not exactly who we think she is. In reality, Angela Merkel is far from the straitlaced, earnest image she often projects to the world. As a youth trapped behind the Iron Curtain, she said that her dream was "to see the Rocky Mountains and drive around in a car, listening to Bruce Springsteen." "She's funny as hell," adds Philip Murphy, former US ambassador to Germany and the current governor of New Jersey. Despite decades on the world stage, Merkel has not lost her talent to be normal. As fellow East German David Gill, Germany's consul general to New York, explains, "If you started your life where she did, behind the wall—which we thought was permanent—you never get over that. Others may forget where she came from, but Angela Merkel does not."

During her entire adult life, Merkel has been sustained by her near-photographic memory, her trained scientific ability to break down problems to their component parts, and her ravenous appetite for work. Add to these qualities the fact that she does not require much sleep (five hours tops) and an iron constitution. Late in learning to walk, Merkel was prone to falls and breaks during childhood. Yet in her sixties, through sheer willpower, she can still hike for six hours at a time. From these strengths—some natural, some nurtured—flows an unshakable confidence that often unnerves her fellow heads of state and fueled her astonishing longevity as chancellor.

Following her conversation with the pastor, Angela Merkel circulates through the small chapel, chatting easily with guests and waitstaff. Some of the servers, who are also members of this church community, have Down syndrome and other disabilities. Having grown up in the company of the disabled, who formed a vital part of her father's parish, the chancellor seems completely at ease, cheerfully sampling canapés they have prepared.

The key to Merkel's achievements and, indeed, to who she is, lies in those beginnings. To survive the East German police state unbroken, as Angela Merkel did, is an accomplishment in itself and offers the key to her personal and political resilience. That half of her life produced the opposite of an idealist. Merkel does not believe that the arc of history bends toward justice. Instead, she is an action-driven optimist with a sharp awareness of human frailty. During her final years as chancellor, she made repeated references to civilizations that disappear because they fail to safeguard their freedom and security. She referred to the fall of the Incan Empire in one speech and more recently invoked the Peace of Augsburg of 1555, a tranquil interlude during Europe's bloody religious wars of the sixteenth and seventeenth centuries. After this period of peace, a new generation without memories of the misery of war plunged back into ruinous conflict, resulting in the deaths of a third of Germany's population.

More than seventy-five years have passed since the end of World War II, but a question haunts Germany to this day: Can a country that produced Auschwitz and engineered the most ruthlessly efficient, systematic genocide in history ever be "normal"? Angela Merkel would likely answer in the affirmative—but with qualifications. *Yes, but* only if Germany continues to shoulder its responsibility as the perpetrator of one of history's darkest chapters. Under her leadership, she has been determined to ensure it has. As a pastor's daughter, she believes in the quiet and persistent work of everyday salvation.

This account—a human rather than a political portrait—sets out to answer how this pastor's daughter, this outsider, became the most powerful woman in the world. In writing this book, I have drawn on candid and often searching interviews Angela Merkel gave from 1990, when the thirty-five-year-old physicist first entered politics, until her 2005 election as Germany's first woman chancellor. I've complemented these interviews—many never before published in English—with scores of personal conversations with her mentors, friends, and colleagues, which provide the flesh and blood of this narrative. Several people in her inner circle were willing to speak with me, circumventing the chancellor's extraordinary need for control, provided that their names were not cited directly. My own encounters with Angela Merkel, dating from 2001, though not formal interviews, have also enhanced my familiarity and understanding of the chancellor.

Having spent my own childhood in Hungary, an Eastern bloc satellite much like Merkel's native East Germany, my upbringing helped me understand her, especially her supreme public reticence, born of a childhood and youth spent in a police state. Only when the entire false edifice of the Soviet Empire crumbled did Merkel embark on her life as a politician. When the chance to serve and to do good, as her Lutheran faith prescribed, presented itself, she seized it. As we shall see, however, her motives in doing so were as complex as the woman herself. She sought and has lived the intellectually challenging and adventuresome life she missed living behind the wall for thirty-five years.

Back in the chapel, Pastor Fichtmuller leans toward the chancellor. "Does it annoy you to still be referred to as the pastor's daughter? At your age?" he asks.

The world's most powerful woman answers without hesitation: "Not at all. That is who I am."

THE CHANCELLOR

Angela Merkel's father, Pastor Horst Kasner—shown here in the woods near Templin, where the future chancellor was raised—moved his family from West to East Germany shortly after the birth of his daughter, in answer to the Lutheran Church's call to preach in the atheist Communist state. Known as a hard man who was overly accommodating to the regime, from him Angela learned logical rigor.

1

AGAINST THE TIDE

Nothing in life is to be feared. It is only to be understood."

—Marie Curie (1867–1934)

Pastor Horst Kasner missed the birth of his firstborn child. On that day, July 17, 1954, he was driving a van filled with his family's furniture to a remote hamlet in East Germany, where he would begin life as the small town's new minister.

"Only Communists or idiots go east voluntarily," the West German movers told Kasner. Well over six feet tall, the sharp-featured twenty-eight-year-old was one of the few to answer Hamburg bishop Hans-Otto Wölber's call to service in the underserved Soviet zone. "I would have travelled anywhere to preach the word of our Lord," Kasner would later say. He and his wife, Herlind, a twenty-six-year-old English teacher, had married only the year before. Horst had warned the fine-boned, blue-eyed, Danzig-born Herlind Jentzch that his duty to the church would always come first. He kept his word.

Kasner, born Kazmierczak, to a Polish father, but raised in Berlin, was seven years old when Adolf Hitler came to power in 1933. A member of the Nazi Party's Hitler Youth organization while in high school and recruited into the Nazi armed forces, or Wehrmacht, at age eighteen, he is said to have been captured a year later by the Allies—though the particulars of that chapter of his life are unavailable to researchers, if they exist at all after so many decades. Following his release, Horst studied theology at the prestigious Heidelberg University and then in Hamburg. And that is the sum total of what is in the public record regarding the background of Angela Merkel's father.

Fortunately, personal interviews tell us more. To this austere, demanding man of God, Angela would never be as important as his faith or his flock. Though she accepted this fact, his oldest daughter was understandably left longing for a more present, more approving father. Kasner was never quite satisfied with his brilliant child—certainly he never explicitly expressed his approval—yet Angela never ceased in her attempt to win his full-hearted support. The connection between her never fully realized desire for her father's approval and her intense drive for achievement is clear. But perhaps none of Horst Kasner's actions was more influential on Angela's early development than his decision to leave West Germany's relative security to face the dangers and volatility of the Soviet-occupied East.

Angela Merkel's birthplace, the once-bustling port city of Hamburg, was a charred, unrecognizable ruin after British and American bombers flattened it in 1943, killing forty thousand people. The Germans coined a new word, *Feuersturm* (firestorm), to describe the city's devastation. Yet by the time of Germany's surrender on May 8, 1945, thousands of desperate survivors— among them newly freed refugees from concentration camps and those fleeing the Soviet Union's merciless Red Army—were drawn to what remained of Hamburg, crowding into the shells of buildings and makeshift shelters.

By 1954, the year Angela Dorothea Kasner was born in Barmbek Hospital, determined citizens had cleared the worst of the devastation. Streets were passable again, buildings were reconstructed under scaffolding, and life gradually began to resume its former rhythms. The Allies, who had dispatched the bombs a decade earlier, now sent millions in aid to rebuild. Hamburg was on its way to becoming the Federal Republic of Germany's center of trade, media, and style, gradually reclaiming the status it had held in the sixteenth and seventeenth centuries as a free imperial city of the Hanseatic League—a Baltic maritime trade group. Survivors of the *Feuersturm* again began to envision the possibilities of a decent life. Eager to bury the past under the rubble, crowds packed the dive bars of the St. Pauli's redlight district, and the city surged with creative energy, including a vibrant concert and theater scene, as well as a lively and irreverent press. Those participating in the revival were as reluctant to recall life during the Third Reich as they were to spare a thought for their once fellow citizens now trapped in the Soviet-occupied East.

For by 1954, it had become clear that the Democratic Republic of Germany was anything but. Founded in 1949, under Soviet military occupation, it was virtually a carbon copy of the other Moscow-run "satellites" (Poland, Hungary, Czechoslovakia, Bulgaria, Romania, and Albania), with effectively only a single legal political party, the Communist Party, in control of civilian and political life. The year before Angela's birth, East German workers had erupted in revolt. On June 16, 1953, thousands of construction workers laid down their tools and marched down East Berlin's main thoroughfare, demanding higher pay, better working conditions, and fair elections. In response, East Germany's Soviet-controlled government declared martial law, killing several hundred protestors and establishing a brutal pattern to be repeated in Hungary in 1956, in Czechoslovakia in 1968, and in Ukraine in 2014.

The government violence and repression turned a steady migration from East to West Germany into a human flood. That year, seven years before the inner German border wall would finally stop the hemorrhaging, 331,000 East Germans abandoned their homes and livelihoods and headed West.

One German family chose to travel in the opposite direction. Two months after her husband left Hamburg for the East, Herlind Kasner, with daughter Angela in a basket, boarded a train for the three-hour journey to Quitzow, in the province of Brandenburg, to join him. The contrast between the reviving bustle of Hamburg and bare-bones life in this small farming town was sobering, even for the ascetic pastor and his wife. Before long, the young family moved to Templin, a small town some ninety miles east, tucked in a region of pristine lakes and pine forests that resembled the backdrop of a German fairy tale. It was here that Angela Kasner took her first steps.

Angela was once asked what image comes to mind when she hears the word *Heimat*—an untranslatable German word that suggests not only the notion of home but also the place where you feel that you belong. She responded with a verbal sketch of the area around Templin: "a lake, some forests and cows, a boulder here and there . . . pines, and hay." There, with very few distractions and the freedom to explore both nature and her own imagination, young Angela Merkel learned to rely on herself. Even today, Merkel maintains that the place where she prefers most to wake up is "at home." Templin.

The train from Berlin to Templin winds through many of the bloodiest stations of Germany's last, troubled century, including Oranienburg, site of one of the first Nazi concentration camps; Sachsenhausen, first a Nazi, then a Soviet concentration camp; and Seelow, where Hitler's and Russian leader Joseph Stalin's troops savaged each other until the bitter end of the war. The Cyrillic road signs that still point the way toward Templin are an undeniable reminder of the Soviet army's occupation. The local soil is still poisoned from weapons testing that was carried out at the nearby former Russian military base. During Angela's childhood, this surreal calm was shattered several times a day by low-flying Soviet aircraft.

Pulling into Templin, a visitor finds a picturesque town of cobblestone streets and redbrick buildings. This is where Merkel grew up, went to school, and first married—and it remained her mother's hometown until her death in 2019. When asked about her family's move in later years, Herlind would explain: "We came as Christians helping other Christians. Some go to Africa. So why could we not go to the other part of our country?" The comparison between East Germany and Africa is revealing, suggesting just how alien the Communist East seemed to those from the West. Herlind paid a high price for their move East: for being a "bourgeois" pastor's wife, she was barred from teaching. Yet Angela has no recollection of her mother ever lamenting their family's move to the Soviet-occupied zone. Horst and Herlind Kasner instilled the values of sacrifice and self-discipline in their daughter from the beginning.

When the Kasner family first arrived at Waldhof—"forest court" in English—an isolated compound of approximately thirty buildings belonging to the Lutheran Church—they were too poor even to afford a stroller for infant Angela. A converted crate served as the future chancellor's crib. "My father had to milk goats, and my mother learned from an old woman how to make nettle soup," Merkel would recall. Her first memory is of running away from horses galloping through their yard. In those years, "My parents shared a small motorcycle for transport," she remembered. Later, when Horst Kasner had become an established, state-approved pastor—when it became clear, that is, that he did not challenge the legitimacy of the Communist state—the family was granted two private cars, a rare privilege in a Soviet satellite.* Many of his fellow churchmen held that he was much

---

*Growing up in Hungary, my sister and I attended Catholic mass every Sunday in our neighborhood church, but the nun who came to our home to instruct us in catechism was not allowed to wear her habit. It was definitely not a plus to be an active Christian in that era. It marked you as bourgeois, a crime that was among the reasons my journalist parents were arrested in early 1955 and charged falsely as American spies.

too accommodating to a malignant regime. Despite the privileges accorded to Kasner as a result of his prominence in the church, his status, as well as his family's, was precarious. The country of Martin Luther was, according to a 1994 official report, de-Christianized under Communist Party rule. Learning to maneuver in such murky waters, however, provided the future chancellor useful lessons in political dexterity.

Part of the Waldhof complex consisted of one of East Germany's most significant seminaries, where Kasner trained clerics. Life there was plain: no frills, no luxuries. Then and now, the parish included a shelter for several hundred children and adults with physical and developmental disabilities, who were taught simple trades. A vital part of the church community, their presence—even at Kasner family celebrations—always seemed normal to Angela.

Surviving neighbors recall Horst Kasner as an intimidating and controversial figure, known well beyond the immediate area. "He was a hard man, who did not strike you as a church man," recalled Angela's childhood friend Ulrich Schöneich, a tall, burly, still-youthful man who was once Templin's mayor. Pastor Kasner may not have been a gentle man of the cloth, but from him Angela learned logical rigor and clarity of argument.

Kasner maintained a demanding regime for Angela. "Everything had to be in perfect order," she explained in an interview early in her political career. Growing up, she had a difficult time understanding her father's priorities: "My father was good at approaching people and getting them to talk. What really made me angry as a child was his way of showing so much understanding for everybody else. But if we children did something wrong, his reaction was completely different." Particularly painful to Merkel was the realization that her beloved father appeared to use work as a reason to stay away from his family duties. "The worst was when he said he would be right back, but then it took hours for him to return," she recalled. Some days she would wait for him in the street outside their home for "a very long time."

Fortunately, there were other adults in Merkel's young life who had time, patience, and the warmth that her chilly father and busy mother often did not provide. "I remember a gardener, a sturdy, older man, who instilled basic trust and great calm in me," Angela recalled much later.

"I learned all kinds of things from him about practical life. I learned how to identify flowers, or when the cyclamen are in season. From him I learned how to talk to the mentally disabled. With him the atmosphere was warm and trusting, and he allowed me to eat carrots fresh from the ground. This man awakened a connection to the earth and to nature for me. . . . Today I recognize how important time is; more important than possessions."

In this unspoiled setting of woods and lakes, Merkel grew to draw comfort from the silence of the countryside. Later, one of her closest aides in the chancellery would refer to Merkel's rambles in these same woods as her "private think tank." One of her oldest friends attributes what he calls the "mellow Merkel" to those early days spent far from the stress and clamor of urban life. She still enjoys the quiet, admitting: "All the talking; that is a problem for me sometimes. . . . It is important for me not to have to say anything and still be together with someone." Angela Merkel's comfort with silence would prove helpful in her future as politician and negotiator—when she would deploy it to unsettle adversaries.

The serene years of Angela Kasner's early childhood ended abruptly on the morning of August 13, 1961. Two days earlier, her father had sensed that something was amiss. As the family drove home from vacation in Bavaria, the pastor noticed large rolls of barbed wire stacked in a pine forest along the highway as their car crossed from West Germany into East Germany. How odd, Kasner remarked to his wife. Two days later, the Kasners were en route to church when the radio announced the news. Those rolls of barbed wire had been used to cut East Germany off from West Germany—and from the rest of Europe. Thereafter, East Germany would become a prison state. Kasner's sacrifice for his God and his church suddenly took on another dimension.

"I was seven when I [first] saw my parents completely helpless. They had no idea what to do or say. My mother cried all day," Merkel recalled. "I wanted to help them, to cheer them up, but it was not possible." Herlind was realizing she might never be able to visit her family in Hamburg again. At least her husband's family lived in East Berlin. The Hamburg family was cut off from the Kasners by Europe's strictest border controls, which henceforth amputated West Germany from the East.

Erecting the roughly seventy-mile Berlin Wall (or the Antifascist Protection Rampart, as it was called officially) and the inner German border wall along the boundary between the two countries was an act of desperation to salvage Communist East Germany. With an open border, up to two thousand East Germans had been leaving for the West each day. Now a concrete barrier four feet wide and thirteen and a half feet tall was topped by barbed wire, while on the ground, land mines, dogs, and guards with automatic weapons made the border between East and West Berlin Europe's deadliest strip of land. Floodlights after sunset discouraged all but the most determined from flight. Later, Merkel would call the country of her youth a *Lager,* a word used generally to describe concentration camps.

Within the sanctuary of the Waldhof, however, life for young Angela did not change materially. She had her parents and her younger siblings, Marcus (born in 1957) and Irene (born 1964). And Angela had access to her parents' wide-ranging collection of books they had brought with them from Hamburg; in a closed-off country, these became the child's means of escape. Even before adolescence, she had a voracious interest in discovering new worlds contained in books. During the long, dark nights in the spartan Waldhof, Angela devoured the Russian classics, beginning her lifelong affection for Russian culture and language. "Russian is a beautiful language, full of emotion, a bit like music, but also a bit melancholy," she observed. She would never confuse Russia's soulful writers and poets—or the Russian people—with their Soviet leaders.

Although Herlind was barred from formal teaching, she taught her daughter serviceable English, which later helped Angela on the global stage. But the Kasners did not have many English books in the house. In East Germany, reading material that was not on the approved Marxist-Leninist list was controlled as carefully as weapons.* The only English-language publication available to young Angela was the official British Communist Party organ, *The Morning Star,* which she would grab on trips to Berlin.

In the stillness of the parish house as she read biographies of great European statesmen and scholars, Angela found her role model: Marie Curie, the first woman to win not just one but two Nobel Prizes. There were a number of reasons for the physicist's appeal. She was born in Poland, as was one of Merkel's grandfathers. "While she was alive, Poland was divided and occupied by Russia. We also had our experience with Russian occupation," Merkel noted in an early interview. But what most impressed the girl were the circumstances that led to Curie's discovering the element radium:

"She made this discovery because she was convinced that she had a good idea. . . . If you believe in an idea—even if you are alone—if you pursue this idea, and suffer through the highs and lows, you will ultimately reach your goal, if the idea was right."

Avid for escape and seeking a role model, Angela was fired by Curie's tenacity and eventual triumph, particularly in a field rife with gender

---

*Crossing from West to East Berlin as a news correspondent in the late 1970s, I recall being asked by the border security guards, "Any contraband, weapons, or newspapers?"

discrimination. "Nothing in life is to be feared, it is only to be understood," Curie had written, a sentiment which deeply impressed the young Angela.

If Curie's life in science offered inspiration, so too did the Bible, which was also Angela's constant childhood companion. Thanks to her father's Sunday sermons in Templin's redbrick St. George's Chapel, the young girl became as familiar with figures from the Old and New Testaments as other children were with characters from *Grimm's Fairy Tales*. Merkel's father encouraged rigorous, critical thinking—even, to an extent he may not have intended, on the subject of God. In an early interview, Angela expressed a rather unorthodox perspective on the afterlife and salvation, saying, "I believe that this world is limited and final, but there is something beyond it, which makes the world endurable. You might call it god or something else . . . but I find it comforting that there is such a thing as the church. The fact that we are allowed to sin and be forgiven is some relief for me. Otherwise you would go crazy." In the Bible, she found bottomless riches that would become a lifelong source of strength for her.*

Merkel's faith is essential to who she is and all she has accomplished. It is very different from her father's more doctrinaire Christianity. "I treat faith cautiously," she noted. "For me, religion belongs in the private sphere. It allows me to be forgiving of myself and of others and prevents me from drowning in my responsibilities. If I were an atheist, it would be more difficult to carry such a heavy burden. . . .

"The most difficult thing, and the most important is . . . love. If you read the Bible, the book of John, it doesn't refer to [love as] sentimental words but rather to actual *deeds*. This love is unconditional and fearless. It is

---

*In her early days as politician, Merkel sometimes allowed biblical language to slip into her speech. On January 17, 2001, for example, she urged then foreign minister Joschka Fischer to "repent" for throwing a stone at a policeman during his days as a student radical in 1968. It was not a mistake she would repeat as a more seasoned politician.

serving," she explained during a Protestant Church convention in 1995, in her most explicit statement of the worldview that would guide her personal and political lives. Deeds carry more weight than words, and demonstrating one's love is less about achieving a particular goal than about doggedly and steadfastly making the attempt. This was Angela Merkel's credo.

Ten years later, in another speech at a Protestant Church convention, regarding her faith, Merkel cited self-knowledge and self-confidence as vital for both giving and receiving love, insisting, "You are only able to love in the first place if you love yourself, if you believe in yourself, if you know your-self. Only then can you approach the *other.* . . . Love can only come if you are clear about who you are." This self-awareness would also lead to the acknowledgment that "I am part of history; I am allowed to and will make mistakes." Such self-acceptance explains a great deal about her composure even under tremendous stress.

In many ways, Merkel's faith was grounded in her exposure to the com-munity of disabled people she lived with at Waldhof. In the same 2005 ad-dress, Merkel quoted the Bible passage Malachi 2.17, saying, "Malachi sees the violence in society against the weak, those who are at the margin of so-ciety, the hired workers, the widows and the orphans treated unjustly. Mala-chi says that this is unacceptable; it goes against God's commandments. . . . The weakest in society must not be wronged. We must focus our attention on them." A decade later, she would put those words into practice as she allowed one million of those "at the margins of society"—refugees fleeing their homelands in the violent Middle East—to enter Germany. Those fa-miliar with her private faith were not altogether surprised.

To achieve her goal of service, Merkel recognized early that she would need power, which she never saw as a dirty word. As she explained it: "Power per se is nothing bad. It is necessary. Power is 'to make'—to do something. If I want to do something, I need the right tools; that is, the support of a group. . . . The opposite of power is *powerless.* What's the use of a good idea if I can't execute it?" To hear a politician, man or woman, express such an explicit perspective on power—and her need for it—is, to say the least, unusual.

She began to exercise her own power early. Childhood friend Ulrich Schöneich described Angela as "a leader, from the beginning. If there was something that needed to be organized, she took care of it." Dispatching her own schoolwork with speed, "I helped others with theirs," she said later. And she took comfort in being prepared. "I started thinking about what gifts to buy two months in advance of Christmas. Structuring my life and avoiding chaos was very important to me."

Even in her youth, she displayed an innate caution and need for control. There are few better illustrations of this than the story her friends tell of Angela on the diving board. With her third-grade teacher coaxing her amid her classmates' jeers and laughter, the nine-year-old climbed the twelve long steps up a ten-foot diving board—and then froze. The water seemed a very long way down. Yet she did not retreat; instead, for forty-five minutes, she paced back and forth on the board, as if calculating cost and benefit. Finally, just as the class bell rang, Angela dove in.

Accommodation—how far to go along with a malignant system for survival—was a question Angela could not escape in East Germany. No country outside the Soviet Union had more Russian troops than East Germany: an estimated 380,000 soldiers and 180,000 civilians occupied the country until 1991. Over time, those Russian occupiers with whom she had chatted on Templin's streets, as well as their German collaborators, became a source of mounting frustration and even rage. When Merkel got home from school each day, she said later, "I had to talk about it to my mother, to get it out of my system first." More than the wall, Angela increasingly encountered invisible boundaries. "You were never allowed to really challenge yourself, to see how far you could go," she recalled. Your background—bourgeois or proletarian—played the largest role in your future prospects.* Despite mounting frustration, however, she made a bargain with herself: "I told myself, if I can't bear to live here anymore, I will not have my life ruined. If I can't bear it anymore, I will go to the West, somehow."†

Standing out was dangerous, so she learned not to call attention to herself. In group photographs from this period, Angela, with pin-straight bangs in a shapeless sweater, smiles from the back row. But she was the first in her school to wear that sartorial symbol of the decadent West: blue jeans, received as contraband from her Hamburg relatives. Merkel soon learned, however, that even a pair of pants could get you in trouble. Her school principal occasionally sent children home for wearing them, telling students, "Choose clothes suitable for the workers' and peasants' state."

It was not Angela Kasner's appearance, however, that people remarked upon; it was her intelligence. "I got to know her when she was a skinny twelve-year-old," remembered Erika Benn, Merkel's one-time Russian teacher. "Today we would call her 'highly gifted.' She was highly motivated, never made mistakes in Russian grammar, and got the top score in the regional Language Olympics, then went on to win the national contest." Benn, a former Communist Party member, said the only problem she had with her star pupil was that Merkel had no stage presence. "She never smiled! She never tried to win you over with charm. 'Eye contact!' I would hiss at her when she looked down at her shoes."

---

*As did your and your family's attitudes toward the all-powerful state. My own parents were deemed "enemies of the state" for their unfriendly attitude toward Communist Hungary; thus, I would not have been able to pursue an academic education there, only a technical one.
†"Going to the West" required extraordinary planning, great courage, usually money to pay "guides," and, of course, luck. The odds of a successful escape were dauntingly slim. Throughout my Hungarian childhood, my parents tried various escape routes from behind the Iron Curtain;—all of them failed for various reasons: internal betrayal, bad weather, a child's fall. (That child was me.)

For winning the Russian Language Olympics, the fifteen-year-old was rewarded with her first trip to a foreign country—to Moscow. Merkel's most vivid memory of the trip is buying her first Western record, although she is no longer certain whether the LP in question was by the Beatles or the Rolling Stones. (Of the Soviet satellites, East Germany was the strictest and most tightly controlled against "imperialist"—Western—cultural and political influences.)

For a clergyman's child to be admitted to an academic secondary school instead of a technical school was highly unusual. And although Merkel was a straight-A student, she was rarely praised or rewarded by her teachers. In fact, her Russian instructor was reprimanded for Angela's prize-winning performances: "At one of the Communist Party assemblies at the school," Benn recalled, "a party official sneered, 'It's not all that tough to get results from the children of the *bourgeoisie*! We need to promote the children of the workers and the peasants!" Angela's offense was always her so-called bourgeois father, who, while far from being a dissident, was nevertheless a Lutheran minister in the atheist state, and thus suspect. "I always had to be better than the others in class," Merkel recalled.

However brilliant, Angela still longed for her peers' company and approval, so she joined the Young Pioneers, a sort of pre–Communist Party preparatory organization. By her own admission, Merkel's motivation for signing up was "seventy percent opportunism." She wanted a social life; she wanted to belong. Thus, Angela learned to navigate between worlds: singing Lutheran hymns in church, and miming Vladimir Lenin's praises in school. "There were people whom I sometimes even envied for simply being able to believe. Not asking, not doubting, simply playing by the rules," she admitted.

Even as she mastered Marxist-Leninist theory, with its sunny prediction of the inevitable triumph of the proletariat, Merkel secretly followed politics in the forbidden half of Germany. "I sneaked into the girls' toilet in 1969 with my transistor radio and listened to the debates prior to the election of the West German president," she recalled. "I was moved by how exciting three rounds of voting could be!" Thanks to her father, that same year, Angela acquired a rare copy of the dissident Soviet nuclear physicist Andrei Sakharov's essay attacking Moscow's dangerous and costly arms race. When Merkel was caught with such forbidden reading, Pastor Kasner was promptly summoned for questioning by the Stasi. He refused to disclose his source, but the episode reminded him that even pastors "friendly" to the state were not immune from the apparatus of terror.

Ulrich Schöneich and others considered Angela's father, whom many referred to as Rote Kasner—Red Kasner—much too accommodating to the regime. Even as he preached the Gospel, the pastor did not push back vigorously against state incursions and regulations of the church. "There was a time when people like Angela's father thought Communists and Christians had an identical goal," Lothar de Maizière, an active member of the East German Lutheran church, told me. "They all believed in the benevolent human being." And so they tried to find common ground. "We don't want to be a church *against* socialism. We don't want to be a church *for* socialism. We want to be Christians within this system and coexist peacefully with the state," explained de Maizière, "This formula was invented by Angela Merkel's father."

Decades after the fall of the wall, there are those whose memories of Pastor Kasner remain fresh and bitter. Reiner Eppelmann is one such clergyman. As an outspoken, dissident pastor in 1980s East Germany, Eppelmann was the target of three failed Stasi assassination attempts. He met Pastor Kasner at the Templin seminary when he was just completing his theological studies. "I was shocked by Kasner's attitude," he recalled in Berlin during our long interview in the fall of 2017. Horst was supposed to guide new pastors through the final steps of their theological training, but, according to Eppelmann, he seemed convinced that this socialist Germany was "free of exploitation" and was truly better than the capitalist Germany. "He made this clear time and again to us pastors. He was arrogant and critical of the Protestant Church even though it was doing all it could under severe pressure." Kasner also told Epplemann that he thought there might not be pastors in East Germany much longer.

"You have to imagine," Epplemann said, "fifteen young people sitting in this pastoral college, waiting to be released to their first parish somewhere in the East. All of a sudden, Kasner tells us, 'You are not going to be pastors in a parish, because the number of pastors in the East will continue to shrink. The church won't be able to afford you any longer. You will need "normal" nine-to-five jobs from Monday to Friday and take care of your church Saturday and Sunday.' You can imagine how demoralized we were." Kasner's blending of political and religious ideology rubbed Epplemann the wrong way—and his behavior sometimes seemed hypocritical: "I thought the way he connected faith and politics was terrible. And the way he did not want to see how much Protestant parents and children were suffering in East Germany. . . . He refused to acknowledge that they were punished *because* they were Christians! Kasner believed all of us, even Christian pastors, were supposed to become 'developed socialists.'"

When Kasner was forced to accommodate and even promote the Stasi state's plan to abolish pastors, one wonders whether he regretted his decision to move to the East. Regardless, Angela's father clung to the hope that some version of his socialist ideal would survive—even as evidence to the contrary continued piling up.

Merkel never publicly criticized her father's politics. "My father tried to shape a church that met the needs of the people in the East," she said, likening his beliefs to those of liberation theologians in Latin America. Her public loyalty did not mean Angela agreed with him in private, however. She remembered one early argument "about how much property you should communize, while still making sure there is enough individual responsibility left." Years later, the pastor would say that his daughter was lost to him early on, commenting somewhat bitterly, "She always does what she wants."

The year 1968 dealt another harsh blow to Kasner's idealized version of socialism—something that made a deep impression on the fourteen-year-old Angela. It was the year of the Prague Spring, a period of political liberalization and mass protest in the Czechoslovak Socialist Republic. Freedoms granted included loosening restrictions on the media, speech, and travel from January until August 1968. "I remember well the spirit of optimism and a fresh start," she reflected years later.

"We were on vacation in the Pec Mountains in Czechoslovakia. Everybody was excited. Then my parents went to Prague for two days to see what was happening in Wenceslas Square," site of the antigovernment protests. "They came back in the highest spirits, hopeful that things within the socialist camp would change and crack open after all . . . and that what was happening in Czechoslovakia might happen in East Germany too. I recall being skeptical as to whether socialism itself could be reformed."

By August 21, Merkel had returned from her vacation in the Czech mountains and was visiting her grandmother in East Berlin. "I can still see myself standing in the kitchen on that morning when it was announced on the radio: Russian troops have marched into Prague." Five hundred thousand soldiers from the fellow Socialist Republics—Poland, Bulgaria, Hungary, and, most painfully for young Angela, East Germany—poured across the Czech border and crushed Prague's Spring. "That was a sharp blow. I was ashamed, and I was very sad," Merkel recalled. When Russian tanks crushed Ukraine's reform movement in 2014, Merkel reacted faster and more forcefully than her fellow heads of state, the brutality undoubtedly triggering the memory of standing in her grandmother's kitchen during that long-ago summer of 1968, listening to the news from Prague.

The Soviet crushing of Czechoslovakia's liberal experiment of

"Socialism with a Human Face," as the Prague Spring was dubbed by its leaders, notably Alexander Dubcek, who headed the Communist Party's Central Committee, made it harder for Pastor Kasner to delude himself about the East German regime's true nature. Yet Kasner never quite gave up on his dream of a "humane" socialism and never fully reconciled himself to capitalism. Long after German unification—when his daughter was already a rising star in that capitalist state—he bemoaned, "All that counts [for capitalists], is *money;* for the producers to make profits, and the consumers to buy, and to buy more than they need. The market economy is being beaten into us and is not supposed to be questioned. Everything is being turned into a 'market,' even nature itself."

Having finished her senior year at her Templin *Gymnasium*—the equivalent of a preparatory high school in the United States—with top honors in mathematics, physics, and Russian, Angela was very nearly prohibited from graduating. Holding her back was nothing more than a youthful prank. Required to profess her love of Marxism-Leninism by staging a skit about its world triumph, Merkel and a few classmates decided to show solidarity not only with the Communist Vietcong (then America's enemy in Southeast Asia, and thus deemed a good choice) but also with the people of Mozambique, who were waging war against their Portuguese colonizers. This latter affiliation was more problematic, given that the struggle there was not strictly pro-Soviet. Worst of all, Merkel's group concluded its act by singing a rousing chorus of "The Internationale," the official anthem of the Communist movement, in *English,* the "language of the imperialists." For these transgressions, the Communist Party planned to withhold the diploma of one of the *Gymnasium*'s—indeed, the whole region's—brightest graduates, who had already been accepted to the acclaimed Leipzig University (renamed Karl Marx University in 1953).

In despair at the consequences of his daughter's rare act of rebellion,

Merkel's father contacted his bishop, who urged the state to be lenient toward the promising student and her classmates. Kasner's daughter was spared but learned another lesson about the brutality of a state that was willing to cut short a potentially bright future for nothing more than a mild act of mischief.

Nineteen-year-old Angela Merkel arrived at this grand train station—where she was greeted by Vladimir Lenin's portrait—in the fall of 1973 to begin her studies in physics at the famed Leipzig University. On her own for the first time, she proved to be a politically careful but fiercely motivated and even brilliant student.

2

LEIPZIG — ON HER OWN

It must look democratic, but we must have everything in our control.

—Walter Ulbricht, first secretary of the Socialist

Party of East Germany, from 1950 to 1971

The fall of 1973, when nineteen-year-old Angela Kasner left home for Leipzig University, was a gloomy time for East Germany. Communists who had been too outspoken in favor of the Prague Spring remained jailed or purged from the country's Communist Party. US president Richard Nixon may have made his dramatic trip to China only the previous year, but back at the Kremlin, geriatric president Leonid Brezhnev was uninterested in nudging East Germany's Walter Ulbricht from his hardline Stalinism. The population retreated deeper into a sullen acceptance of *things as they are*.

Following her brush with the all-seeing state, Merkel escaped into the safer province of science. "I chose physics because I wanted to understand Einstein's theory of relativity and because even East Germany wasn't capable of suspending basic arithmetic and the rules of nature," she said later. Why pursue the humanities when, despite German author Heinrich Böll's recent Nobel Prize for literature, "You had to get permission to read Boll's *The Clown* and could not get foreign books or newspapers," Merkel recalled. Her goal was a PhD in physics. She chose the University of Leipzig not only because of its prestige as one of Germany's high temples of science, but also on account of its distance of 168 miles from Templin. It was time to strike out on her own. "I wanted to get away, to get out of this small town," Merkel explained. No doubt she also longed for some distance from her impossible-to-please father and his unfailingly loyal wife.

Stepping off the Templin-Leipzig train, Merkel arrived at the Hauptbahnhof, with its high, vaulted ceiling, one of Europe's grandiose train stations; a remnant of the golden age of rail travel. Gigantic portraits of the Communist heroes—Marx, Lenin, Ulbricht—greeted the nineteen-year-old. Still, not even propaganda could diminish this city's grandeur. Leipzig boasted a proud history and still possessed traces of international flair. Composer Johann Sebastian Bach, poet Friedrich von Schiller, the dramatist Johann Wolfgang von Goethe, and artist Max Beckmann had all either studied or lived there. What's more, as host of the annual Leipzig Trade Fair and home of a fabled university, the city was, by satellite standards, a lively place.

Merkel hopped the tram to Karl Marx Platz (today restored to its previous name, Augustusplatz) to register for classes in the university's soulless concrete administration building. Angela surely experienced a thrill as she first walked the austere corridors to take her place in the amphitheaters and seminar rooms, altered little since the philosopher Friedrich Nietzsche, the composer Richard Wagner, and Nobel Prize–winning physicists Werner Heisenberg and Gustav Hertz preceded her here.

Of the seventy freshmen in Leipzig's physics program, Merkel was one of only seven women. "She was the first woman in my class," her thermodynamics professor, Reinhold Haberlandt, recalled. A tall, grave man, now in his eighties, four decades later he has vivid memories of his student—despite her best effort not to stand out in class. "Angela was very quiet and precise when she spoke. There were eighty students in my lecture hall, and only when asked did Angela speak," Haberlandt said. But she was brilliant. "When she spoke in class," remembered classmate Frank Mieszkalski, "it was as if she and the professor were speaking a language of their own, foreign to the rest of us. I think she has a few extra wires in her brain."

One night in the students' club in the basement of the sprawling university, Mieszkalski asked Angela to dance. As he described to me many years later:

"She looked pleased—until I revealed my real motive. I needed her help to prepare for our upcoming finals, in a class that was a forerunner to IT [information technology]. I had attended the first class and then cut the rest of the semester. She looked a bit disappointed for just a moment. But then she got over it, and we sat down, and I took notes while she summarized a semester. She had amazing recall. She is so structured and organized in her thinking. It was all in her head!"

Mieszkalski passed the exam. Angela herself would post only one poor grade as an undergraduate. That was in the compulsory study of Marxism-Leninism, for which Merkel received the lowest passing grade possible: *genugend*, or average.

Even in the sciences, the Communist state erected barriers to learning. "We weren't allowed to read English-language scientific studies; to do so was dangerous," Professor Haberlandt recalled. "We had to translate all English material into Russian. Only then were we allowed to read them, as if to read in English would infect us with a virus of some sort. What a colossal waste of human effort!" he said, shaking his head at the memory. When I asked for his reaction to his remarkable student's decision to change her profession from science to politics, he replied, "She would have made a good scientist. But there are many of those. There are very few good politicians."

Merkel's master's degree thesis supervisor, Ralf Der, professor of neuroinformatics and robotics, recalled his first impressions of his celebrated former pupil being "young, open, lively, short haircut. I liked her immediately." Student and teacher soon became friends, and in 1980 the two coauthored a paper titled "On the Influence of Spatial Correlations on the Rate of Chemical Reactions in Dense Systems." Yet the quality that Der found most memorable about Merkel wasn't directly related to her academic achievements. "She seemed to have a strong inner life all her own," he said, "That impressed all of us,"

"I remember asking her once," Mieszkalski recalled, "how she reconciles her Christian faith—I mean, we all knew she was a pastor's daughter—with being a scientist. Angela said, 'God to me means living an ethical life.' She said her goal was to merge Christian ethics and science."

Navigating between church and state, between independent thinking and Marxist-Leninist dogma, required mental and emotional finesse. Merkel was already a shrewd survivor, managing to simultaneously stay both a faithful Lutheran and a member of the Communist Youth. She was not going to jeopardize her future by coming down hard on either side. She had mastered the tricky business of adaptation and compromise—and learned the importance of keeping her own counsel.

Not everyone in her circle was as circumspect. Among her friends in Leipzig was a fellow physicist named Reinhard Wulfert, who, unlike Merkel, was openly opposed to the East German regime. In 1982, some years after graduation, he joined a silent peace march through Jena, a city in the province of Thuringia. The demonstration was, of course, monitored by both uniformed and plainclothes Stasi agents, and, shortly afterward, Wulfert was arrested. After pressure from scientists and academics worldwide, he was released from custody and eventually managed to escape to the West. When he wrote later to Angela, she requested that he stop their correspondence, assuming that she was under surveillance too. Wulfert's bold but high-risk actions were precisely the sort of behavior that Merkel would never permit herself.

In 1989, following the fall of the wall, Merkel reached out to her old friend. This time, however, it was Wulfert, living in West Germany, who declined to resume the friendship.

Merkel's first exposure to the free market economy was as a bartender at the university's student union. Her specialty was a concoction of whiskey and cherry juice that she sold to her fellow students for a profit, taking the streetcar each week to the other end of Leipzig to buy the canned cherries and cheap whiskey. Her classmates recalled a cheerful and skilled bartender—with an eye toward her bottom line. "I was always the girl who eats the peanuts and doesn't dance," she said. Nor was she inspired by the pop music choices, in yet another example of state control. "The state imposed a precise quota, of sixty percent East German, and forty percent Western music for student gatherings," Merkel remembered. She would have preferred the opposite ratio.

Well into her first year at university, Angela was also a member of the Club der Ungekussten (Club of the Unkissed, or CDU—ironically, the name of her future political party). If men were not especially drawn to the rather androgynous-appearing young woman who preferred baggy pants and a well-scrubbed face, the feeling was mutual; more often than not, she found men annoying. "In class, I always preferred doing my experiments with women," she recalled. "When we started using laboratory equipment, the men went right away for the burners and other machinery, while I took my time to think about my experiment first. But by then, all the equipment was occupied by the men, and they had already broken many parts."

Eventually Merkel did fall in love. In 1974, at the age of twenty, she met Ulrich Merkel, a fellow Leipzig physics student, on an exchange trip to Moscow and Leningrad. Ulrich was "a regular guy, a man you could steal horses with," Mieszkalski joked, using a German expression. "I noticed Angela because she was a friendly, open, natural girl," Ulrich Merkel recalled in a rare 2004 interview. After dating for almost two years, they moved in together. "We shared a bath and toilet with fellow students," he said. "Each of us paid ten marks a month. We had one bed, two desks, and one closet. That was it. It sounds Spartan, but it was enough for us.

"We were committed to a future together," he reflected, although he admitted that "there was another, more practical motive for early marriage: if you were married, you were more likely to get an apartment." They wed the next year: Angela was twenty-three; Ulrich, twenty-four. The ceremony took place in her father's little church in Templin, at Angela's behest, though Pastor Kasner did not perform the wedding service. The bride wore blue.

The newlyweds skipped a honeymoon in order to resume their studies immediately, as both had to prepare for final exams. Merkel's master's thesis, titled "Aspects of Nuclear Physics," was published in the English scientific journal *Chemical Physics*, a remarkable achievement for an East German PhD candidate. Even with her stellar academic record, however, Merkel's career choices were limited. Teaching was out of the question, given her "bourgeois" background, and even if it had been an option, the state's ideological principles would have made it distasteful for her. "I would have had to act like all the other teachers. . . . I would have had to make students who attended Christian religious instruction stand up and identify themselves," Merkel said later. "If I had lived in the West, chances are good I would have become a teacher," the future chancellor has said.

It's hard to imagine either teaching or science long containing this brilliant and quietly ambitious young woman en route to the Cold War's front line: Berlin.

Flanked by her close friend Michael Schindhelm and her future husband, Joachim Sauer, Angela celebrated receiving her PhD in physics in 1986 in Berlin.

3

BERLIN

Angela and I lived an absurd life in this city in the eighties.

—Michael Schindhelm

Angela Merkel's passage from Leipzig to the capital was not uneventful. Berlin had not been her first choice for post-university life. She had applied for a job at Technical University Ilmenau in Thüringen, a mountainous, heavily forested region that she loved. Once the refuge of Martin Luther, Ilmenau was a prestigious center for scientific study. But when Merkel arrived at what she thought was a job interview, she was greeted by two Stasi agents. Leading her into an office, the agents peppered Merkel with questions meant to intimidate her: "How often do you listen to Western broadcasts?"

"Do you love your country?"

"How do you guard against infiltration by imperialist agents?"

Their goal was to *persuade* her to do "her patriotic duty" and inform on future colleagues.

Angela was as well prepared for this encounter as any East German could be. "My parents always told me to tell Stasi officers that I was a chatterbox and simply couldn't keep my mouth shut. I also told the agents I couldn't keep being an informant secret from my husband," she recalled. It seemed a credible answer from a naïve academic, and the agents dismissed her with a shrug—and doubtless a black mark in her dossier. She didn't get the job at the university.

Instead of the cozy comfort of small-town Ilmenau, both husband and wife accepted positions at the prestigious East German Academy of Sciences in East Berlin. In the late 1970s, though the divided city's most historic landmarks were in the East, it was still largely unrestored. Three decades after World War II, the Soviet-occupied city still felt raw and neglected, with weeds proliferating in the rutted fields surrounding the blackened wreck of the Reichstag, the former home of the German parliament, technically in West Berlin but looming next to the wall. The once-glittering Hotel Adlon on the now-shabby boulevard Unter den Linden had emerged slowly from the rubble as hostelry to Soviet officers. Twice daily, Angela's S-Bahn commuter train snaked by the wall, en route to the Academy of Sciences, located in a charmless compound on the city's periphery. Passing the well-raked sand of no man's land—with its watchtowers and guard dog patrols—never failed to depress her. From November until late March, twilight arrived in the early afternoon, casting an even deeper pall over Berlin. At night, the city's Eastern half was nearly pitch black.

Angela and Ulrich settled into a tiny flat at 24 Marienstrasse, near the Brandenburg Gate, the forbidding barrier between East and West. Several times an hour, the Merkels' one-room apartment trembled as the S-Bahn rattled past. From the window, they could see the gloomy Tränenpalast (Palace of Tears), a border-control station so named because, in this squalid depot, East Germans said good-byes to friends and relatives visiting from West Berlin.

Still working on her PhD in physics, Merkel was putting in the three years she owed the state in exchange for her education. Despite this being the premier research institution of East Germany, Angela labored in a bare-bones lab housed in a former construction workers' bungalow and stocked with outdated equipment. There was a single central processor in the so-called computer center; all twelve scientists on Merkel's team had to do their own programming. As would often be the case in her professional life, she was the only woman.

Almost as depressing as her daily commute was her work: carrying out repetitive experiments separating carbon and hydrogen atoms at high temperatures. Soon enough, Merkel was bored, realizing that she preferred abstract and theoretical thinking. She spoke later about her frustration at her professional limitations in those years, calling "the prospect of another twenty-five years of carrying out scientific research on a shoestring budget," in her typically understated way, "not enticing."

Things at home weren't much better. Within three years, Merkel realized that her marriage had been a mistake. "We married because everybody else was getting married. I did not treat marriage with the necessary seriousness," Angela admitted later. Ulrich claimed he did not see their separation coming. "Angela packed up her things and moved out. She made the decision on her own," he said. Still, the divorce, though a disappointment, was amicable. "There was not much to divide between the two of us. She took the washing machine; I kept the furniture," he recalled. The last time Ulrich saw Angela was at the Academy of Sciences in 1989, just before the wall fell. Though she kept his name, Merkel rarely mentions this brief marriage.

Angela celebrated her thirtieth birthday newly divorced and living in a barely furnished apartment on Templiner Strasse (Street) in Prenzlauer Berg, a neighborhood of gutted, war-damaged buildings occupied primarily by illegal squatters—Merkel among them. Friends helped her "break in" to and fix up an abandoned flat. Angela's most vivid memory of that year was a visit from her father. Surveying his daughter's threadbare, not-quite-legal new home, he remarked acidly, "Well, Angela, you certainly haven't come very far." Such a rebuke from the parent she had worked hard to please must have stung, but Merkel neither protested nor disagreed with his judgment; confrontation was not her style, then or later. As with other powerful men who underestimated her, Merkel would bide her time and ultimately prove him wrong.

To keep her mind and spirit alive in these years, she attended performances at the government-run Berliner Ensemble Theater on nearby Bertolt-Brecht Platz. She also widened her circle of friends, a move that would prove dangerous. Unknown to Merkel, her lab partner and confidant, Frank Schneider, had been assigned by the Stasi to inform on her. And while Schneider rarely had anything political to report, he did seem to take a salacious interest in the young divorcée's love life. "Sometimes, when I picked her up for work, one of her lovers greets me at the door, in a bathrobe. Her love affairs seldom last more than six months," Schneider informed the Stasi on August 30, 1980. (Schneider is the only documented source for Angela Merkel's "love affairs" during this period of sudden and welcome freedom. Merkel has never commented on the more personal aspects of her life as a single woman in Berlin.)

Merkel's trust in the informer seemed total. She enlisted Schneider's help in fixing up her apartment, befriended his Georgian-born wife, and occasionally babysat for the couple's child. She even invited Schneider to her most private sanctuary: her family's home in Templin, where he met and subsequently reported on the pastor and his wife. Schneider found the Kasners guilty of nothing more subversive than a reliance on packages of food and clothing from Herlind's sister in Hamburg.

More politically relevant was his report on Merkel's September 1981 trip to Poland, which she returned from with photographs and enthusiastic descriptions of Solidarity, Poland's first independent labor union, under the leadership of Lech Walesa. The electrician-turned union-activist and his allies would soon shake the Polish People's Republic and then the entire Soviet Empire: demanding better working conditions, free speech, and other rights. "She isn't a dissident, but she sometimes thinks a little too loudly," Schneider informed the Stasi. Merkel didn't learn of her friend's betrayal until 2005, from published reports. "I'm not angry," she said, "but it's a bitter disappointment." *Disappointment* is a strong word in Angela Merkel's vocabulary.

In 1985 Merkel's dreary days in Berlin were lit up by the arrival of a man of sparkling intelligence who would soon become one of her closest friends. Michael Schindhelm had just returned from spending four years studying quantum chemistry in Voronezh, in southwestern Russia. (Quantum chemistry, also called molecular quantum mechanics, is a branch of chemistry that focuses on applying quantum mechanics to chemical systems.)

Schindhelm brought firsthand news of exciting stirrings of change in the long-frozen Soviet Empire. Fifty-four-year-old Communist Party chairman Mikhail Gorbachev had succeeded a series of geriatric Soviet leaders and seemed to be a new species of Soviet Man. Britain's prime minster, Margaret Thatcher, observed, "Gorbachev is a man we can do business with," and US president Ronald Reagan would soon engage with him during summit meetings in Geneva, Switzerland, and Reykjavik, Iceland. The two leaders—Gorbachev and Reagan—seemed mutually charmed. Having assessed the perilous state of the Soviet economy, hemorrhaging from a protracted war in Afghanistan and from an arms race accelerated by Reagan's Strategic Defense Initiative (dubbed Star Wars), "Gorby," as he was universally known, was impatient for reforms. East Germany may have been stuck in the Stalinist Ice Age, but, elsewhere in the empire, the ice was beginning to crack.

Eager for unfiltered news of a rapidly shifting world, Merkel was entranced by Schindhelm's stories of life in the Soviet Union. Moscow was miserable, he told her. There was often no water, no heat, and people were hungry. "You could feel that it was the final act of the Cold War,"

Schindhelm said to his new friend. Angela pressed Schindhelm for details on how Gorbachev's reforms, known in Russian as *perestroika* and *glasnost*—respectively, restructuring the centrally planned Soviet economy and opening up to market forces—would affect East Germany. The divided city where Merkel and Schindhelm lived and worked was still the Cold War's most volatile front line, where the two sides continued to eye each other warily—with the tanks and troops of the East and West separated only by that narrow strip of no-man's-land.*

"Angela and I met for an hour or so, at the day's end, and she would make Turkish coffee, and we talked about everything," Schindhelm recalled during the first of our several meetings in Berlin. An elegant man in a Leonard Cohen–esque fedora, he would restart his life after the fall of the wall as opera impresario and dramatist. As their friendship blossomed, Schindhelm and Merkel discovered that they had a great deal in common. They had both learned, he said, "from our Protestant parents how to keep our distance from the state, to put on disguises when the state came too close, and to take off the disguises when the state was absent. Between Angela and me, the state was absent. Angela had a wonderful sense of humor, but she was, even then, a rather enigmatic person. For me, she has really not changed." Angela introduced Michael to her brother, Marcus, three years her junior, who had also become a physicist. Schindhelm recalled her brother being "just like his sister. I could see there was something in their upbringing that made them both very calm and rather opaque."

The Merkel that Schindhelm knew in the eighties was also a lost soul. He would include her as a character in a roman à clef that he penned later, under the name Renate, painting a clear picture of her lack of enthusiasm

---

*There were three hundred thousand US troops stationed in Germany during the Cold War, thousands of them deployed in and around Berlin. During the Cuban Missile crisis of 1962, President John F. Kennedy's greatest fear was that the Russians would seize all of Berlin, igniting war in Europe.

for life under the East German state. He called her "the model of a young scientist without any illusions. She had been working on her doctorate for several years without a clear goal in sight. The only time she showed any enthusiasm was talking about biking in Brandenburg." One other thing seemed to excite her: the thought of the West. "We shared an admiration for the system on the other side of the wall that we passed by each day on our commute from Prenzlauer Berg to Adlershof," Schindhelm wrote. "The magic cast by the other system held us captive."

Though she felt stymied throughout her decade living in East Berlin, Merkel was having life experiences that would define the type of leader she would become. Hers was not just a political education but also a moral one. In 1985 Angela was profoundly moved by a speech that few East Germans were allowed to hear. Through friends in the Lutheran Church, she got hold of West German president Richard von Weizsäcker's commemoration of the fortieth anniversary of the end of World War II. Its honesty about Germany's past stunned her. Von Weizsäcker's blunt reckoning with the Holocaust was dramatically at odds with what she had been taught at school.

In the years following the war, East Germany spun its own mythology of its history as an anti-Fascist Socialist Republic—the part of Germany that had resisted Hitler. In the classroom in Templin and even during field trips to the Sachsenhausen concentration camp near Berlin, the focus remained on East German communists and the twenty-two million Soviets who were killed in combat while fighting the Fascists. East Germans regarded themselves as victims—not perpetrators—of war crimes. "There was not a single week in school when we did not talk about National Socialism," Merkel recalled. "Since second grade we regularly visited concentration camps. Still, in class, we only talked about *Communist* victims. Jews were hardly mentioned—and if they were, it was usually Jews who were friends of Communists."

Now she was hearing a completely different version of history. "We need to look unblinkered at the truth; the greater honesty we show, the freer we are to face the consequences. The root of the tyranny was Hitler's immeasurable hatred of our Jewish compatriots. Hitler never concealed this hatred from the public but made the entire nation a tool of it," the newly elected West German president was saying. Von Weizsäcker urged his fellow Germans, "Remember especially the six million Jews who were murdered in German concentration camps—a genocide unique in history."

The president's plea for Germany to confront its past was an important milestone in Merkel's political and moral evolution, affecting her deeply. "Angela and I spent many hours discussing the speech," Schindhelm said.* As we shall see, for the rest of her life, the Shoah—as she has always referred to the Holocaust—would be central to her leadership and to her conviction that Germany's debt to the Jewish people was permanent.

Several events the following year disrupted the thirty-two-year-old Angela's monotonous routine. For the first time, she was given permission to travel to the West, a sign that her cautious lifestyle had paid off. She visited Hamburg, her birthplace, for a cousin's wedding. She felt nervous. "I had travelled alone to Budapest, Moscow, Leningrad, and Poland, and yet this trip seemed different," Merkel recalled. She wasn't sure how even the most basic things were done in the West. For instance, "It wasn't clear to me if

---

*For several decades after the war, West Germany was similarly reluctant to confront its darkest history. Shocking as this sounds now, the country's first broad exposure to the Holocaust came from a fictional American television drama, *Holocaust*. As the ABC News correspondent in West Germany, I reported from Bonn in 1977 that the show "has been nothing short of a thunderbolt . . . an American TV series, seen by twenty million Germans, provoked a long-overdue national debate on the past. Foreign observers, this reporter included, have been astonished at the overwhelming reaction to the broadcast. As one German put it, "I don't feel personal guilt for all those things that I had nothing to do with. What I do feel now is shame."

a woman could simply book a room in a hotel. My anxiety may have had something to do with the crime shows I had watched on television," she said.

Instead of criminals, she encountered West Germany's high-speed transportation system. "What technological wonder!" she remarked later. The trains not only ran on time but also provided a smooth and pleasant ride. There was no way, she realized, the East could ever compete with such advanced technology. With her modest allowance of deutschmarks, Merkel purchased a few precious items of Western clothing, including "two shirts for my boyfriend." She returned from this adventure convinced that the German Democratic Republic was doomed.

The boyfriend, Joachim Sauer, was one reason Merkel returned to her seemingly dead-end life in East Berlin. "I think they were already in love by then," Schindhelm said. Sauer, five years Merkel's senior, was a distinguished quantum chemist still married to a fellow chemist. He and Angela had travelled to Prague together two years before, when she was a fellow at the J. Heyrovsky Institute of Physical Chemistry. According to Frank Schneider, still a zealous informer, the couple "had grown a bit close" in the Czech capital.

Sauer's marriage might have been effectively over, but his sons were twelve and fourteen; he couldn't attempt to steal out of the country and leave them behind. "I also did not want to go to prison in the East, unlike others, who were willing to risk that," Sauer admitted in a rare interview with the *Berliner Zeitung* newspaper in 2017. And so he and Angela stayed in East Berlin, accommodated to a system they abhorred but without ever crossing the line into collaboration, hoping but not yet knowing that this terrible existence of compromise and calculation would end in three years' time, when the Berlin Wall fell on a chilly night in November 1989.

In November 1989 West and East Berliners—Angela Merkel among them—surged around the suddenly opened wall that had divided the capital for nearly three decades. The union of the two Germanies was the transformative event in the life of Angela Merkel, enabling her to restart her life as a politician.

4

1989

I was never tired because it was all so incredibly exciting. . . . I had a great thirst for action.

—Angela Merkel

The Berlin Wall fell almost casually. With a single word, an East German government spokesman flung open the gates of the prison state.

When asked during a televised press conference if permission was still required to travel to the West, the spokesman replied matter-of-factly, "No." "Starting when?" came the incredulous follow up. "*Sofort*," he answered. "Immediately." *Sofort* became the word that turned a page in history. It may have been a single word uttered in the confusion and chaos of a crowded news conference, but months of mounting protests by captive populations from "Stettin on the Baltic, to Trieste on the Adriatic," to quote British prime minister Winston Churchill's unforgettable Iron Curtain speech of 1946— and with Mikhail Gorbachev's tacit support—finally broke open the dam.[*]

[*]It must be added that "Trieste on the Adriatic" was, by 1989, part of Yugoslavia, which, while still a one-party Communist dictatorship—under nationalist Josip Broz Tito—had long since broken from Moscow's rule.

"I called my mother when I heard," Angela would reflect later. "We always had a saying at home: 'If the wall should ever fall, we'll go to the Kempinski for oysters'"—Kempinski being West Berlin's most luxurious hotel. "I told my mother, 'The time has come.' Then I went to the sauna," just as she did every Thursday. (Germans, East and West, love a good sauna, and, in the East, it was one of a few sybaritic pleasures still available under Communism). The East German physicist was not one to get carried away, even as the tectonic plates of history shifted beneath her.

After the sauna, but skipping her usual beer at the nearby pub (where her photograph still hangs over the bar), Merkel joined exuberant throngs at the Bornholmer Bridge, surging toward the long-forbidden West. The way she tells the story, "I met a few people, and at some point, we were all sitting in the apartment of a happy West German family. Everybody wanted to go to the Ku'damm," West Berlin's most fashionable boulevard, the Kurfurstendamm. But Angela, ever practical even in the midst of history in the making, decided to head home. "I had to get up early the next morning," she explained. "And this much foreign company was enough for the time being." For Angela Merkel, having spent her entire life on the wrong side of the wall, West Berliners were foreigners.

Angela's first glimpse of West Berlin was a shock. When she did get around to visiting the Kurfurstendamm, the glittering shops and sleek, new apartment buildings—without a trace of war damage—dazzled the young woman. Equally disorienting was the speed with which events around her were spinning. A state enforced by hundreds of thousands of uniformed and plainclothes agents had collapsed like a sandcastle overnight. Angela, who had long dreamed of travelling to the West, suddenly saw unexpected and still vague possibilities shimmering before her. Given her upbringing, however, she was also cautious.

In the days and weeks that followed, no one—not in Moscow, not in

Washington, DC, and, most of all, not in the once-powerful East German Communist Party politburo—could envision the future. Would the so-called German Democratic Republic survive? No shots had been fired, no arrests made, no curfews imposed, no tear gas or tanks released to contain the crowds protesting against the Stasi state in East German cities, particularly in Leipzig and East Berlin, emboldened by their new freedom. For once, the regime issued no stern televised warnings to the population to beware of Western "saboteurs" in their midst; none of the familiar techniques to "restore order" were imposed. With each day, fear dissipated along with the smashed slabs of concrete that had once comprised the Antifascist Protection Rampart. In the ultimate sign that anything was now possible, bananas were suddenly available in East German grocery stores.

It was a thrilling but uncertain time, and yet apart from a few jaunts through West Berlin, Merkel's life continued almost as normal. "A few days after the fall of the wall, I went to a science conference in Poland. There, someone said that the next step would be German unity. That amazed me! I had not thought that far ahead," Merkel admitted. But by late 1989, her job as a theoretical researcher at the academy struck her as increasingly meaningless. Her career as a physicist had been a safe outlet for her inquiring mind, but in this new era of freedom, she had little interest in spending her days cooped up in a lab. "What I disliked was not having a chance to speak to people during the day," she would say later. She began thinking about her new life and a new occupation.

Within weeks, the Western nations, led by US president George H. W. Bush and his secretary of state, James A. Baker, took charge of the historic merger of the two Germanies. Unification would be based on West German chancellor Helmut Kohl's plan, which included elections in the East open to all parties, not merely Communists, and the dismantling of the East's centrally planned economy. Like many marriages, the union of East and West turned out to be more complex than had been anticipated during those exhilarating, early days.

Euphoria is not a sustainable emotion; reality could not match four decades of dreams about freedom and the West. The habits of obedience, distrust, austerity, and loss of personal initiative were not easily shed. Acts of betrayal, both trivial and consequential—covert services in exchange for admission to university, an apartment, or a job—marred much of the population's permanent record and stained its conscience. Because universities, health care, hospitals, factories, and cultural life were all state run in East Germany, almost 40 percent of the people had been directly part of the system. A generation of Germans had been brainwashed into thinking they were part of the first country of "peasants and workers" on German ground. Suddenly they were told they were no different from the people inhabiting that *other* Germany.

"We were refugees," said Michael Schindhelm, "without having fled our country." East Germans were required to accept a cascade of alien practices and priorities, from health care (no longer state provided and free), to education (based on competition and merit, not devotion to Marxism-Leninism and a "proletarian" background), to social life, to rock groups. They even lost Pittiplatsch and Schnatterinchen, beloved puppets on a children's television show that were moved back and forth on a piece of green felt using wires. The West was supposed to be freer, but the Federal Republic of Germany struck many from the East as overregulated. In the East, you could park wherever you found a place—and not pay. You could move into an unclaimed apartment. *Ossis,* as people from the East were informally known, suddenly felt like the poor cousins: clumsy, slow moving, provincial.

The speed of change was disorienting—and sometimes even disturbing. On October 3, 1990, at a special celebration of unification, a jubilant

Angela Merkel bounded up the steps of the Berlin Philharmonic's concert hall, glimpsed a policeman wearing the uniform of the newly unified state, and froze. "To me, he looked like an East German, suddenly wearing a different uniform. I felt the same when I saw certain people wearing the Bundeswehr [West German armed forces] uniform. Yesterday they were still part of the East German army. I still recognized them as such. Do the West Germans know what kind of people they will be living with side by side in one country? Do they understand the difference between the East Germans and themselves?" she wondered. She feared that the West did not fully comprehend the cruelty of the system and how it had hardened its most loyal servants—now citizens, and even policemen, of an open, liberal West.

Angela Merkel was keen to understand and overcome those differences. Volker Schlöndorff, an Oscar-winning film director, was among her first friends in the West. They met at a Berlin dinner party and struck up an immediate friendship—so much so that she soon invited Volker to her country home. "I remember a long walk near her dacha, where we roamed across an open field," Schlöndorff recalled. Interrogating each other about their lives soon thereafter, Merkel told him cheerfully, "We can learn to be like *you*. But you can never figure *us* out. Because our master [she used the German word, *Lehrmeister*] is dead." She was referring, of course, to Marx, Lenin, Stalin, and the rest of Communism's fallen idols, and she seemed pleased by the revelation. We will always be inscrutable to you, she implied, but you are transparent to us.

Within weeks of unification, the East German economy crumbled, and a third of East Germans were suddenly unemployed—as the dilapidated factories and run-down businesses of a centrally planned economy were unable to compete in the free market. Reflecting on this tumultuous time, Lothar de Maizière, East Germany's transitional prime minister from April to October 1990, said, "I always say that we have a ten-ten generation:

people who were ten years too old to relaunch their careers when the wall fell, but ten years too young to retire. They were the 'leftovers.'"

Angela Merkel was determined not to be a leftover. "We in the East decided voluntarily to join the Federal Republic of Germany," she told Herlinde Koelbl, a well-known German photographer who began taking photos of Merkel in 1991 and, over the next seven years, gained the future chancellor's trust. "The reasons were simple and convincing: the economic and political order in the West was more successful, efficient, and reasonable, and on top of that, freer. No ands, ifs, or buts. We wanted to join this system." She was impatient with those *Ossis* who were less nimble, less adaptable than she herself.

"I am sometimes shocked," she said, "how comfortable some people in East Germany feel, as if they should still be taken care of . . . without an awareness that East Germany was economically ruined. . . . For [many East Germans] nothing has changed, except maybe they took down Honecker's picture." Erich Honecker, the much-loathed longtime head of the East German Communist Party, resigned just two months before the dismantling of the Berlin Wall. Merkel, then thirty-five, was more emotionally and intellectually prepared than most. Unlike many of her fellow countrymen, she had never fully resigned herself to the Stasi state. Long before November 1989, she had decided that a system based on fear and the total surveillance of its own people could not survive long—it was just a question of time.

Her time had arrived.

Merkel's entrance into politics in December 1989 was low-key. Many East Germans who had kept their heads down for forty years of Communist oppression following twelve years of Nazi terror were now eager to form or join new political parties, Merkel among them. "I knew that the time had come to become active politically," she said. Bored in her dead-end laboratory job, she was no doubt exhilarated by the prospect of helping to shape the future of her newly liberated country, combined with a more adventure-some life for herself.

She'd had her fill of socialist experiments, so the West German Social Democratic Party was out. "They were too ideological for me," she said. And, though she would never say so publicly, choosing a more right-leaning party may have been another way of declaring her independence from her socialist father.

One of the new East German parties was the Demokratischer Aufbruch (DA), which would soon merge with the powerful West German Christian Democratic Union (CDU). The DA was mostly male, Catholic, and conservative, but Angela liked the serious-minded, nonideological people she met there. They struck her as less dogmatic and more open to ideas than the socialists. She also liked the party's name, which translated as Democratic Awakening.

"I remember well when Angela came to our first meeting," said Andreas Apelt, a DA leader. "She was very reserved, very modest, and looked younger than thirty-five. She wore a shapeless corduroy skirt and sort of Jesus sandals. Her hair was cut in a Dutch boy bob." As would be repeated throughout her political life, Merkel saw an opening and seized it. Noticing sealed crates in the corner of the DA's modest office, the scientist rolled up her sleeves and assembled the party's first computers. Observing her, the neophyte East German politicians were impressed and offered her a seat at the table. "Angela said she worked for the Academy of Sciences. She never mentioned that she had a doctorate. At first she only listened." Apelt recalled. When she returned a few days later, she joined in the conversation. Angela Merkel was smitten by politics.

Her life in the sciences was over. "I had been a good physicist, but not an outstanding one who would ever win a Nobel Prize," she reflected later. The comment is revealing: she wanted to pursue only a field in which she could reach the very top—and was prepared to wait decades to get there.

Yet her years in science had not been wasted: "My thinking was shaped by a scientific education," she would say. "I try to bring rational thinking to any debate. This surprised some men who like to say that women aren't capable of this."

By the spring of 1990, Merkel had formally resigned from her position at the academy to work full-time in politics. Having observed her methodical approach and calm in chaos, Apelt asked Angela to be the DA's spokesperson—dealing with the press, shaping the party's messaging, and briefing its leaders on press coverage. "Her response surprised me: 'I have to think about it first,' she told me." Angela Merkel refuses to be rushed. At the same time, Apelt noted that once she was on board, "If you told Merkel you needed something by seven o'clock tomorrow, it would be on your desk at six fifty-nine."

Another pattern soon emerged in Merkel's political ascent. Over the course of the 1990s, powerful men—her mentors included—would fall by the wayside while she plowed ahead. And although she may not have torched her rivals directly, she also never ran for the firehose as they were self-immolating. She stood back and waited. Though cautious by nature, she would soon reveal an instinct for a bold move when things opened up.

Chancellor Helmut Kohl smiles benignly at his protégé—whom he called his *Mädchen*—at a CDU Party conference in December 1991 in Dresden. In choosing her as his minister for women and youth and then as minister for the environment, Kohl, more than anyone else, launched her political ascent.

5

THE APPRENTICE

Angela and I weren't so different politically. That which really differenti-
ated us is her background. She is from the East.

—Former British prime minister Tony Blair

During the period following reunification, Angela Merkel benefitted enormously from being a woman from the East, at a time when Chancellor
Helmut Kohl needed to fold both categories of people into the leadership
of the new Federal Republic of Germany. Very few other East German politicians were female, and none were as single minded, ambitious, and canny
as Angela Merkel. Her political rise would be fueled by self-control, strategic thinking, and, when necessary, passive aggression.

Luck, too, played a role in her success, but good fortune always found
her well prepared. Merkel would have three East German mentors, all male,
who each fell victim to rumors of previous Stasi connections or corruption.
Their demise cleared her path as the *Ossi* best positioned for a bright political future in the West.

The Stasi took down her first two party chiefs. First, the cofounder of the
Democratic Awakening, Wolfgang Schnur, a well-known East German

civil rights lawyer, was exposed as having been a Stasi informer. His fellow DA leaders, shocked at Schnur's betrayal, panicked and feared that in this fevered environment—with new freedoms literally exploding—they, too, might be exposed as onetime informants or for some long forgotten act of carelessness. While Angela's political elders wrung their hands, the new press spokesperson stayed calm and coolly evicted Western journalists from the DA's headquarters, so that the new party could put out its first political fire behind closed doors.

Next to go was a man who really did not deserve the political beheading. Lothar de Maizière, a well-known and popular figure in East German reformist circles, was a professional violist from a distinguished Huguenot—originally French Protestant—family. Merkel was only a few months into her job as DA spokesperson, when de Maizière offered her the position of deputy spokesperson of East Germany's first and last democratically elected government. Today his Berlin office is crammed with mementoes of German unification, in which he played a historic role. Photographs and menus signed by George H. W. Bush, Helmut Kohl, and Mikhail Gorbachev line his walls.

"When I made her the offer, Angela told me she was going to London for the weekend and would let me know after she returned," he recalled. Merkel was making up for lost time. She had fantasized about visiting London on one of her trips to Budapest; standing in front of the sprawling Hungarian parliament, she conjured up Westminster Palace. De Maizière and her next step up the political ladder could wait until after the weekend.

Of course, she accepted de Maizière's offer—in hindsight, an especially wise move, given that in October 1990 the Democratic Awakening Party merged with the CDU—and proved adept in her new role. Unlike most politicians, Angela spoke to the press with scientific precision and in easy-to-understand sentences. "She hardly used adjectives and said things as they were, without flourishes. She presented twice as much information as her colleagues," praised de Maizière. A scientist who spoke plainly was indeed a treasure, and the fact that she crammed her briefings with a great deal of information was also a plus, particularly for an East German public hungry for facts. "What surprised me later was her assertiveness," de Maizière said. "That, I did not expect." Nor did the mentor count on cold political calculation from his protégé.

By late 1990, rumors swirled that Lothar de Maizière, too, had been a Stasi informer; the stories were false, but they would soon end his political career. "It was Merkel who got rid of me when things got difficult," de Maizière noted bitterly—quite an exaggeration, although his protégé did not leap to his defense when he was under fire. The young woman from the East demonstrated an unsentimental streak that would speed her ascent.

De Maizière was all the more shocked by her lack of staunch support considering that, shortly prior to his own fall from grace, he had helped ensure Angela Merkel's political future. Helmut Kohl, then in his eighth year as chancellor, approached de Maizière "wanting to fill a 'soft' Cabinet position with an East German woman, whom he named. 'That woman is not qualified,' I told him, 'Pick Dr. Merkel. She is the most intelligent.'" Kohl soon followed de Maizière's advice.*

And so, on January 18, 1991, only a year after she'd sauntered into the cluttered offices of a political start-up in her East Berlin neighborhood and offered to assemble the computers, Angela Merkel took her place in the Cabinet of Helmut Kohl, chancellor of a newly united Federal Republic of

---

*Kohl was a historic figure who ruled supremely over Germany from 1982 to 1998 and over the Christian Democrats for even longer (1973 until 1998). Strongly pro-American, his friendship with President Bill Clinton was as real as it was high in calories. (Their Italian dinners out in Washington, DC, were a favorite subject of journalists in the 1990s). Both were, in some ways, good old boys. I recall my husband, Richard Holbrooke, ambassador to Germany in the early Clinton years, telling me of Kohl's ribald anecdotes when in all-male company.

Germany. He had appointed her as minister for women and youth—"two subjects Angela really did not care about at all," de Maizière noted wryly.

The youngest and least experienced member of Kohl's Cabinet was aware of the tokenism that had gotten her there. "This would not have happened if I had grown up in West Germany with the same capabilities," she admitted, as clear eyed and analytical about herself as about others. Nor would Merkel waste the opportunity.

Bonn, a small town on the Rhine River most notable for being the birthplace of composer Ludwig van Beethoven, was chosen as the postwar West German capital partly due to its proximity to the home of Konrad Adenauer, the Federal Republic's first chancellor, from 1949 to 1963. With the historic capital of Berlin under partial Soviet occupation, Bonn had the provisional feel of a capital in exile. Angela Merkel's base between 1990 and 1998, Bonn was an unapologetically masculine environment. Its prevalent color was gray: the Rhine, the coldly modern office buildings, and the men's suits were all the same shade. Women were assistants to the (male) government officials, diplomats, and journalists who filled the halls, cafeterias, and three decent restaurants (two Italian, and one French). During the nineties, to be a young woman in a nonservice job in Bonn was to feel perpetually self-conscious.* Though Merkel had often been the lone woman among academics and scientists in the East, politics in the West played out in an atmosphere where intelligence and hard work, were, in Merkel's words, "no match for a male voice and physical size."

Merkel's apartment in a four-story building faced the Siebengebirge, the mountain range that rises above the Rhine, and the famous hill known

---

*Out of Kohl's 17 Cabinet members, there were only 2—sometimes 3—women, including Angela Merkel. In the Bundestag, women held 20 percent of the seats, or 136 out of 662, in the same period, 1990 to 1995. Women today make up roughly one-third of the Bundestag.

as Drachenfels (Dragon Rock). The freshly anointed minister was rarely home in time to enjoy the view, however, as she applied herself to mastering a new profession and a new identity.

Merkel had admirers already. Former American secretary of state Henry Kissinger called on her when she joined Kohl's Cabinet. "Angela was amazed that someone of 'my renown,' as she put it, would visit her. I told her I was interested in how someone whose formation and formative years were in the East would perform in the West," Kissinger said. The pair became fast friends. In addition to their shared love of German *kultur*—the great writers, philosophers, and composers on whom they were raised—the planet's two most famous Germans share an understanding of the tragic components to life. Kissinger's Jewish family was forced into exile by the Nazis, while Merkel's youth under the Stasi regime pushed her into a form of internal exile, with science serving as her refuge. Both had to reinvent themselves in strange new lands: Kissinger in America, Merkel in the former West Germany. But while Kissinger's sense of tragedy made him the pessimistic prophet of Realpolitik, Merkel's led her to a determined optimism.

Kissinger recognized something different about his new mentee. "She has never fallen into the trap of most German politicians, who play games and talk only to each other," he said. Kissinger took it upon himself to introduce her to influential Americans but did not envision a great future for the plain-looking scientist-turned-politician without much charisma. No one else did either, except perhaps Angela Merkel herself. In June 2005 she approached Tony Blair, who was visiting Berlin, and went straight to the point.

"I have the following problems: I am a woman, I have no charisma, and I'm not good at communicating." Merkel was seeking the British prime minister's advice on how to compensate for those deficits. At the same time, Blair's chief of staff recalled, "She was confident she would win."

• • •

As Germany's youngest minister in history at the age of just thirty-six—and a woman from the East, to boot—Merkel knew that all eyes were on her. But even for someone as avid to learn new ways as Merkel, the passage from East to West Germany was sometimes rough.

Angela was particularly shocked at the attention focused on her appearance. In East Germany, there were few outlets for vanity. "Fashion" was not really on offer in the Peoples' Department stores, which generally featured two new styles of coats per season. The population may have been shabby, but they were uniformly so. Suddenly Angela's unfashionable haircuts, flat shoes, and shapeless coats were all scrutinized. The only other East German in Kohl's Cabinet, Paul Krüger, the new minister of research and technology, recalled, "I had noticed Angela at political events and was struck by how little she cared about her appearance. That was striking. And yet she had *presence*. It's hard to explain this, but from the outset, I had the feeling that she was different. She had an authority." *Mehr sein als schein*— to *be* more than to be *seen to be*—was one of Angela's Lutheran edicts; now that was being challenged by the demands of her new profession, which put a premium on appearance. De Maizière and, later, Helmut Kohl, pleaded with their female assistants (and, in Kohl's case, his wife) to work on Merkel's nonexistent fashion sense. "Angela dressed like a student in those days: sandals, baggy pants," de Maizière recalled. Before their first official trip to Moscow, he asked his office manager, "Please talk to Dr. Merkel. I can't travel with her if she looks like that." When Merkel showed up in a new outfit for the trip, he attempted to encourage her, saying, "Wow! You look great, Angela!" Instead of seeming pleased by the compliment, "She turned beet red. The entire situation was very embarrassing for her." The challenges of the situation were summed up in a lame joke that made the rounds back in the 1990s:

"What does Merkel do with her old clothes?"

"She wears them."

"For a man, it's no problem at all to wear a dark-blue suit a hundred days in a row," Merkel grumbled. "But if I wear the same jacket four times, I receive letters from citizens. . . . I once had a photographer lying under the table to take a picture of my crooked heels." But, as always, she adapted. Merkel made her appearance a nonstory by building a wardrobe that was her equivalent of a man's dark suit: a closetful of boxy, colorful jackets designed by a reputable Hamburg fashion house, comfortable black pants, and black flats. Eventually she even accepted the daily intervention of a hair stylist as part of the price of doing her job. Her old friend Michael Schindhelm recalled his surprise at once seeing Merkel wearing a dirndl—the frilly, full-skirted Bavarian folk costume—at the Salzburg Music Festival. "Angela, that's the first time I've ever seen you in a dress!" he exclaimed, to Merkel's visible discomfort.

Nevertheless, when British diplomat Paul Lever complimented her on the glamourous evening gown she wore to the Oslo Opera House, saying, "Madame Chancellor, you look great!" Merkel seemed pleased, and went into some detail regarding the dress and its designer. However, the media's excited coverage of her departure from her predictable "uniform" discouraged her from ever wearing the dress again.

Merkel also struggled with other aspects of public presentation; what to do with her hands when she stood at a lectern, for instance. She understood that her fidgeting sent the wrong message. After trial and error, she landed on the "Merkel rhombus": fingertips pressed together in what has since become her signature. (Years later, her party would use the emoticon in political campaigns, along with the slogan "Germany's future in good hands.")

Despite such awkwardness, there was a widespread feeling in Bonn in the nineties that the young woman from the East was rising too fast—indeed, a Cabinet post within a year of entering politics was unusual, to say the least. Chancellor Kohl had begun treating her as a protégé, which disturbed others in his circle as well as those in the CDU who regarded her as an unwelcome and unqualified interloper from the East who had not earned her political stripes. Who would stop her was a topic of after-hours conversations in the capital's political watering holes. Merkel was oblivious to the fact that twelve promising young men in her party had created a "working group" from which women (a rare species in the CDU hierarchy) were excluded. Called the Andes Pact, the men—all from rich, industrial German *Länder* (states)—pledged to support one another's rise, a pointed reminder that women were unwelcome in the party's higher echelons.

Wise enough to build her own base independent of powerful male patrons, she campaigned for and won a seat in the Bundestag, the German federal parliament (though not a requirement for a cabinet position, most ministers are members of the Bundestag), representing the formerly East German region of Mecklenburg Vorpommern. The path had been cleared for her by Gunther Krause, a prominent local politician who also fell from grace as a result of his Stasi connections. Though Merkel wasn't from the rugged Baltic region, while campaigning, she gamely knocked back shots of the local schnapps with fishermen and won support with her simple affect and youthful optimism. As a campaigner, she did not patronize or pretend to have all the answers, but mostly listened, sympathized, and expressed herself in her characteristic plain style, convincing locals that she was one of *them.* They reelected her their representative in every federal election since 1990.

Merkel may not have been aware of a secret network of CDU men seeking to outshine her and may have appeared to be the wide-eyed innocent, but she was increasingly alert to the danger. "[I]f someone rises faster than normal, greed and envy soon rear their heads," she noted in 1991. "You are under close scrutiny, and every little mistake will be registered and followed by a sharp reaction." She resented the idea that Kohl gave her special treatment and bridled at the frequent references to her as his *Mädchen,* or young lady. "I find it annoying, to put it mildly. Our relationship . . . is not characterized by continuous goodwill. Kohl carefully and critically observes my work," she insisted.

She did admit, however, that it was the German chancellor who launched her on the world stage by taking her to America in 1991, where he introduced Merkel to her hero Ronald Reagan. (By then, sadly, the former president was much diminished by Alzheimer's disease.) Her first time in the White House, then occupied by George H. W. Bush, "there was a look of wonderment on her face when she shook hands with the president in the Cabinet Room," recalled Robert Kimmitt, the US ambassador to Germany at the time.

On that trip, Kohl asked Merkel how he was regarded by East Germans. Not willing to be "inauthentic"—a sin by her lights—Merkel resisted the easy appeal of flattery. She admitted that, after years of propaganda, they generally saw him as a cartoonish figure—depicted as a pear-shaped capitalist with Uncle Sam propping him up.* Authenticity was more important to her than stroking needy egos. She wasn't much good at faking emotions, nor interested in learning how.

She *was* interested, however, in doing the opposite: it was during those sometimes rocky early years that Merkel mastered steely composure. On a trip to Israel in the spring of 1991, she was all but ignored by her hosts, who assumed she was a ministerial assistant. Some in the media reported on her tears of frustration. "I have to be tougher," she acknowledged to Herlinde Koelbl at the time.

If the trip to Israel started with tears, Merkel recalled how differently it ended, with a visit to a monastery on the Sea of Galilee:

---

*There was nothing subtle about Kremlin-inspired propaganda: my Budapest kindergarten teacher taught me an untranslatable Hungarian ditty, which I can still recite, depicting US president Dwight Eisenhower as a human time bomb ready to explode.

"We stood overlooking the countryside with its hills. We saw the ground where the Sea of Galilee is located. Then a monk said, 'This is where Jesus came down the hill, and, at this lake, Jesus met Peter, the fisherman. . . . And a bit farther, he fed the five thousand, and then he had the experience with the storm.' I am familiar with the Bible and with what happened at the Sea of Galilee. But to hear someone simply assert that this is what happened, right here, was something quite startling."

Searching for grounding amid disorienting change, Merkel found inspiration at the Sea of Galilee. "I am not always clear and sure in my faith. I sometimes have doubts," she admitted, unusual for a politician. But there, by the Sea of Galilee, in a monastery where Benedictine brothers worked with youth with disabilities, she found the monk she was speaking with "had a source of strength in his difficult work that I envied."

As chancellor, Merkel would return many times to Israel, making the still-fraught topic of the German-Jewish relationship one of the core issues of her administration—and one of the foundations of modern Germany. But on this first trip, it was inner strength she sought. In the space of two years, the ground had shifted beneath her. She had transformed herself—as her country had been transformed. Now her ambition needed a stronger anchor. Her private faith, and the Bible, would steady her sometimes rocky path.

Germany, the heavily armed frontier between East and West, had long stood at the epicenter of America's effort to avert nuclear Armageddon. In the 1990s, under Chancellor Kohl, the country enjoyed a breathing spell after years of high tension. With unification achieved, Germany felt safe as part of a network of postwar institutions that bound it to the United States and, beginning in 1993, to the new European Union. The Atlantic alliance enjoyed its peak years, embodied by the warm friendship between Helmut Kohl and Bill Clinton—two men of remarkably similar gifts and vulnerabilities. Kohl's goal was the merger of East and West Germany into a single nation—in more than name. When Clinton and Kohl walked together through the Brandenburg Gate from West to East Berlin on a cloudless day in July 1994, it seemed the perfect finale to the high drama of the last fifty years: the Berlin Airlift in 1948, when the United States airlifted food, water, and medicine to the desperate citizens of the besieged city in response to a Soviet blockade; the building of the wall, and the confrontation between American and Soviet tanks at Checkpoint Charlie in 1961; President Kennedy's *"Ich bin ein Berliner"* address in 1963; and Ronald Reagan's plea "Mr. Gorbachev, tear down this wall!" in June 1987. Under Kohl, Germany became Europe's largest country and soon the Continent's economic powerhouse.

Angela Merkel, the most prominent East German in Kohl's government, was part of the chancellor's plan to merge the two parts into a whole. Stefan Kornelius, the author of an early political biography of Merkel, noted that Kohl treated her as "a kind of trophy" of German unification. What the garrulous and normally shrewd Kohl did not calculate was that his "trophy" had plans and ambitions of her own and was willing to bide her time to realize them.

As minister for women and youth, Merkel broke no ground, but she proved a supple, nonideological politician able to compromise on controversial matters. For instance, regarding abortion, she opposed legalizing it, but was in favor of decriminalizing it. She often kept her own rather conservative views to herself and basically punted on the issue.

With Markel having demonstrated her capacity for hard word, loyalty, and discretion, Kohl soon offered her the more prestigious environment portfolio in 1994. Instead of an immediate, enthusiastic "Yes!" for this obvious promotion, Angela once again requested time to think it over. For several weeks, she kept the news to herself—a departure from Bonn's general political custom of self-promotion. Kohl wondered if she was actually even interested. But Merkel was merely attempting to get a feel for what lay ahead for her in such a high-profile position. Championing the government's relatively new environmental protection policies in the industrial powerhouse of Europe was far from a "quota Frau" responsibility.

Merkel had long been determined not to be pigeonholed into any fixed identity: neither *Ossi nor Wessi* (as Germans from the West are known). She also resisted the "Frau" label, as she felt that aspect of her identity was self-evident. In May 1993 she found a way to make clear that she was fundamentally, if quietly, a feminist. In a book review of Susan Faludi's *Backlash: The Undeclared War Against American Women* for a mainstream German woman's journal, she wrote:

> As long as women aren't represented in leadership positions, in the media, in political parties, in interest groups, in business, as long as they don't belong to the ranks of top fashion designers, and top chefs, role models for women will be determined by men. . . . What are my chances of getting married if I'm in a leadership position? What are my chances of having a miscarriage? How will my children suffer if I try to combine career and family? These questions are discussed time and again using negative examples that discourage women. It's the attempt by men to keep positions they currently occupy. . . . In my opinion, equality means the equal right for women to shape their own lives.

There is nothing ambiguous about this: Angela Merkel was a feminist. Nevertheless, she would face criticism over the years from those who felt she was insufficiently committed to the advancement of women—that she was too low-key in her advocacy. Though she bristles at sexist humor, she would not embarrass the joke teller in public. "I give him an angry look, and, later, when we are alone, I'll tell him that was not okay," she once said, explaining her strategy. She insisted that her most powerful weapon against sexism was achieving success in her own life, as a spur for others to follow.

Her approach to leadership—in this and other areas—does not lean heavily on the bully pulpit.

Now, as minister of the environment, Merkel had to master German politics and media relations under a far more relentless glare than before. With just two years' experience in government, she was aware of rumors circulating in the capital that she was simply not up to the job. "Why Angela?" some wondered out loud. Her English isn't good enough to face international audiences, her rivals groused. She soon silenced that particular rumor by taking evening English classes. Then, six weeks into the job, she fired her much-respected second in command, Clemens Stroetmann. Bonn was a small town, and the environmentalist had been too vocal regarding Merkel's dependence on him to run the department. Whatever Stroetmann's qualifications, her decision demonstrated that the new minister was not afraid to wield power.

Photographs of Merkel from those days often show a smiling woman, looking much younger than her forty years, gazing at politicians long since forgotten, who often have one arm draped casually around the young minister's shoulder. She may be smiling, but she was also analyzing them, working out which of them was successful at his job, and why. She had to learn to control her low tolerance for blustering male peacocks. "I often feel physically bothered in the presence of men, for whom the discussion isn't about facts but only who can threaten the other more effectively," she admitted. That was something else she'd learn to hide.

It wasn't easy being minister for environment of an industrial giant such as Germany. "I am often in the firing line, from the packing industry, the states, the Bundestag, and, of course, the economists who know everything better! I have the EU, and the monopolies, and mergers commission, and the Constitutional Court on top of it. For one side, the regulations aren't enough; for the other side, too much; the third side doesn't want any regulation at all; the fourth wants it all. In such a situation, it isn't easy to get up in a good mood in the morning," she said, summarizing her tough new portfolio. As usual, she walked a tightrope—in search of consensus—sometimes succeeding, sometimes not.

In one particularly frustrating Cabinet meeting, Merkel inadvertently provided her detractors something to savor with their evening stein of beer: she allowed tears to flow. "It might have been better to shout, like the men," she admitted later. The issue that had provoked such emotion was air quality. "Summer was coming, and they wanted to send me out for another round of talks, to god, and the world! I knew exactly how this would end. So, I simply stated that . . . many parents had the impression that they couldn't send their children out to play, that people were afraid, and demanded action." Her tears of frustration shocked the Cabinet into action, passing a set of tough clean air regulations. Her outburst, born of exhaustion and frustration, was a human reaction to the Cabinet's evasive and rather belittling behavior—endlessly dispatching her on useless public relations exercises—but it worked. It was, however, the last time she was seen crying in the Cabinet.

Social Democratic Party leader Gerhard Schröder, who would succeed Kohl as chancellor, sometimes baited her on various issues, calling her "not commanding, pathetic." Schröder was playing hardball politics, but, instead of tears, Merkel responded with anger and defiance. "I told him that the time would come when I would put him in a corner too," she told Koelbl. "I still need time for that. But I'm looking forward to it." The once timid and somewhat bewildered *Mädchen* from the East was learning fast.

Avid to master the ways of the West, and eager for role models outside of Kohl's Cabinet, Merkel reached out to statesmen well beyond the Rhine. "She asked me a lot of questions about the workings of the British political system," said Paul Lever, British ambassador to Germany from 1997 to 2003, "about how much time British ministers spend in their constituencies, about the relationship between the prime minister and the backbench MPs [members of Parliament]. I sensed that she was preparing herself for an international role."*

"Hers was a blend of curiosity and purposeful ambition," recalled American ambassador Robert Kimmitt. Merkel invited him and his wife to her and Joachim's modest country house in Uckermark, where, after a lunch of goulash prepared by Angela, the two couples set off for a hike. "In what struck me as a preplanned move, Joachim took my wife one way, while Angela and I continued another way. For the next couple of hours, she questioned me. 'Tell me about NATO.' 'What is US's role in various security arrangements?'—the sort of questions anyone who had spent their lives in the East wouldn't have access to but would need in the next step up the political ladder," Kimmitt said. It was obvious to him that a small town on the Rhine was not going to be Merkel's final destination.

For all Angela's frustrations during her four years as minister for the environment, there were also triumphs. In 1995 the formerly sheltered Eastern bloc scientist stood beneath an enormous blue globe and welcomed more than one thousand delegates from 160 nations to Berlin's Natural History Museum for a historic United Nations Climate Conference. Former Colorado senator Timothy Wirth, head of the American delegation, admitted that his first reaction upon meeting Merkel was, "Well, Chancellor Kohl checked off a lot of boxes when he picked this dowdy woman from the East!" After a few days of observing her, though, Wirth changed his tune.

*In September 2001 Schlöndorff arranged for Merkel to meet Richard Holbrooke— then US ambassador to the United Nations (and my husband)—who had recently negotiated an end to the war in Bosnia. I joined Richard for the meeting, my first encounter with the future chancellor. As it happened, the writer Susan Sontag was also part of this lunch at Schlöndorff's home. Sontag and Merkel were a study in contrasts: Sontag, expansive; Merkel, the active listener.

Merkel was still feeling her way, trying out her very basic English in small groups. When she addressed the audience of one thousand delegates, she spoke in German. As always, she reached out to those who could be helpful to her. Advised by a seasoned Indian delegate, Kamal Nath, she divided the delegations into teams of developing and developed countries, shuttling between the two. Undogmatic, she was bent on achieving results through compromise. For the first time, Merkel also demonstrated a quality that would be among her strengths as chancellor: phenomenal stamina. After a night of relentless diplomacy ending in the early morning hours, most delegates were reeling from exhaustion. Not Angela Merkel, who was ready to chair another session the next morning. The conference ultimately brought about an accord called the Berlin Mandate, which called on governments to establish specific, legally binding targets and timetables for reducing emissions of greenhouse gases. Two years later, this agreement led to the landmark Kyoto Protocol.

For Merkel, the Berlin Climate Conference was "one of my greatest achievements," although she typically backtracked to say, "Maybe we shouldn't call them *my* achievements. Let's call them experiences." Whatever the deliberately self-effacing Merkel called her debut on the world stage, she acknowledged, "For the first time, I had the opportunity to get to know the different cultures of the world and their various ways of working. I really came alive." Merkel also made many friends at that 1995 Climate Conference, establishing herself as a particular friend of the developing world, which would serve her well in the future. Her self-confidence was growing.

It is in small groups that Angela Merkel reveals a warmth she rarely displays in public. A few years after the Berlin Climate Conference, she asked the then US secretary of the Treasury, Henry "Hank" Paulson, to help prepare her for her first meeting with President George W. Bush. "I put together a high-powered group to meet her," Paulson recalled. "CEOs, bank presidents, financial leaders who got to ask her questions and vice versa. And she did this really endearing thing: she periodically squeezed my hand under the table when she was taking their questions. I've never forgotten that gesture." Paulson smiled at the memory of the supremely serious Merkel's unexpected warmth.

Merkel revealed other—tougher—qualities to Paulson, as they got to know each other. "I was having a hard time with her finance minister, Peer Steinbrück," he recalled. "Angela said, 'Look, we have a coalition government, and he's with the SPD and has a big ego and probably wants to be chancellor. So, just pay him a lot of attention, make a big fuss over him, listen to him, and things will get better.' Well, I did all those things, and she was right. Things did get better with the finance minister. Unlike most men, she does not try to dominate or score points, nor does she defer to others. I never saw a woman with her style: seeking consensus, playing her cards very close to the chest, but with strong convictions."

Lawrence Bacow, president of Harvard University, was similarly unprepared for the humanity the chancellor rarely shows in public. During their private conversation prior to Merkel's delivery of Harvard's June 2019 commencement address, she asked about his mother. Angela Merkel—as usual—had done her homework. She knew that Bacow's mother came from a small village outside Frankfurt. Many members of Bacow's family had been murdered during the Holocaust. Her hand on his arm, the chancellor asked if he had ever visited his mother's village. "Yes," Bacow replied, describing a painful encounter with the elderly woman who had lived in his family's former home since the Nazis seized it. "It was a very awkward visit," Bacow admitted to the chancellor.

"Is there any other way such a visit could have gone?" Merkel asked.

"She had clearly given a great deal of thought to the human cost of such an encounter," Bacow reflected. "She was obviously interested in both sides, and in the possibility of reconciliation. I was very touched by her interest and her genuine emotion."

Still, Merkel's natural warmth one-on-one doesn't prevent her from being tough when circumstances demand it. During her tenure as minister for the environment, the influential Cardinal Joachim Meisner of Cologne remarked to the tabloid *Bild*, "Apparently there is a female minister of the Christian faith who is living in sin." Merkel did not take kindly to the cardinal's public scolding. "I drove to his place and explained to him why I believe it is important to be *careful* if you've been married once," she said. She turned his attack to her advantage—as if she, not the cardinal, was the Lord's chastening servant.

And yet on December 30, 1998, the *Frankfurter Allgemeine Zeitung*, a high-circulation daily newspaper, published the following item, as terse as the couple themselves: "We have married, Angela Merkel and Joachim Sauer." The low-key ceremony reflected the couple's obsession with privacy, without even her parents or the groom's two sons in attendance. "We got married just when no one was expecting it anymore," Merkel said. Acting when no one is expecting it is her way. In doing so, Merkel, well aware that Germany remains a socially conservative society, cleared a potential obstacle toward her next step up the political ladder.

Once, when asked what she contributed to German political life, Merkel answered, "Someone who lived thirty-five years of her life in a system without freedom, and who therefore understands the unique value of freedom . . . the CDU would also be lacking someone who longs to experience the unexpected, to build bridges in society, who has an urge for change." The next stage of Merkel's ascent would not involve building bridges but rather burning one.

In 1998 Helmut Kohl was defeated in his fifth run for chancellor after sixteen years in power. The following year, he was caught in a financial scandal involving allegations of illegal and anonymous cash donations to his campaigns, stretching back to 1982. Though the Social Democrat Gerhard Schröder was the new chancellor, Kohl, still the powerful leader of the Christian Democrats, was stonewalling investigations by withholding his donors' names. It was "a matter of honor," he claimed.

Angela Merkel was by now a familiar figure in the CDU leadership, and, as a recent minister and member of the Bundestag, a fairly well-known politician. But both the party and Germany itself were about to learn that she was not exactly the accommodating *Mädchen* many had assumed her to be.

On December 2 Germans awoke to find a story headlined "Helmut Kohl's Actions Have Damaged the Party" in the *Frankfurter Allgemeine Zeitung*, under Angela Merkel's byline. "The King Is Dead, Long Live the Queen" might have served as an alternate headline. The article was as much of a shock to Merkel's former mentor and his likeliest heir, Wolfgang Schäuble, as it was to the entire German political class. Calling the scandal a "tragedy," Merkel made clear that her loyalty was not to one man but to the future of the party. "The time of Party Chairman Kohl is irreversibly over," she proclaimed coolly. Merkel implied audaciously that she was doing Kohl a favor by relieving him of the burden of power during his advanced years, writing, "The party needs to learn to walk, must dare to take on its political opponents without its Old Warhorse."

No one else in the party had had the courage to put down the "Old Warhorse" and thereby rescue the Christian Democrats. "Kohl's attitude was very David and Goliath," said Volker Schlöndorff, "as in, 'How dare this street kid throw a stone at me?'" Asked if she wasn't a little afraid of taking on such a daunting figure, Merkel replied with feigned incomprehension: "Why should I be afraid of him? We worked together for eight years." Her message: there are no giants among us, just politicians.

In daring to suggest that the CDU could get by without its chairman of more than twenty years, Merkel committed one of the boldest acts in contemporary German politics. For nearly a decade, her placid manner had lulled her colleagues into underestimating her capacity for guile. Now she had demonstrated that beneath her stolid façade lay a fierce will. For Merkel, writing the article was a necessary act of personal and political liberation. When asked about her motivations in later years, she was honest, explaining, "First and foremost, I wanted to get out of this captivity, to create space for myself."

In a stroke, Merkel's article also eliminated her probable competitor to lead the CDU: Schäuble, who had also been implicated in the slush fund scandal and who stayed loyal to Kohl. A brilliant and popular politician whose ministerial career began in 1984, Schäuble was known to be devoted to Kohl. In 1990, while attending a campaign rally, an assassin's bullet shattered Shäuble's spine. Kohl stood by him, while many in the CDU wrote off the wheelchair-bound Schäuble as too disabled for an active political life. Merkel had not warned him of her upcoming article denouncing their mutual chief and mentor, whom Schäuble had succeeded as CDU chairman. In the wake of the scandal, Schäuble, himself compromised, resigned that post.

With her newly acquired stature and proven courage, Merkel put herself forward for the CDU's chairmanship in early 2000 and was elected without opposition. Untouched by scandal, the forty-five-year-old physicist turned politician presented a fresh image and the chance for a new start for the post–Cold War Party. Liberated from Kohl, Merkel had become, for the first time, the master of her political destiny. Now she had to consolidate her grip on this party of conservative men.

On April 10, her first day as CDU chair, Angela Merkel strode into the conference room of the Bonn headquarters where the party leaders awaited her. Surveying the room, she requested that everyone stand up and disperse randomly around the long table where they had already settled. Her message was clear: Don't bother plotting against me. I'm watching you. This was Angela Merkel's party now.

That year, Berlin assumed its historic place as the Federal Republic's official capital. Merkel left the small town on the Rhine with few regrets. Bonn—provincial, conservative, predominantly male—had never really been her home. Relieved to be done with her political apprenticeship, she returned to a city familiar to her since her childhood visits to her grandmother in East Berlin. Not for her one of the city's elegant, leafy neighborhoods with their gracious mansions; not Grunewald or Dahlem or Charlottenburg. No, she and Joaquim settled in a modest apartment in the heart of the former East Berlin—across the street from the Pergamon Museum—territory as familiar to her as the Waldhof in Templin. Instead of the slow-moving Rhine, she now overlooked a city feverishly rebuilding to suit its new status as a world metropolis—its skyline crowded with cranes, the former no-man's-land with remnants of the hideous wall still visible here and there, and the war-scarred Reichstag still under construction. In Berlin, Angela Merkel felt at home, sure-footed and no longer in need of life lessons.

Devouring egos are generally slow to forgive injury. Helmut Kohl eventually reconciled with his protégé, however. By 2005, he would endorse Angela Merkel as candidate for chancellor. Four years later, Merkel paid Kohl a visit at his home for a ritual public burying of the hatchet. Regardless of their true feelings, they both knew the rules of politics, gamely hiding their disappointment and hurt. In 2012 US ambassador Philip Murphy hosted a small dinner in honor of the thirtieth anniversary of Kohl's ascension to office. Arriving to the dinner straight from a flight from China, Chancellor Merkel warmly toasted her former mentor. "As she spoke of her trip, I kept my eyes on Kohl. He had a proud, parental smile on his face," said former ambassador Kimmitt, who was also present. "But it was clear who was chancellor."

In 2014, on her sixtieth birthday, Kohl sent Merkel his double-edged greetings. "When you look back today, you can do so safe in the knowledge that you seized opportunities that your varied life has offered you," he wrote. Seizing opportunities was indeed her strength, and the Old Warhorse—from whom she had learned much about power—could not help but admire her for it.

Though Merkel often acknowledges Kohl's role in her life, she frames what she owes him as a political, not personal, debt. Merkel's greater debt was to the country that, in unification, gave her a second chance.

On November 22, 2005, Angela Merkel made history. This triple outsider—a woman, a scientist, and a German from the East—was sworn in as Germany's first woman chancellor, and her portrait hung alongside her male predecessors in the chancellery's portrait gallery.

6

TO THE CHANCELLERY
AT LAST

Germans wanted someone who wasn't looking in the mirror but looking
at their problems. She's perfected a style of politics where the focus is
not on her.

—Karl-Theodor von Guttenberg

I'm not good at speaking. I can only tell the truth.

—Socrates

In 2005, when Chancellor Gerhard Schröder called for early elections, no
one in the Christian Democratic Union seriously contested that Angela
Merkel's time had arrived. The once patriarchal party chose a pragmatic
leader who would maintain its centrist, moderate profile and strong transatlantic ties, yet offer a fresh start—and even a chance to make history as
the country's first woman chancellor. Germans liked her humility, her plain
but direct style, her absence of theatrics, and the fact that she had made
the transition from the East to the West with seeming ease. Little more was
really known about her beyond the remarkable sangfroid with which she
dispatched Kohl, who had let down both the party and the country. But

neither Merkel nor her rival—the moderately left of center Social Democrat, Gerhard Schröder—advocated a departure from Germany's polite politics of consensus. With its long history of anything but boring politics, boring was considered desirable in post–World War II Germany.

Based on polls in the weeks leading up to the September elections, a Merkel victory seemed ensured. She and her party were far ahead of the garrulous Schröder, despite the media's fondness for a leader who loved to share his private life with the press and made excellent copy. But the tide turned quickly, and she very nearly lost. In the process, Angela Merkel learned a valuable lesson about the importance of whom she chose to surround herself with—and to always keep one eye on the mood of the country she was determined to lead.

The problem had to do with taxes. During her campaign, Merkel picked as her future finance minister Paul Kirchhof, a professor of jurisprudence at the famed Heidelberg University. Kirchhof, a politically tone-deaf academic, advocated for all Germans to pay the same level of income tax,* a generally unpopular idea that gave the struggling Chancellor Schröder some badly needed ammunition. Merkel, Schröder proclaimed, was an out-of-touch conservative radical who would deliver a fatal blow to Germany's economy. Soon, Merkel's lead shrank from double digits to single numbers.

Germany has a parliamentary system of government, with citizens voting for the legislators who will represent them in Berlin; those legislators then choose the chancellor. The party with the most votes forms a coalition with the next highest vote-getting party or parties, in complicated negotiations for distributing ministries in the Cabinet that can take weeks and sometimes even months. On election night in 2005, Schröder's and Merkel's parties were in a virtual tie—neither had won the necessary

---

*The German tax system operates a progressive tax rate in which taxes increase with taxable income.

majority to be declared chancellor without forming a coalition with the other. The election was simply too close to call. Following a German ritual for candidates, they met on TV that evening to submit to a journalistic grilling before setting off to try to form a coalition. Merkel, baking under the hot klieg lights, looked drawn and exhausted. Next to her, Schröder, filling every inch of his armchair, assured the audience boldly, "I will continue to be chancellor. Do you really believe that my party would take up an offer from Merkel to talk?" his expression midway between gloat and sneer. Just then, the camera panned to Merkel, as an almost imperceptible smile began to lift her sagging features. Keeping silent, she let Schröder bluster on. This is her power move: letting an alpha male keep talking and waiting patiently as he self-destructs.

Finally, Merkel leaned into her microphone and said calmly: "Quite simply, you did not win today." Turning from the raging Schröder to the audience, she added, "I promise, we will not turn democratic norms upside down." The audience erupted in applause. Merkel allowed herself a smile of satisfaction. She had delivered on her promise to herself that, one day, she would, "put Schröder in a corner." In the process, she had made history.

Two months later, on November 22, Angela Merkel was sworn in as Germany's first female chancellor. The ceremony took place in the Reichstag building, destroyed during the famous fire in 1933 that had enabled Adolf Hitler to consolidate absolute power, now gloriously renovated.* Berlin was resplendent as the capital of a now-united Germany. Light poured through the Reichstag's glass-enclosed dome, its transparency intended to

---

*The Reichstag fire was an arson attack on the Reichstag building on February 27, 1933, four weeks after Adolf Hitler was sworn in as chancellor. Hitler's government claimed the arsonist was a Communist agitator, and the Nazis used the fire as pretext to claim that Germany was under threat from Communists. Mass arrests of Hitler's perceived enemies followed.

symbolize Germany's redemptive democracy. Unsmiling, the fifty-year-old Angela Merkel, somber in a black suit, raised her right hand and swore "to dedicate my efforts to the well-being of the German people, promote their welfare, protect them from harm, and uphold and defend the Constitution. So help me God." When she looked up to accept the applause of the audience, Merkel smiled shyly and blinked back tears at this most improbable development in her life. Her parents and siblings in the gallery showed barely a trace of emotion, but, then, they were not people who emote easily. What went through the mind of Pastor Horst Kasner as his quietly independent daughter took the oath of office to lead a country whose politics he did not fully condone?

Astonishingly, Merkel's husband was absent from this history-making ceremony. Sauer was, as usual, busy in the laboratory with his own work as quantum chemist. His wife did not seem to mind. "It's more important that he supports me when it matters," the new chancellor said. She would soon need that support.

Among the first to congratulate Germany's eighth chancellor was its seventh. "Dear Madame Chancellor," Schröder said, reaching for her hand following the ceremony. "We wish you success in your work for our country."

"I thank you for all you have done for our country. I will treat your legacy responsibly," Merkel replied graciously. But even in a mature democracy where such transitions are executed smoothly and free of controversy, old grudges can linger. When Schröder returned to the chancellery for the unveiling of his official portrait in July 2007, Chancellor Merkel said to her predecessor, "Well, we all end up on this wall." To which Schröder replied, "Some of us sooner than others."

The swearing in dispensed with, Chancellor Angela Merkel strode through the great colonnaded Reichstag portal, engraved with the famous words *"Dem Deutchen Volke"* ("To the German People"), carved during the

First World War; the letters were filled with melted French cannons. Walking briskly across the wide lawn to her new office, she was impatient to get to work. But first, she had to face the world media.

Most Germans can think of only once or twice when their supremely self-possessed chancellor has been dumbstruck in public. The first time was during the news conference following her swearing in. The question that rendered her speechless could not have been more mundane. "Madame Chancellor, how do you *feel?*" Judy Dempsey of the *International Herald Tribune* asked, perhaps the one question that could catch the new chancellor unprepared. Merkel was not one to dwell on feelings, particularly not her own. "Well, yes, well, under the circumstances . . ." she mumbled, in a small, telling moment before she regained her habitual composure, her mantra (*"In der Ruhe liegt die Kraft"*—"There is strength in calm") fully operational once again. Ten years would pass before her composure slipped again in public.

The chancellor of the Federal Republic is not a powerful executive. Power in the Federal Republic—especially in domestic matters—is deliberately dispersed among the sixteen *Länder* (states) and a robust Constitutional Court. The chancellor thus rules mostly by consensus and persuasion, with far more leeway in foreign affairs than in domestic policy. Rather than a program or specific policies, Merkel brought a set of core values to the office: her deep but private faith, an unshakable creed of duty and service; a belief in Germany's permanent debt to Jews for what she has always referred to as the Shoah; her scientist's devotion to precise, evidence-based decision-making; and a visceral loathing of dictators who imprison their own people. Freedom of expression and movement are more than hackneyed phrases for a politician who spent her first thirty-five years lacking both.

Despite her deeply held beliefs, Angela Merkel is not a bold leader but proceeds at a speed that people can follow, using polling to confirm her own instincts for what is politically feasible. When—in very rare instances—she departs from her habitual caution, it jolts her country, as, later, it would the world.

Merkel's goal upon taking office was a Germany strong enough to stand up to the newly aggressive Russia, and self-aware enough to resist the ever-present virus of racism and xenophobia. NATO and the transatlantic relationship formed the bedrock of Merkel's foreign policy. Her Germany would be part of Europe—neither leading the Continent nor threatening it. Merkel's heroes, Presidents Reagan and George H. W. Bush, as well as her mentor Helmut Kohl, had worked hard at the time of unification to overcome British and French fears of a newly expanded and economically powerful Federal Republic. She would try to emulate them and make Germany a nation among nations, self-confident but modest, very much like the woman who now led it.

From her first day in office, an almost hospital-like calm reigned over Merkel's chancellery. The modernist building, so much glass and steel, was a place of business, not ceremony. The navy-blue uniformed guards at the front gate do not look as if they spend their free time at a shooting range or working out. They, too, are businesslike; it's hard to picture them marching in unison. Inside, the pale-green walls are stripped of the emblems of power and history, bare of heroic portraits of emperors and generals. This is the center of power of a nation neither quite at ease with its history, nor comfortable with its recent status as world power.

Daylight was usually just breaking over Berlin as Chancellor Merkel arrived at the office—"as God made her," in the words of one aide. No makeup, no hairdo, dressed plainly, and ready for work. While Petra Keller—the chancellor's stylist for more than a decade, who traveled with her but has not yet been to Merkel's home—transformed Merkel into the image of the chancellor familiar to the world, the politician had breakfast and read a file of overnight cable traffic and news reports on her tablet. Even as multiple crises roiled, her team would make sure that the atmosphere in the chancellery felt as sheltered from turbulence as the Templin vicarage of her childhood.

With her absolute need to control information and messaging from her chancellery, Angela Merkel scrupulously avoided social media, alive to its power to spread misinformation and turn even innocent interactions into ammunition against her. Her awareness of the internet's power was on display at an EU conference on the Balkans, held in Paris's resplendent Élysée Palace in July 2016. To celebrate the conclusion of the talks, the deputy prime minister of Montenegro, Ivica Dacic, broke into his favorite song, "O Sole Mio." As the Montenegrin crooned, other EU leaders reached for their phones. While the moment provided great comic material for their social media accounts, Merkel saw only potential danger. Rising from the table, she pleaded, "Please, put away your phones! These pictures will go viral, and they will give a very bad impression of our conference." Obediently, the other European leaders turned off their devices, cutting off the deputy prime minister midsong. Such was Angela Merkel's quiet authority over a roomful of her fellow heads of state.

Among the first changes Merkel made in the chancellery was rearranging the furniture in her vast, 475-foot office. Even as a schoolgirl, she did not like sitting in the front row, preferring somewhere in the middle so that she could observe the rest of the class. Now, instead of using her predecessor's battleship-sized desk at the back of the immense chamber, she positioned her worktable close to the door, enabling her to see visitors before she is seen. Her office in the gleaming hypermodern chancellery felt more like the headquarters of a successful start-up than the hub of a world power. Evident in the spartan décor were Merkel's Lutheran edicts of humility and simplicity. Stepping out on her terrace—which she did often, to show visitors the view of a city that was still *becoming*—she faced the Reichstag, with all its powerful resonance. Both she and the modern capital have been dramatically transformed by recent history.

Before diving into the day's jammed agenda, Merkel would pick up the phone to make some calls (she prides herself on making her own calls)—anything from speaking with presidents to thanking the gardener responsible for providing fresh flowers for her desk, as he did each morning. Merkel had turned her predecessor's closet into a kitchenette, where she often made coffee for her visitors. (The smell of coffee gradually replaced the lingering aroma of Schröder's Cuban cigars.)

Brewing drinks for her guests is about more than attending to their caffeination needs: it's about not allowing the trappings of the office to prevent human interaction. While the chancellor made coffee, she would pepper her visitors with questions, trying to glean something from each she did not know before. Michael Keating, an aide to the former secretary-general of the United Nations, Kofi Annan, recalled that when Annan arrived for his first appointment with the chancellor in 2006, "She was disarming as she listened attentively as to why Africa should be a priority for Germany. Between discussing the impact of climate change, Africa's economic potential, migration, and terrorism, there was much humor."

A small, silver-framed portrait on her desk caught the visitor's eye. It was of Catherine the Great, the German princess who began her life as Princess Sophie of Anhalt-Zest, a Lutheran from Stettin, a town not far from Merkel's Templin. Following her arranged marriage to the future Russian emperor Peter III, grandson of Czar Peter the Great, Sophie (who Russified her German name to Ekaterina, or Catherine), became Russian czarina in 1762. Shrewd and determined, she toppled many men who underestimated her, Catherine ruled for thirty-four years. Among the czarina's bolder feats was seizing Ukraine from the Ottomans; Merkel herself would soon struggle to wrest the region from the latter-day Russian czar Vladimir Putin.

Decorating her walls was a large, framed photograph of Helmut Kohl with President George H. W. Bush at the Berlin Wall and a portrait by the Austrian expressionist Oskar Kokoschka, of the first post–World War II German chancellor, Konrad Adenauer. It was Adenauer who tied his ruined nation's destiny to that of the West, and particularly to Washington. On her desk, a Plexiglas cube was engraved with the chancellor's mantra, *"In der Ruhe liegt die Kraft"* ("There is strength in calm"). A giant wooden chess figure dominated another corner of Merkel's office. It was, of course, a queen.

With her every move shadowed by a battery of security agents and her daily schedule distributed to various government branches, Merkel drew an ever-sharper line between her work and her private life. None of her close aides have ever visited her home, a rent-controlled apartment in a fairly nondescript building minutes from the chancellery. They also soon learned that the new chancellor preferred to sleep in her own bed—even if just for a few hours—even after a day in another European capital.

Merkel's routine changed little in her sixteen years as chancellor. By eight thirty, in full "chancellor armor," as her staff referred to it, she held her daily meeting with Beate Baumann, her chief of staff; Steffen Seibert, her spokesman; Eva Christiansen, her long-standing jack-of-all-trades; and, in her final term, Jan Hecker, her national security advisor. Of this small circle, Baumann was by far the most important—possibly the second most powerful figure in German politics during Merkel's time in office. Apart from her husband, no one knows Merkel better or is more trusted by the chancellor.

A decade Merkel's junior, Cambridge-educated, and unmarried, Baumann has had much to do with shaping Merkel's political formation and her near-reverential belief in America. Invisible to the public, Baumann's anonymity is something Merkel can only dream of. Merkel hired Baumann in 1995 as her private secretary and office manager, a title she bore through

2021—while filling a role that defies a job description. After two and a half decades of a near symbiotic relationship, Merkel and Baumann still use the formal "*Sie*" with each other. As a sign of her privileged status, however, Baumann would address her boss as "Frau Merkel" rather than "Frau Bundeskanzlerin"—Madame Chancellor—the title used by the rest of the staff. Bernd Ulrich, who has covered Merkel for the journal *Die Zeit* for decades, described their relationship as "like sisters. They interrupt each other. They disagree with each other. There are no barriers between them. Just trust." During Merkel's first years as chancellor, Baumann was sometimes caught giving her hand signals from the front row to suggest "Pick up the pace," "Wind it up," or "Now a little smile"—the sort of cues few would dare offer.

If Baumann was a slightly younger version of her boss, Eva Christiansen was their more glamorous sister. In charge of digitalization—especially upgrading internet access in the former East—Eva, two decades younger than the chancellor, is blonde and slim, with the wholesome good looks of a yoga instructor. All three women—as well as Merkel's former defense minister and current president of the European Commission, Ursula von der Leyen—shrugged off the German media's references to their "girls' camp."

Visiting the chancellery in June 2018, I observed just how intellectually aligned Merkel, Baumann, and Christiansen are. Without prior consultation, all three women were reading *A Culture of Ambiguity: An Alternate History of Islam*, by German historian Thomas Bauer—a reconsideration of classical and modern Islam and the tension contained in its various threads.

Merkel has always expected her inner circle to be candid. "There are no flatterers on her staff. We can criticize her," said one of the "girls." One of Angela's longest-serving ambassadors, Wolfgang Ischinger, affirmed just how tight Merkel's entourage is—and how careful she is to let people know when they're being allowed in and what's expected of them. "En route to the White House during the Obama presidency, the chancellor's phone rang," he remembered. "She put her hand on the receiver and said to me, 'Of course, this is confidential.' That my chancellor felt she needed to tell me, her ambassador, such a thing, that was astonishing." Given the chancellor's experience of life in a police state where trusting could land you in trouble, perhaps it's not that astonishing.

Not everyone the chancellor worked with was a long-standing member of this inner circle. In 2017, in a characteristic Merkel gambit, she invited Frank-Walter Steinmeier, whom she'd just defeated to win her second term, to become president of the Federal Republic—a prestigious but largely ceremonial office. "Keep your friends close but your rivals closer" might be another mantra of hers. She repeated the same maneuver to tame two other potentially dangerous rivals: Jens Spahn, who became her health minister, and Horst Seehofer, her final minister of the interior. Most notably, Merkel made Wolfgang Schäuble—the victim of Kohl's slush fund scandal and another potential rival—her first minister of the interior and, in 2009, her minister of finance, where he remained for eight turbulent years.

Anyone who failed to live up to her standards did not long survive. "You always have to be precise with her," acknowledged Thomas de Maizière, her former defense minister and later interior minister, and a cousin of her onetime mentor Lothar de Maizière. She holds those around her to the same standard of precision as she does herself. De Maizière recounted the story of how "Once, I cited a figure for her, which I only knew approximately. Days later, she used this figure in a public speech, and it turned out to be wrong—that is, not exact. When later I asked her where she got it from, she said, 'You told me that a week ago!' Which I had, in casual conversation. Of course, she recalled it quite precisely. . . . Her memory is extraordinary. You have to be on your toes with her at all times."

That precision has made working with her an intense experience but not always a pleasant one. When asked if he enjoyed working for the chancellor for two decades, Thomas de Maizière replied, "No!" with surprising vehemence. The experience "was very challenging, every minute was challenging. . . . But there was one consolation: she has a great sense of humor, which she does not let the public see," de Maizière conceded.

Humor is Merkel's way to defuse moments of high tension. On a flight to inspect German troops deployed in Afghanistan in December 2010, the government Airbus's electronic warning system—intended to confuse a potential attack—set off flares on the aircraft's tail as it approached the war zone. As the pilot took evasive action, the plane juddered, smoke from its defensive missiles blowing through the open gun hatches. When all clear was announced, the chancellor turned to her military escort and asked coolly, "So, what other entertainment do you have planned for me?"

Merkel can find mirth in strange places. One of the regulars on the chancellor's plane recalled, "Once, she was telling us about the sale of a German submarine. The buyer country just didn't want to pay, Merkel said, and kept coming up with new excuses. Their final excuse for refusing to pay was that the submarine wasn't straight, but crooked, like a banana. When the chancellor told us this, she literally doubled over laughing."

Merkel's also been known to do a comic imitation of Vladimir Putin when riled up, scribbling frantically on a piece of paper. "There! There!" Merkel mimics Putin squealing, jabbing her finger at the sheet as he does—a hilarious contrast to the inscrutable visage the Russian presents the world.

The chancellery houses five hundred civil servants and a hundred policy advisors, but Angela Merkel did not make all these civil servants happy in their posts. One speechwriter groused, "She resists rhetorical flourishes. Grand ideas, soaring phrases, are all taboo." The speechwriter dreamed of penning an impassioned, eloquent speech like the one President Obama delivered in Selma, Alabama, on March 7, 2015, the fiftieth anniversary of the bloody civil rights protest march led there by Dr. Martin Luther King.

"Angela Merkel would never accept such a speech; even if I were to write it, she could not deliver it, not the way Obama did."

Merkel rarely practices her speeches, certainly not in front of a mirror, and often reads them straight from the text presented to her. "Why does she use such bureaucratic language in her speeches?" former foreign minister Joschka Fischer grumbled sometimes. But for Merkel, the facility to excite a crowd is a dangerous gift. Her insistence on plainspoken communication reflects more than a deficit of oratorical talent. Hitler's fiery rhetoric is still recent history for many Germans. In her experience, language cannot be trusted. Words are weapons to be deployed cautiously. Merkel prefers being the uninspiring but wise custodian of the liberal West to playing with the fire of demagogy. Even Obama's rhetorical brilliance was not a point in his favor in Merkel's estimation.

Angela Merkel is not the only modern German politician to shy away from inspiring oratory. Chancellor Konrad Adenauer, a stern figure of iron-clad democratic values, too, was known for his dry-as-sawdust speeches. When contemporary pundits complained that Adenauer seemed to have a vocabulary of but two hundred words, his defenders shot back, "If he knew more, he would be clever enough not to use them." The same might be said of Merkel.

One of the chancellor's essential survival mechanisms has been her singular ability to detach emotionally; to *depersonalize* politics, parking her ego outside. It has enabled her to withstand attacks from even rivals within her own coalition who took a very long time to accept a woman as their leader. Domestic affairs have rarely inspired Angela Merkel. And no wonder, when they involved dealing with sometimes uncooperative coalition partners; the Bundestag, with its hundreds of members; the *Länder*, each with its own interests—inside a hyperregulated system where laws cover every inch of life.* So, it's no surprise that Merkel preferred foreign policy, with its greater scope for creativity and the freedom to deploy her exceptional powers of analysis. This has been the case for most chancellors, but especially so for Angela Merkel, who had a narrow margin for creativity and action during her East German formation.

Though not her passion, she kept Germany's economy humming along, and, under her watch, the country grew even more prosperous, replacing France as Europe's most competitive economy. Much of the credit for that goes to changes put in place by her predecessor, Gerhard Schröder. There is no question, however, that she guided Germany's economy with a sure hand, and, as we shall soon see, in the global recession, virtually rescued the euro.

It was, however, the world beyond Germany's borders that fascinated Angela Merkel—and where she made singular contributions. Two events from her relatively peaceful early years as chancellor are particularly noteworthy for what they reveal about Angela Merkel's character and leadership. Neither occurred on German soil, but both impacted deeply the country she led.

The first such event occurred in a land that—apart from the United States—holds the greatest meaning for Angela Merkel: Israel.

In the early spring of 2008, with plodding steps and frequent pauses to catch their breath, a collection of elderly Holocaust survivors climbed the hill to the Knesset, Israel's cube-shaped, modernist parliament building in Jerusalem. The men wore *kippahs* and open-necked shirts, the women were in their Sabbath finery, as they climbed this hill to hear a speech from the

---

*While I was living in Bonn, my landlord alerted me not to take overlong showers on Sunday, the day of enforced quiet. He helpfully posted the local ordinance spelling that out on my front door.

chancellor of Germany—the country that, only sixty years before, had tried to wipe out their people. Six of the Knesset's 120 members had walked out in protest against Merkel's being selected to speak to the Israeli body, "in the language of the murderers." The sight of Israel's blue-and-white banner snapping in the breeze next to the black, red, and gold flag of Germany was too much for them.

The first German chancellor to address the Israeli legislative body did not begin her speech in the "language of the murderers." Standing beside the Israeli flag, a black-suited Merkel began softly, in Hebrew, "*Anni modda lachem* . . . I thank God for allowing me to speak to you, here, in the Knesset." Only then did she switch to German.

"Thank you too for allowing me to speak in my mother tongue. I bow before the victims. I bow before the survivors and before those who helped them survive. The Shoah fills us Germans with shame. It means that for me, as a German chancellor, Israel's security is nonnegotiable."

Looking squarely at the unsmiling faces of hundreds of survivors, and the children and grandchildren of those who did not survive, her humility and her plain words struck the right note. Minutes before starting the speech, Merkel, head bowed, had mounted the narrow spiral staircase from the candle-lit cave at the Yad Vashem World Holocaust Remembrance Center, with its stark memorial to one and a half million children murdered during the Holocaust. The impact of having just seen all those names was visible on her drawn features.

"The break with civilization that was the Shoah left wounds that have not healed to this day," she noted grimly. "It seemed to make relations between Israel and Germany impossible. Israeli passports long contained the words 'valid for all countries except Germany.'" Then, in a reference she mostly avoids at home, she said:

"I spent the first thirty-five years of my life in a part of Germany where national socialism was considered a *West* German problem. . . . It took more than forty years before Germany as a whole acknowledged and embraced its historic responsibility and the state of Israel. . . . Here, of all places, I want to explicitly stress . . . this historic responsibility is part of my country's raison d'etre."

To so explicitly and publicly link her nation's purpose for existing to that of another nation was a bold and unprecedented statement.

But Merkel was not finished. Having identified Israel's security as nonnegotiable, the chancellor switched to speaking of Iran. "If Iran ever acquires nuclear weapons, the consequences will be disastrous—first and foremost for the security and existence of Israel, secondly to the entire region, and ultimately for all of us in Europe and the world. . . . This must be prevented," she concluded. Merkel would repeat this plea in every speech she delivered to the United Nations until the international agreement to curb Iran's nuclear weapons program was finally signed in 2015.

The chancellor closed her remarks with some more words in Hebrew: "Mazel tov . . . on the sixtieth anniversary of Israel. Shalom!" The audience of Knesset members and Holocaust survivors leapt to their feet in applause.

Merkel would form a friendship with Israeli prime minister Ehud Olmert, with whom she spoke almost daily during his time in office from 2006 until 2009. She soon gave up, however, on having a productive partnership with Prime Minister Benjamin Netanyahu—who struck her as unserious about negotiating with Palestinians and dismissive of the two-state solution. But she never swerved from her conviction expressed that spring day in Jerusalem in 2008 that Israel is part of Germany's reason for being.

Merkel was also attentive to Germany's responsibility toward its own Jewish population. Charlotte Knobloch, the leader of a thriving Jewish community in Munich, accompanied the chancellor to Jerusalem and played a part in shaping Merkel's thinking on the subject. As she recalled: "When Angela Merkel reached out to me in the early 2000s, she really didn't know much about the Holocaust. But she was hungry to learn. As the daughter of a theologian, she is very aware of Judaism's and Christianity's shared roots." Knobloch attributed Merkel's particular concern for the well-being of Germany's Jewish citizens to her Lutheran roots, saying, "Her policies are guided by ethical standards that are based in the Torah, later adopted by the founders of Christianity."

Knobloch wanted the chancellor to understand that "We don't want anti-Semitism to be *our* problem." Under Merkel, it became Germany's burden too. In 2009 she even scolded an authority unaccustomed to public rebuke: the Pope—indeed a German Pope, Benedict XVI—whom the chancellor condemned for reinstating four excommunicated bishops who were Holocaust deniers. "I believe that a fundamental question is at stake when a Vatican decision conveys the impression that one can conceivably lie about the Holocaust," the pastor's daughter said forcefully. The bishops in question were once again excommunicated from the Church.

No one realized yet just how important Merkel's commitment to combatting anti-Semitism in Germany would become during her later years in office, as racism spread like lava in Europe and across the Atlantic.

The next time Merkel acted boldly, the impetus would not be her Lutheran faith but her years of scientific training—as well as her political opportunism.

On March 11, 2011, Japan was hit by the most devastating earthquake in its history. The 8.9-magnitude quake gave rise to a powerful tsunami that cost thousands of lives and destroyed homes and even whole villages. It was the presence of two nuclear power plants in the earthquake's zone, however, that transformed the storm from a devastating natural disaster into a horrifying emergency that the Japanese government called the nation's gravest crisis since World War II. Approximately 160,000 people in the vicinity of the Fukushima Daichi nuclear plant, where one overheated reactor had already exploded, were evacuated just before another explosion rocked the region. Ten thousand people were reported dead days after the tsunami; the human cost of radiation exposure will take decades to fully assess, in the worst nuclear accident since Chernobyl, in the Soviet Union, in 1986.

From faraway Berlin, the only head of state who is also a trained physicist was horrified by the unfolding disaster. Glued to her iPad, Angela Merkel watched the spectacular nuclear explosions in Fukushima with mounting dread. Three months later, on June 9, a grim-faced chancellor told the Bundestag, "The risks inherent in nuclear energy cannot be mastered and are only acceptable if you believe that human error will never occur. When it does, the consequences are so devastating and so permanent that they completely surpass all other risks of all other forms of power combined." Without real debate, and dispensing with the usual studies from government ministries, Merkel—who had long stood with business leaders *against* the powerful antinuclear movements—now called for the immediate phaseout of German nuclear energy. She announced that six plants would cease operation by 2021, while three more would shut down by the following year.

She won plaudits for this decision from one of her frequent critics: Nobel Prize–winning economist Joseph Stiglitz. Merkel may have framed her motivation for eliminating nuclear power as vigilant concern, but Stiglitz noted that her plan also made economic sense: "No nuclear facility has ever survived without government subsidies in the marketplace. And when they blow up, governments and society bear the cost. Nor can we figure out what to do with nuclear waste. People who don't look at the full societal cost of nuclear energy miss the hidden costs," Stiglitz said.

Joachim Gauck, soon to become Germany's president, agreed that Merkel's reversal on nuclear power was more than a science-based decision; it was a canny political move as well. As he told me later:

"I pointed out to Merkel that her decision was a bit odd, coming from a scientist. I mentioned that our neighbors in France and Poland have scientists, too. For some reason, they are able to support keeping nuclear power plants open. Without saying so explicitly, she implied that, of course, it was also a question of politics. I believe it was a strategic call to make sure she would win the next election."

Merkel understood that she had a window while she had public support—and moved fast. Her commitment to climate change runs deep, but she is also a tactician whose pollsters provided her with weekly figures regarding the mood of the nation on major issues. Beyond her pollsters, Angela Merkel had people on the ground telling her what citizens in North-Rhine Westphalia or Bavaria are saying, feeling, and worrying about. Merkel factors all of that intelligence into her final calculation.

By closing down nuclear power plants, Merkel robbed the Green Party of one of its most potent rallying cries: *"Atomkraft? Nein Danke!"* Nuclear power? No thanks!

In opting out of nuclear energy, Merkel the politician and Merkel the moralist were aligned. That's how she operates: daring to boldly do what she thinks right when she senses her boldness will be welcomed. Six years into her role as chancellor, she wasn't yet willing to put her career on the line for her principles. But she'd get to a point where she would be.

President George W. Bush, shown here at a barbecue in the chancellor's home district of Mecklenburg–West Pomerania in July 2005—was fascinated by Merkel's youth spent in the Stasi state. She, for her part, found him "authentic" and genuinely enjoyed his company.

7

HER FIRST AMERICAN PRESIDENT

Angie, you are so smart!

—President George W. Bush

Angela Merkel's two most important relationships in her first term were with two dramatically different personalities: Vladimir Putin and George W. Bush. Putin was a familiar species, given Merkel's experience with macho men. In many ways, she had more in common with the scrappy former Soviet intelligence operative than she did with the scion of a privileged American political dynasty. But to the surprise of both, Angela and George (as the informal forty-third president of the United States insisted they address each other from the beginning) bonded. The swaggering, born-again Texan and the understated scientist-turned-politician from the East were an unlikely pair. But Bush had a huge advantage: Angela revered America and its values, and attributed both Germany's and her own second chance in large measure to America's intervention. George W. Bush's father, POTUS forty-one, was one of Merkel's Cold War heroes for his role in the peaceful unification of her divided country. The elder Bush's portrait, standing next to Kohl at the wall, hung in the chancellor's office.

Personal rapport between heads of state does not necessarily determine good relations between their countries, but Merkel worked hard at this part of her job. Throughout her time as chancellor, she never criticized a fellow head of state in public, be it Putin, Erdogan, Xi or even Trump, without first trying to establish a relationship of trust. In her first term in office, Merkel tested out on George W. Bush what would soon become standard practice for her: build a rapport and then use that mutual affection—or, at a minimum, trust—to try to change her fellow leader's mind.

It certainly didn't hurt Germany's relationship with one of its most important allies that Merkel, if not a wholehearted supporter of the US-led Iraq War launched in March 2003, was more inclined to support Bush in this ultimately disastrous campaign than her predecessor had been. In an opinion piece published in the *Washington Post* in February 2003, two years before her election, Merkel criticized Chancellor Schröder for his stance against the invasion.

Criticizing your own head of state in a foreign newspaper is unusual, to say the least, and spoke to Merkel's near obsessional commitment to the transatlantic relationship and her fear of Germany again becoming an outlier nation. Germany alone is a frightening prospect for Angela Merkel. The past—both the Holocaust and the police state that was her foundation—are not chapters out of dusty tomes but part of her DNA. Thus, she would go to great lengths to avoid a clash with Washington, even briefly overcoming her aversion to the use of force as a solution to an intractable problem.

Still, she wasn't in lockstep with her American counterpart. Just before going to DC to meet Bush in January 2006, two months into her first term, Merkel gave an interview to *Der Spiegel* magazine in which she called for closing the detention camp at the US Guantanamo Bay Naval Base in Cuba. Other ways of dealing with prisoners accused of terrorism must be found, she said. While some might consider publicly criticizing the policies of the country you're about to visit awkward, for Merkel the move was intentional; she has always preferred not to spring the unexpected on her interlocutors.

The chancellor made other preparations for the historic meeting, even submitting to a makeover. "I've never looked like this before," she marvelled, sufficiently impressed by her new highlights to return to Udo Walz's fashionable Kurfurstendamm salon, a month later for another cut and color, a routine she has since continued. Another change she made before the trip would be just as long lasting. Up until then, Merkel had used interpreters in meetings with foreign dignitaries. Ambassador Ischinger, who briefed the chancellor for her visit to the Oval Office, proposed a different course. "She protested, 'My English isn't that good!'" Ischinger recalled. 'Neither is Bush's,' I assured her." And so, following Ischinger's advice, she didn't use an interpreter—and she and Bush clicked. W. was fascinated by her life story. "You really grew up in a police state?" he asked in wonder. He could not get enough details of her East German youth.

The new chancellor found the Texan "authentic," one of her highest words of praise. She appreciated that he didn't try too hard to impress, nor profess to know things when he didn't. And he was unafraid to ask questions. That W. is a man of faith—as Merkel is in her very private way—also helped connect the pair.

Merkel deftly turned her Eastern bloc experiences into a policy advantage, helping Bush see things from her point of view. During conversations about the need to sanction Iran to halt its nuclear weapons build-up, Merkel noted that after the United States imposed widespread sanctions on the Soviet Union as punishment for its invasion of Afghanistan, the price of oranges in her hometown spiked. "We felt this was unfair," she explained. "She really got Bush to think about the need for targeted sanctions against Iran with those personal stories," Ischinger said. "Angie, you are so smart!" the president exclaimed.

That summer's viral sensation was a video of Merkel seated at the G8 summit roundtable in St. Petersburg, Russia, as President Bush saunters in from behind her and casually greets her with a shoulder squeeze. The chancellor, startled by this very un-Teutonic act of intimacy, flings up her hands in response. When Bush gives her a wink after she turns her head, Merkel, realizing who had taken such liberties, responds with a conspiratorial smile. Observing this rare spontaneous moment in an otherwise tightly scripted setting, the six other leaders of the Western democracies got the message: their two most important colleagues were now friends.

By that point, Merkel, Bush, and their spouses had already spent two days in Merkel's electoral district of Mecklenburg-Vorpommern on the Baltic Sea. Bush gamely sampled the local specialty, wild boar, and accepted a barrel of native herring from a local fisherman. Merkel appreciated that Bush didn't take himself too seriously in casual contexts and was able to laugh at his gaffe-prone nature—as, for example, when he referred to the wild boar as a "pig."

In November 2007 further signs of the deepening bond between the leaders came when Merkel and her mostly invisible husband accepted an invitation to the Bush's ranch in Crawford, Texas. "It was a fantastic trip," recalled Christoph Heusgen, Merkel's foreign policy advisor, calling it "one of the best state visits ever." Greeting his German visitors in blue jeans, shirtsleeves, and, naturally, cowboy boots, the president quickly established an ease and informality rare during state visits. Even Sauer traded his suit for casual clothing, though the chancellor still wore a jacket. "When you invite someone to your home," Bush told the travelling media, "it's a sign of warmth and of respect." With a light pat on the chancellor's back, he and the First Lady, Laura, led the visitors to their pickup truck. Bush got in behind the wheel, Merkel slid in next to him, and Laura and Joachim sat in the back—just four country folks, seemingly in their element. (This is likely the closest Angela Merkel has come to realizing her youthful dream of driving through the Rockies listening to Springsteen on the radio.) Early the next morning, the chancellor and the president set off on a long walk, mixing the business of state with the proud rancher's chance to show off his property. Bush explained to Merkel how he had personally cleared much of the 1,600-acre retreat and, along with Laura, had planted native cypresses, bluebonnets, and Indian paintbrush flowers throughout the grounds of Prairie Chapel Ranch. The president pointed to the breezeway, where he liked to set up his easel in good weather and paint. That evening, the group lingered at the dinner table late into the star-filled Texas night. Condoleezza Rice, the first African American secretary of state, circulated copies of the menu for everyone to sign and keep as souvenirs. Each person in attendance still has one, a framed reminder of a time that now seems from the distant past. For the chancellor, the simplicity of Bush's home and his love of nature gave her a different image of the American president. Having her husband along—a rare occurrence—likely also enhanced the visit for Merkel.

After making a brief effort at being the "First Gentleman," Sauer would soon decide he was not cut out for the role. Perhaps he made the decision after his state visit to Vienna, Austria, in early 2006, when protocol dictated that he sit behind his wife during a concert. After that humbling event, on the rare occasion when Sauer chose to accompany his wife on official visits, he mostly kept his own schedule. The chancellor may have envied her husband when they arrived in London for a visit rich in royal pomp, yet Sauer was able to jump out of the official limousine and head for the Piccadilly Circus tube station to keep his own appointments.

In 2006 the sun was shining on Angela Merkel and her brand of collective leadership among the Western democracies. The qualities the German public admired in its chancellor: her low-key style, the absence of ego or theatrics, her diligence, and a genuine interest in achieving results, not scoring points, endeared Angela Merkel to her fellow heads of state, too. A less well-known quality also won her friends. Angela, in the words of New

Jersey Governor Philip Murphy, formerly the US ambassador to Germany, "is funny as hell." Then, too, the fact that her legendary stamina did not evaporate at the end of a long day, also helped in forging personal relationships. The chancellor enjoyed staying up late over drinks with those heads of state with whom she shared a rapport. The normally caustic *Economist* featured a photograph of the smiling chancellor raising a glass, under the headline "Angela Merkel Charms the World."

"Less than 100 days after taking the oath," the weekly newspaper reported, "Ms. Merkel has touched some unprecedented pinnacles. In a series of foreign forays, she has won plaudits from Washington, to Brussels, to Jerusalem. . . . To cap it all, last weekend a German opinion poll gave her an 89 percent popularity rating, the highest ever recorded by a chancellor. . . . The German economy, once the sickest in Europe, is bouncing back, business confidence is high, exports are breaking records, and even consumers are at last perking up." With a casual sexism that was still acceptable at the time, the article also applauded her physical transformation, commenting, "Even Ms. Merkel's dowdiness has been swept away."

That summer, Berlin suddenly exploded with the rarely seen German tricolors. The black, red, and gold banner flew from windows, was draped over car hoods, poked out of backpacks, and was smeared with makeup on the faces of children. The burst of national pride coincided with Merkel's early golden days and a general sense that she was now widely deemed Europe's most admired and effective leader. (As with Barack Obama, awarded the Nobel Peace Prize during his first year as president, Merkel's accolade was based more on image than substance. But substance would soon follow.) Yet it was not Merkel the nation was celebrating, but the World Cup, in which the German team was a top contender and Berlin the host. It was an astonishing event, even for those indifferent to soccer. "Arriba! Arriba!" sang the million-strong crowd from every corner of the globe, gathered on Berlin's so-called fan mile along the Tiergarten park. German soccer fans were more familiar with the words of the World Soccer Association anthem than with their own, rarely played anthem—the words to which only 51 percent of Germans even know. But they soon learned the words and sang them whenever their team took to the field. Germany came in third, but it hardly mattered; soccer had finally made it acceptable to show pride in being German.

Though an avid soccer fan, *proud* is not a word the chancellor herself uses to describe her feelings toward her homeland, generally preferring to say she is "happy" to be German. "When I use a word like *fatherland,* I don't mean it in an elevated sense," she has said.

"I don't think Germans are particularly bad, or outstandingly wonderful. I am fond of kebabs, and pizza, I think Italians have a nicer outdoor café culture, and I think there is more sunshine in Switzerland. I grew up here. I like living here. I have confidence in this country, I am part of its history, with all its pain and all the good things."

Reading this statement in an era of rising xenophobia and fevered populism, Merkel sounds almost radical in her moderation; a voice from another era.

Merkel's personal rapport with Bush paid off. At the June 2007 G8 summit in Heiligendamm, Germany, President Bush recognized publicly that climate change was real for the first time, acknowledging that halving emissions by 2050 should be "seriously considered." On this key issue, Merkel had won the American president, initially a climate skeptic, to her side.

Their rapport also made it far easier to disagree without creating a diplomatic crisis. Aware of Russian sensitivity to too-deep Western encroachment into its former empire, she opposed Bush's plan to offer NATO membership to Ukraine and the Republic of Georgia—an argument she won. As with climate change, Merkel's calm recitation of facts and history prevailed over the sometimes impulsive Bush.

Angela Merkel's facial expressions often reveal more than her words. The chancellor is shown here with Chinese president Xi Jinping, Russian president Vladimir Putin, and Turkey's Recep Tayyip Erdogan at the G20 Leaders' Summit in Hamburg, Germany, on July 7, 2017. (India's prime minister, Narendra Modi, and Japan's prime minister, Shinzo Abe, stand in the row behind her.)

8

DICTATORS

The secret of politics? Make a good treaty with Russia.

—Otto von Bismarck, first chancellor of
the German Empire, 1871–1890

Merkel's approach to authoritarian regimes, whether Russian or Chinese, has been pragmatic. She scorns bombastic public shaming of dictators as counterproductive. Merkel would likely agree with this advice from fictional mob boss Michael Corleone in the film *The Godfather: Part III:* "Never hate your enemies; it affects your judgment." Her approach with rivals combines patience and persistence to pursue even a sliver of common ground. Threading the needle between her values, political calculations, and Germany's longer-term interests was sometimes excruciatingly difficult—if not impossible.

Unsurprisingly, Vladimir Putin was the first leader to challenge her.

On February 10, 2007, the somber prime minister of a resurgent Russia strode onto a stage in Munich to deliver a scorching diatribe against democracy, the West, and everything for which Angela Merkel stands. "Russians are constantly being taught about democracy, when those who teach us do not want to learn themselves," he rebuked the gathering of transatlantic security specialists and government officials. Gone was the accommodating Putin of just a few years earlier, grateful to be a part of the European family and proud that the German chancellor spoke good Russian. His stated goal had become to reclaim Russia's place as a formidable global player by any means necessary. Blending lies with threats, he taunted the audience, deflected hard questions, and punctured the West's moral superiority.

"Wars have not diminished," he charged, in spite of the West's attempts to broker peace around the globe. "More are dying than before." Though Putin had not yet thrown his support behind Syrian dictator Bashar al-Assad's genocidal war against his own people, he scolded Washington for its wars in the Middle East and referred to the Cold War as a "stable" era. Merkel, sitting in the front row, was visibly shaken by the Russian's venomous performance—and his description of the system that had kept her its prisoner for thirty-five years.

Not since Soviet leader Nikita Khrushchev pounded the UN podium with his shoe in 1960 and earlier proclaimed, "We will bury you!" had the world heard such vitriol from a Russian head of state. But Khrushchev thundered at the height of the Cold War; this was 2007. Things were supposed to be different now. Yet for the next decade and a half, Angela Merkel's relationship with Putin would be her most frustrating and dangerous. It would also be her longest relationship with a fellow head of state, its roots reaching back to November 9, 1989.

Stationed as a KGB officer in Dresden, a mere two-hour train ride from Berlin, thirty-seven-year-old Vladimir Putin did not share Merkel's euphoria on the night the wall came down. "When the Berlin Wall fell, it was clear this was the end. We had this horrible feeling that the country that had almost become our home would soon cease to exist," Putin's then wife, Lyudmila, said. Putin had spent four productive and contented years as a Soviet spy in East Germany's second largest city. Once a glittering center of arts and music, Dresden was rich territory for KGB agent recruitment—aided by the fact that it was the one East German town that did not receive Western television. The Allies' devastating bombing raids of this formerly magnificent Baroque city three months before Germany's surrender in World War II had created lingering resentment toward the West, including West Germany, which was seen as America's "puppet." The East German regime deliberately left the gaping ruin of the great domed Frauenkirche Lutheran church in the city's heart as a memorial "to the tens of thousands of dead, and an inspiration to the living in their struggle against imperialist barbarism."

This city was Lieutenant Colonel Vladimir Putin's home, and he thrived spying on Germans on both sides of the East-West divide. "An important part of our work was gathering information about the citizens," Putin would later recall. After being awarded a bronze medal for Extraordinary Merit to the German Democratic People's Army while serving in Dresden, Putin, along with Lyudmila and their two daughters (the youngest of whom, Ekaterina, was born in Dresden) enjoyed the city and quickly mastered the language. Putin's only regret was the twenty-five pounds he gained while there, blaming his new girth on the excellent local beer.

While Dresden lacked the cloak-and-dagger drama of East Berlin, it was well placed for the KGB's high-tech smuggling operation from West Germany. The Soviet Union was lagging ever further behind Western technology, and part of Putin's brief was to lure scientists and businessmen from major companies such as Siemens, the industrial and technology giant; Bayer pharmaceuticals; and the steel manufacturer Thyssen. Agent Putin frequented a dimly lit bar called Am Tor in central Dresden, where he would meet potential recruits. Nearby, the Bellevue Hotel on the banks of the Elbe was owned by the Stasi, its elegant restaurants and bedrooms fitted out with hidden cameras. In these operations, which frequently involved blackmail, the Stasi and the KGB collaborated.

One month after the fall of the wall, on December 5, 1989, Putin—bristling with barely contained rage—stepped outside the three-story villa on Angelikastrasse 4, headquarters of the Dresden KGB. A gated iron fence separated him from a small but determined group of hostile East German demonstrators. "Move back! This is Soviet territory. My comrades are armed and authorized to shoot," Putin bluffed. There was no armed militia inside; the lieutenant colonel was playing for time. Earlier, in civilian clothes, he'd observed angry demonstrators ransack Dresden's Stasi headquarters, near his own. Seething at the sight but helpless to stop it, Putin was not going to let them breach the KGB's iron gate.

"Who are you? Your German is too good!" one of the demonstrators challenged Putin. "I'm an interpreter," the agent lied. Though the unarmed protestors soon dispersed, Putin felt betrayed by both Moscow and its once-loyal satellite. He was also certain that the emboldened demonstrators would soon return, likely in greater numbers. Desperate, Putin dialed the local Soviet military headquarters. "We cannot do anything until we get orders from Moscow—and Moscow is silent," the local tank commander informed Putin.

Alone now, Putin prepared for the worst. He began to shovel hundreds of KGB documents and files into a small wood-burning stove—better to destroy four years' worth of intelligence than have it fall into the hands of the mob. He tossed in files from informants inside Kohl's government, threw in agent reports on West German high-tech firms, and trashed transcripts of conversations with Latin American and African students he had recruited at the nearby University of Leipzig (still called Karl Marx University for another two years). "We threw things in the fire day and night, all contacts were cut, any cooperation with informants was ended, and all material whatsoever was either destroyed or archived," back in Moscow, he would later say. So fast and furiously did Putin work that the stove exploded in a black, charred mess.

A few months later, in 1990, the very year of Angela Merkel's rebirth as a German politician, Vladimir Putin, behind the wheel of a used Trabant—the cheap East German answer to West Germany's Volkswagen—fled Dresden as street protests exploded into revolution. With their two little girls and a twenty-year-old washing machine, the Putins returned to Leningrad—soon to be reborn as St. Petersburg. "The Soviets simply dropped everything and left. We would have avoided a lot of problems if Moscow had not made such a hasty exit from Eastern Europe," Putin noted bitterly of the empire's fall.

Vladimir Putin, once a proud standard-bearer of the humiliated Soviet Union, had learned a lesson he would not soon forget. Unchecked demonstrations and sudden eruptions of freedom can topple even the world's most heavily armed empire. His battle to reverse what he considered to be "the greatest geopolitical catastrophe of the twentieth century" would ensnare Angela Merkel, a product of the same failed state. Their convoluted relationship would zigzag between faint hope and despair on her side, and dogged determination on both their parts. She was chancellor of Germany, and he was the modern-era czar of Russia. Divorce was not an option.

For Merkel, the scenario Putin outlined in Munich of the world as an arena for combat among the most powerful nations represented a terrible regression. "Never again," Germany's post-Holocaust mantra, was quickly followed by "Never alone" for subsequent Cold War chancellors, Merkel included. Secure inside the Western alliance, with Washington as the ultimate guarantor of its security, Germany thrived as an economic powerhouse. A rules-based international order and the European Union, which was an actual commonwealth of nations with shared democratic values rather than a mere giant bureaucracy—that was Merkel's vision. Now it was being threatened by Putin.

Neither Merkel nor Putin needed to be reminded that she had become chancellor as a result of the same events that had swept away the cause he'd served. As contemporaries only two years apart in age, Putin and Merkel emerged from similar backgrounds with radically different world views. From his perspective, the Cold War did not end in 1989; it merely took a short breather. Since then, Russia's tactics had evolved. While the Soviets brandished nuclear-tipped missiles, Putin opts for weapons that are less conventional and less visible but ultimately more flexible and effective, such as spreading discord in the West through disinformation and cyber warfare, Putin sees himself, in his own words, as "the last great nationalist." His ultimate goal is to weaken the European Union and its ally the United States. "The main enemy was NATO," Putin said of his KGB service in Dresden. It remains so today.

In Angela Merkel, Putin knew he had met his match. More than merely speaking Putin's language, Merkel has experienced the Russia that very few heads of state ever see. Her trip to Moscow in her early teens to receive a prize in a Russian language competition left a deep impression: on the one hand, there was its overwhelming size, the heroic scale of the capital's architecture, and the remnants of a civilization she's so admired, from the Bolshoi Ballet to the still sublime concert halls and theaters. These features contrasted sharply with Soviet society's near-total surveillance—the model for East Germany's regime of terror. Later, during a vacation in 1984, Angela hitchhiked to parts of the Soviet Union that were closed to foreigners. After being picked up by police in Sochi and charged with travelling without a permit, she was forced to write an essay titled "Why I Broke the Law, Even Though I Have a University Degree and Know the Law." Merkel's command of Russian so impressed the local police that she and her companions were released from custody and allowed to fly back to Berlin. The next time Angela visited Sochi, she arrived in her capacity as chancellor of Germany, under heavy security and accompanied by an entourage of aides and journalists for a meeting with the Russian prime minister, Vladimir Putin.

Her best preparation for Putin, of course, was her decades of living under Soviet rule. Having herself suffered the police state he served, Merkel has a bone-deep sense of his capacity for calculation and cruelty. The two are also intimately familiar with each other's personal histories. To appreciate how radically different these two products of the same socialist foundation had become, one need only compare Merkel's simple, even austere, lifestyle and her disdain for the elaborate trappings of power with the imperial grandeur Putin strives to convey. Though he has spent his entire career in government, the Russian leader is believed to be among the world's wealthiest men. "They have a perfect understanding of each other," said K. T. von Guttenberg, Merkel's former minister of defense.

Throughout her tenure as chancellor, Merkel continued to speak regularly with Putin (increasingly in German, as her Russian grew rusty, while his German is still fluent). Typically, for the first half hour or so of their conversation, she'd hang back, letting him vent his list of grievances—some real, most imagined—inflicted on Russia by the West. Merkel saw this as therapeutic for Putin. Then, when he was at last done, she'd tell him, "Look, Vladimir, this is not how the rest of the world sees things. This is not in your interest." According to Merkel's longtime Cabinet member Thomas de Maizière, who was frequently in the room with the two leaders, "She is the only head of state that Putin actually respects. With her, he knows he can't pull off any of his usual tricks." De Maizière was referring, of course, to Putin's habitual deceit and the fantasies he spins to confuse less shrewd interlocutors.

The Putin-Merkel relationship is based on profound differences but also on the grudging mutual respect of two battle-tested warriors. Each respects the other's culture and language; Putin certainly appreciates Merkel's fondness for the great Russian writers Fyodor Dostoyevsky and Nikolay Gogol. And the chancellor feels the burden of their intertwined histories: Russia suffered unspeakable human losses in the war that Adolf Hitler started, betraying his then ally with a massive surprise attack in 1941. The conflict left twenty-seven million dead, including Putin's older brother Viktor, who died during the thousand-day Nazi siege of Leningrad. Early in their time in office, Merkel and Putin may have hoped for something better between their nations—and perhaps even between themselves.

A portentous event in their relationship occurred in 2001. That year, a gawky and seemingly humble President Putin addressed the German parliament in flawless German, expressing his desire for warmer ties with the West and assuring the Bundestag that their two nations were on the same team. "Stalinist totalitarian ideology could no longer oppose the ideas of freedom and democracy. . . . The political choice of the people of Russia enabled the USSR . . . to raze the Berlin Wall," he said—astonishingly taking credit for opening the wall. "Russia is a friendly, European nation," he pledged.

The German lawmakers leapt to their feet, applauding enthusiastically. Did Putin notice that in the second row of the Bundestag chamber, an unsmiling future chancellor remained seated? Angela Merkel barely clapped. She knew something that West German parliamentarians perhaps did not: the KGB's values, loyalties, and training are not so easily shed.

If Merkel nurtured the faintest hopes for a more moderate Putin, reality dispelled them. Foundry workers in the Ural Mountains were soon casting Putin's likeness in bronze, while entire Russian factories received orders to produce rugs, watches, and plates bearing the presidential mug. Following Putin's visit to Magnitogorsk, the overalls he'd worn that day were displayed in the industrial city's museum. Merkel understood the man she'd be dealing with: Putin's role model was not the reformist Mikhail Gorbachev but rather dictator Joseph Stalin.

In 2006, shortly after Merkel became chancellor, Putin told the press proudly, "Mrs. Merkel devotes a lot of attention to Russia. And she speaks Russian!"

The good feelings did not last long, after Putin observed Merkel placing human rights high on her agenda. In KGB style, he began to probe for her vulnerabilities. During their first Kremlin meeting, Putin subjected Merkel to the KGB's well-known staring contest. She did not blink. At their next meeting on the Black Sea, knowing Merkel's fear of dogs (she had been bitten twice), he unleashed his black Labrador retriever, Koni. As Koni circled and sniffed the chancellor, a smile of satisfaction spread on Putin face's. Merkel, however, did not flinch. "He has to do this, to show his manhood. Russia has no successful politics or economy," she told her furious staff later.

Undaunted, Putin kept trying to throw Merkel off her game. In a typical attempt to assert his power, he arrived late to their meetings. When the German chancellor once reproached his tardiness, Putin replied with a shrug, "Well, this is just the way we are," to which she replied, "It is not the way *we* are." Along with modesty and a sense of duty, the virtue of punctuality had been drilled into the pastor's daughter from childhood; she finds its absence in others intolerable.

Merkel has paid Putin back for his pettiness in her own small ways. "Vladimir, have you been praying again?" she would tease him, knowing he had built a chapel near his office, inside the Kremlin. But Putin's slouch, his wide-legged sprawl, and the permanent smirk that so annoyed President Obama that he said the Russian reminded him of the "bored kid at the back of the classroom"—Merkel brushed off all of it as childish and transparent. Putin, she told her aides, "is a man who uses others' weakness. He tests you all day. If you don't resist, you become smaller and smaller," she said, illustrating the diminishment by moving her index finger closer to her thumb.

But he failed to intimidate her. In Dresden, the site of Putin's deepest humiliation, Merkel even flipped his script. It was she who both diminished and humiliated him. The leaders met in his former town in October 2006, three days after the Moscow murder of Anna Politkovskaya, a reporter and human rights advocate whose coverage of Russia's savage proxy war in the republic of Chechnya had gotten under the president's skin. When Polit-kovskaya was shot dead in the elevator of her Moscow apartment building on Putin's fifty-fourth birthday, some observers felt the timing of her murder was not a coincidence.

Putin had remained silent on the subject of this brazen killing. As he alighted from his black limousine in front of Dresden Castle, Merkel caught her guest by surprise. She told the assembled media that she was "shocked at this act of violence" and that "Politkovskaya's murder must be solved." His lips pursed, a blindsided Putin mumbled incoherently, "That journalist was indeed a harsh critic of the Russian government. But I think her political influence in our country was extremely insignificant. . . . This murder does more harm to Russia . . . than any of her articles," he said, absurdly trying to make himself the real victim of the crime.

Merkel's support of a free press kept getting under his skin. In September 2010, after dozens of people were killed during protests following the publication of twelve cartoons of the prophet Muhammad in the Danish newspaper *Jyllands-Posten* (published on September 30th 2005), Merkel honored one of the cartoonists, Kurt Westergaard, who'd been receiving death threats. Rooftop snipers and more security than Potsdam had seen since Stalin, Churchill, and US president Harry S. Truman met there in 1945 greeted the chancellor at the ceremony. Merkel concluded her speech by declaring, "The secret of freedom is courage." She also took the opportunity to lash out at a planned book burning by Christian fundamentalists in a Florida church, calling the act "repugnant." Even though Merkel was talking about an incident in the United States, Putin saw her comments as giving Western leaders license to meddle in the internal affairs of sovereign nations.

"He always has this stony face when he's around Merkel," observed Ukrainian human rights advocate Maxim Eristavi. "He can be humorous and even animated when he wants to be. But not with her. She knows how to shame him—not by appealing to his humanitarian instincts; that would be useless—but by reminding Putin that human rights violations and atrocities are taking place under his watch. She reminds him that he is responsible." History, she implied, and perhaps even the International Criminal Court, might yet hold this murderous cynic to account.

By the end of Merkel's sixteen-year chancellorship, the two of them had spent hundreds of hours in each other's company. Yet Putin and Merkel would not discuss personal subjects. Merkel, for example, did not even know that Putin's two daughters had attended German schools in Moscow. She and Putin are a pair of professionals who know it wasn't personal when Putin released disinformation about Merkel to weaken her electoral chances; for example, planting fake stories about a Russian German girl named Lisa who was alleged to have been raped by Muslim refugees in Berlin in 2016. "Our Lisa," Putin's foreign minister, Sergei Lavrov, called her, charging Merkel with a "cover-up." Soon hundreds of German citizens marched in front of the chancellery, demanding "Justice for Lisa." But after conducting an exhaustive investigation, Berlin police found that what really happened was that the girl had argued with her parents and spent the night with a male friend. By then, however, confusion and doubt had been sewn. Merkel, of course, despises such crude KGB disinformation tactics—now amplified by the power of social media—but accepts them as part of Putin's authoritarian toolbox. For her, it's not personal.

Part of *her* toolbox would always be supporting dissidents, whether Putin liked it or not. But she knew it would always be an uphill battle against a tyrant as brutal and implacable as the Russian leader.

Merkel kept Catherine the Great's portrait in her office. The German-born Russian Empress tried to rouse Russia from feudal torpor, to "Go out in the open!" (A line that Merkel often invokes to encourage her fellow East Germans to open themselves to other peoples, other experiences, and other ways of life—as she herself did after thirty-five years behind barbed wire and the wall.) Such encouragement is still needed today—not only for Germans but also for Russians.

In June 2020, against a backdrop of monuments to Soviet soldiers killed fighting Nazi Germany, Putin announced he would be extending his rule until 2036. Whatever frail hopes Merkel still held for a different Russia were dashed. Through manipulated voting, fear, coercion, and assassinating his foes, Putin installed himself as dictator for life. Putin aims to best Stalin's thirty-three-year record for holding power. To Merkel's distress, Putin has cut off the oxygen of democracy to a country whose culture, history, and language she deeply admires.

Two months later, in a tragic replay of the assassination of journalist Anna Politkovskaya and countless others who have criticized Putin, opposition figure Aleksei A. Navalny collapsed after being poisoned with a toxic nerve agent. The same method had been tried on Politkovskaya, who survived and was then shot. Navalny, too, survived—due in part to Angela Merkel's intervention. Medivacked from Siberia to the Charité hospital in Berlin, Navalny was fighting for his life when the chancellor warned Putin, "We insist that this case be cleared up quickly. What we have heard so far is very disturbing." Even more powerful was the message of Merkel's bedside visit to Navalny after he emerged from his coma.

Following his recovery, in a breathtaking act of courage, Navalny returned to Moscow, only to be jailed immediately on trumped-up charges. From prison, the opposition leader launched his most potent weapon against the dictator's kleptocracy. Navalny released a two-hour film showing Putin's billion-dollar secret palace on the Black Sea, complete with an underground ice hockey rink, a casino, a red velvet hookah lounge, and a dance pole—all bought, the jailed activist claimed, "with the biggest bribe in history." Within a single day, the video clocked twenty million viewers on YouTube and provoked nationwide street protests.

"You have three choices under Putin: shut up, praise him, or die," said filmmaker Oleg Sentsov, a Russian Ukrainian jailed for activism by Putin. Angela Merkel, a foe as dangerous as Navalny, would neither shut up nor praise him. Nor could Putin silence her.

The assassination attempt on Navalny, however, also revealed a troubling aspect of Angela Merkel's pragmatism. On the one hand, she has called for European solidarity and has led the way in calling out Putin's human rights violations. But even as Putin's most vocal domestic adversary lay in a coma in a Berlin hospital, Merkel declined to cancel the Nord Stream 2 pipeline project, which will pump gas directly from Russia, across the Baltic Sea, and into Germany. When finished, the project will pour billions into the Kremlin's coffers and provide fuel for only one member of the EU: Germany.

Allowing Nord Stream to proceed exposed in Merkel's record a blind spot that is hard to square with her many principled positions, but it serves as a reminder that she is also a calculating politician. It is true that Europe's energy landscape has been dramatically altered by a recent shift away from Russian to US and Norwegian natural gas, and by antitrust cases against Gazprom, the Russian state-owned gas company. The EU under Merkel has become far more interconnected in this and other areas. But her professed ambition of a Europe that behaves as a mature bloc, with a united foreign policy, is undermined by this unilateral act. Moreover, the country that will most suffer if Nord Stream is completed is one where the chancellor has spent a great deal of time and effort: Ukraine. Kyiv will lose over $1 billion a year in transit fees once the pipeline is completed under the Baltic Sea. Merkel no doubt weighed all these factors, including how bad the optics would be if she proceeded.

The issue, long predating the Navalny episode, has perplexed some of her staunchest allies. "Every time Obama asked Merkel why she was going ahead with Nord Stream, Merkel gave a different answer," Charles

Kupchan, an Obama administration national security advisor told me. "Pressures from the business community, domestic politics, keeping her coalition together, this is not her decision to make, and so on—always a different answer." The true answer was likely all of these factors combined. One of Merkel's favorite explanations in complex circumstances is "The advantages outweigh the disadvantages."

A less personally intense but increasingly troubling relationship with another dictatorship has also taken up much of Merkel's attention. Like Putin, the leaders of the Chinese Communist Party studied carefully the collapse of the Soviet Union, determined not to repeat its fate. Though Mao Tse-tung's portrait still looms over Tiananmen Square in the heart of Beijing, the party has jettisoned his scripture. The largest consumer of energy, movies, and beer in the world, China has built more high-speed railroads and airports than the rest of the world combined. The Chinese Communist Party will also soon pass the Soviet record as history's longest-lasting one-party state. The world's newest superpower is already the largest and most populous authoritarian country. Its power arises not from its comparatively small nuclear arsenal but from its fast-growing economic might—and its stated goal to be the world leader in the race for key technologies.

Well before President Barack Obama's much ballyhooed "pivot" to Asia, Angela Merkel was making yearly trips to Beijing and deepening her relationships with its rulers. "She said as early as 2005 that China was a rising star, and we have to have good relations with her. She has invested time with Jiang Zemin, Hu Jintao, and Xi Jinping," said her former national security advisor Christoph Heusgen, naming China's current leader, Xi, and his two predecessors. "China—both its lessons and the danger it poses the world—never strayed from Angela Merkel's radar."

During her early years as chancellor, Merkel was exhilarated by her visits to China. She returned to Berlin energized from meeting new people—cultural figures, scientists, and entrepreneurs, as well as officials—and marvelled at the remarkable progress made by the globe's emerging giant. How, she wondered out loud, had a centrally planned, one-party state lifted millions of its population out of poverty and continued to accelerate its global reach? It seemed an unprecedented trajectory. The chancellor generally returned from Beijing with a packet of lucrative trade deals for German businesses—eventually making China one of the top three markets for German cars.

But in November 2007 Merkel came back from a three-day trip to Beijing with no trade deals and a reminder of the dark side of the Chinese "miracle." The sudden chill in relations was payback for the chancellor's recent meeting with the Dalai Lama in Berlin, as well as her conversation with nongovernmental organizations, dissidents, and independent journalists while in the Chinese capital. "She raised human rights in every conversation," said her then spokesman, Ulrich Wilhelm, who accompanied Merkel on the visit. "I admire your progress, but I cannot start our talks without raising these issues," she told President Hu Jintao at their first encounter.

The Chinese always bristled at this and deemed it unacceptable meddling in their internal affairs. As proof of their displeasure, Beijing rewarded French president Nicolas Sarkozy, visiting China the same week as Merkel, with $30 billion in contracts, while the German chancellor returned home empty-handed. Sarkozy, Merkel couldn't help but notice, treaded much lighter on the sensitive topic of Chinese human rights violations. Ever since, she has walked a tightrope between sticking to her values—mostly behind closed doors with Chinese leaders—and championing Germany's commercial interests. Her dogged pursuit of good relations with Beijing has earned her a level of trust with successive leaders. But that trust was earned at a moral price.

President Xi Jinping, who took office in 2013, once told Merkel that the best way to support human rights, in China and elsewhere, is to fight poverty. Though she did not entirely disagree, as an openly admiring critic, Merkel continued to feel she had the right to speak her mind regarding Beijing's ruthless repression of minorities and of basic human rights. "If you crack down, you will force us to publicly support the protestors," she reportedly told Xi. While calling his increasingly hard line and cult of personality "disappointing," she views China through a more complicated lens than the usual binary of free versus unfree. And so Merkel has also switched to using soft power—not as a substitute for tough negotiations but as a way of signalling her respect for an ancient and, in the West, often ignored civilization.

On most diplomatic trips, Merkel would tend to rush through the customary ceremonial greetings, formal exchange of views, and press briefings. In China, however, she took her time. On one recent visit, she was determined to see for herself how Shenzhen, long just a small village next to Hong Kong, had transformed itself into a high-tech hub of twelve and a half million people, even as the German auto industry failed to develop its own battery cells. After a dozen trips, she knew who to reach out to, beyond Xi Jinping, and who to carefully distance. Xi may make all the important decisions, but he listens to his vice premier, Liu He, so he too was included in her schedule. "We are celebrating the fifth birthday of simultaneous translation!" she informed her entourage cheerfully during a recent visit, recalling a time when Chinese politicians read their answers from laboriously translated index cards. Nor was it lost on the Chinese leadership that Angela Merkel chose to celebrate her fifty-sixth birthday, in July 2010, admiring the seven thousand terra-cotta funerary warriors of the first Chinese emperor, Qin Shi Huang Ti, in Xi'an, capital of Shanxi Province, accompanied by her rarely seen husband.

Merkel loves history, and her special fascination with China's makes its current global aspirations less mysterious and perhaps less threatening to her. As a scientist, she is well aware of its remarkable record of technological inventions—gunpowder, for instance—as well as being among the first countries to have conducted astronomical research (at the time of the Qing dynasty in the seventeenth century). "I often speak with President Xi about how we can learn from each other regarding what each of us does well," she once said. "When I visit China, its leaders tell me that for seventeen hundred of the last two thousand years, they were the leading economy. 'Don't get upset,' they say, 'if we return to the place where we traditionally were.'" Merkel has compared China's remarkable progress in one generation to her own country's rise from the ashes of World War II. "As was the case with Germany, China's rise is largely based on hard work, creativity, and technical skills," she noted. During her time in office, the Chinese economy grew 202 percent. "In ten years," she warned, "we will need people who can read patents in Chinese, because they will no longer feel like writing them in English."

China, she reminded her Cabinet, aims to be at the forefront of artificial intelligence; in 2017 the country invested €12 billion in AI research, while Germany spent only €500 million. She sees China's example of breathtaking progress as less a direct threat than a spur for Europe to move faster, saying, "I believe that chips should be manufactured in the European Union and that Europe should have its own hyperscalers and produce battery cells." Very few heads of state speak with Merkel's level of confidence on such technical subjects. Due to her experience living under a surveillance state, she also feels that Europe should set standards for privacy protection and become a rule maker in setting global digital standards—an alternative to both the United States and China. "I firmly believe that personal data does not belong to the state or to companies," she has said. Pragmatist that she is, even as she negotiated with Chinese telecom giant Huawei, Merkel pushed for tighter German control of such providers. Her refusal to view China through the prism of ideology is all the more remarkable given her personal experience with the reality of life under Communist rule. Still, she also acknowledges that, unlike East Germany or the Soviet Union, China has reformed its economy to the benefit of millions of its people.

To a great many people on both sides of the Atlantic, Merkel's determined pragmatism rang hollow by 2019, as China continued its repression of Hong Kong reformists and Uighur Muslims. Typically, Merkel had weighed her options carefully and chosen what she saw as the lesser evil. She simply did not intend to have Germany's all-important trade with China held hostage to the country's politics. For the chancellor, who observes trends from a historian's perspective, the writing is very much on the wall. If the West doesn't start learning from China, it risks falling behind. She often refers to the fact that, for centuries, China represented the pinnacle of world culture. What was Europe up to in 210 BC, when Chinese artisans sculpted those lifelike funerary warriors? Civilizations rise and—if they grow smug, careless, and decadent—fall. The West, she warned in nearly every speech during her final years in office, is declining in hope and purpose. She wanted to rekindle that hope, but her instruments for doing so were limited. Rousing people to action was not among Angela Merkel's strengths.

An unusually glamourous Merkel arrives with her husband to the opera house in Bayreuth, Germany, for the annual Wagner Festival. Joachim Sauer (known as the "Phantom of the Opera" for his passion for opera and his aversion to the media's attention) and his wife have successfully guarded their private lives to an almost unbelievable degree. Sauer has never given an interview regarding his famous wife.

9

THE PRIVATE CHANCELLOR

I have made very sure that there are boundaries, so certain areas of my life are not open to the public.

—Angela Merkel

Long before Angela Merkel was dubbed the most powerful woman in the world, she was a well-grounded person, with interests well beyond politics and politicians. To a remarkable extent, she has remained the same person throughout her sixteen years in office. This is in great part due to the fact that, more than any successful politician in our time, Merkel has asserted her right to a private life and used a series of stratagems to keep the world at bay. This other life—this private life—has enabled Angela Merkel to sustain the sometimes crushing burdens of her office.

"I have tried to maintain spaces where I can be happy or sad without explanation to the public," she explained in 2019. "Otherwise it's very hard to be happy in public. I don't make exceptions to this rule." Not even to her most devoted staff, none of whom have ever been invited to her home, either in Berlin or to her Brandenburg sanctuary.

Equal distance from Berlin and the Polish border, amid the lakes and forests of Uckermark, near the village of Hohenwalde, sits Angela and

Joachim's plain white cottage, with its red tile roof. The cottage is "very simply furnished," said a sometime guest, filmmaker Volker Schlöndorff. "It feels East German, since it was built by Angela and her husband in the days when you had to scrounge for every piece of wood in the East. It still feels unfinished."

A policeman sitting in a tiny white cube across the road is the only sign that this is the weekend home of the chancellor of Germany. While Angela arrives in her official black Audi, her husband often drives his old red VW Golf. Merkel tries hard to ignore her security guards, but when she emerges from a dip in the nearby lake, she does so under the watchful eyes of a pair of armed agents, whom she has instructed to stay 200 meters from her—150 meters more than is officially recommended. When she goes for a walk in the nearby woods there is always a single SUV at the edge of the forest, with a security agent pretending to be reading a newspaper behind the wheel. "C'mon, I know you aren't really reading that," the chancellor once teased her security man, who had been instructed to make himself as invisible as possible with his most private charge.

Inside their house, friends say Merkel assumes the traditional role of hausfrau. She relaxes by listening to opera and cooking very simple meals—her specialty is potato soup—even insisting on cleaning up afterward. At around four o'clock on Sunday afternoon, however, the weekend hausfrau resumed her weekday routine and started texting her staff regarding the week ahead.

Sauer hardly seems in awe of the league in which his partner now plays. At her fiftieth birthday party (which, in typical Merkel fashion, featured as "entertainment" a long lecture by a scientist entitled "The Brain: Complex System Without Conductor, Consequences for our Self Image"), Sauer turned to his wife at the stroke of midnight and said, "Come, Angela. I'm not a politician. I have to be at work early in the morning." In June 2011, after President Obama presented Merkel with the presidential Medal of Freedom—America's highest civilian honor—he and Michelle invited Merkel and Sauer to dinner in the White House's private quarters. Sauer sent his regrets, explaining that he already made plans to dine with a colleague in Chicago.

Once, before she stopped talking about her private life, Merkel revealed just how vital her husband is to her ability to shoulder the pressures of her position. "I would rather cancel three appointments than endanger our relationship," she told Herlinde Koelbl. "He plays a very important role in my political life. He tells me how a certain decision will affect the common man or woman. He brings me the outsider's view." Andreas Apelt, Merkel's boss when she was just beginning her political career, witnessed how closely the couple collaborated. "When she was our spokesperson, and there was chaos, and Merkel didn't know what to do, she would call Sauer. He would immediately send over a few sentences for her to use in our press release," Apelt told me.

Not only does Sauer act as her political sounding board, but he also provides a safe harbor to which she can retreat. "Sometimes all the talking is a problem for me," Merkel confessed to Koelbl, referring to the relentless sociability imposed by a political life. "With [Joachim], I don't have to say anything; we can just be together." Perhaps Sauer's greatest contribution is to help one of the world's most exposed public figures maintain emotional balance. "Our relationship provides me with security," she has said. Asked if she could manage without such a partner, she replied, "I would say, no."

Berliners have nicknamed Sauer the "Phantom of the Opera," because of his love of opera and his aversion to the media's attention. He is unapologetic about his right to maintain privacy. "I am a scientist. No one is interested in me," he (wrongly) insists.

Despite the strict boundaries she has erected between her public and private lives, Angela Merkel does occasionally—perhaps inadvertently—reveal how "normal" her marriage is. While attending a tech conference in

2020, the chancellor was asked if she had "smart" appliances in her home or if she turns on the washing machine herself. "Actually, my husband does the laundry," she replied matter-of-factly. The Merkel-Sauers, she thus made clear—like most other modern, professional couples—share household chores.

As to why such a well-suited and devoted couple chose not to have children, Merkel has said, "I cannot imagine this in combination with being politically active." At age thirty-six, years before she had remarried, Merkel explained her belief that "a marriage would not change my life. But the way I see it, having a child would require me to give up politics. At the moment, this just isn't an issue for me. And maybe it never will be." And it never was. By the time she and Sauer married, she was well into her forties.

As for her Berlin residence, it looks nothing like those inhabited by other heads of state. It's a modest apartment in an ordinary, four-story prewar rent controlled apartment building in the heart of former East Berlin; her husband's is the name on the house buzzer. Snaking along the narrow Spree River are familiar streets and cafes—joined, since she first moved to Berlin as a young scientist in the late seventies, by body-piercing shops, internet cafes, and Vietnamese, falafel, and vegan restaurants. This is the same neighborhood where, three decades earlier, Angela had been a "squatter"—where, on her thirtieth birthday, her father had noted bitterly, "Well, Angela, you certainly haven't come very far." Merkel still attends performances at the nearby Berliner Ensemble Theater on Bertolt-Brecht Platz. While she no longer takes the S-Bahn from the Friedrichstrasse Station, as she used to, she would likely prefer the train over her current commute in a black sedan, trailed by a follow car. When advisor Eva Christiansen returned from spending Christmas in New York in 2019, she noted the chancellor's wistfulness as she described her carefree and anonymous visit to Manhattan, an experience out of reach for the most powerful woman in the world—and one that will remain so even now that she has left office.

Though privacy and time alone are essential for Merkel, she is nearly always surrounded. From the beginning of her tenure, she not only kept her security detail two hundred meters away; but whenever she and her husband planned to attend concerts or the opera, she informed them only a half hour before departure, to prevent their arrival from disrupting the venue with security searches, barriers, dogs, or other conspicuous signs of their presence. During her early days as chancellor, Merkel once attempted to evade her security detail with a hasty exit through the chancellery's kitchen elevator, which had neither a camera nor a guard. Her freedom lasted only minutes, though: she arrived at the parking garage to find security guards and their dogs standing in formation.

Like an ordinary shopper, Merkel can be seen buying multiple pairs of the same black flats at a French department store on Berlin's Friedrich-strasse, with her security detail doing its best to remain invisible. Or dining with her husband in the small Italian restaurant she likes, in the quiet Char-lottenburg district. No matter how simply she lives, or how ordinary she appears—pushing a cart in "her" grocery store (Ullrich Verbrauchermarkt on Mohrenstrasse, as most Berliners are aware)—in the eyes of the world, "She has an aura, which, of course, comes from power," said Schlöndorff. Or, as Lady Catherine Ashton, former EU foreign minister, put it, "She's Angela Merkel! Of course you know when she is in the room." Her words, her quips, her frown—even just her arched eyebrows—all carry weight. Years ago, as Merkel was en route to her country house, her car hit a bump on the rutted road leading to her cottage. The chancellor emitted a single sound: "Oops!" The next day, work crews laid asphalt to smooth the road.

Public life not being her most natural environment, Merkel tends to escape into friendships with people who work outside the political sphere. They, too, however, are subject to her ironclad need for privacy. Schlöndorff recalled a memorable weekend at his house in Tuscany, Italy, where, along with his wife, Angelica, and Angela's husband, the friendship was sealed over rounds of grappa. The amity cooled however, after the director wrote a warm but somewhat teasing profile of the chancellor, playfully urging her to return to her life as scientist after her second four-year term. "Don't you sometimes miss teaching and doing research? Don't you yearn for the precision of science again, after the imprecision of politics and economics?"

For Merkel, a published profile—however glowing—is a breach of her privacy. Nor does she have any interest in returning to the laboratory. She may be an unorthodox politician, but she is utterly absorbed by politics. "It's the way to get things done," she has said. What lab could possibly match the electricity of life at the very center of the modern political world? In the thick of it for three decades, she is rarely bored.

Merkel's preferred company remains creative people in fields unrelated to her own. "Politicians are expected to repeat the same things pretty often," she once remarked slyly. "In my previous job as physicist, that was a mortal sin. In science, the task is never to tell the same thing twice, because it would indicate that you haven't done anything at all." Politicians, she implied, are boringly repetitive. A politician with a mind as lively and curiosity as far flung as hers is more interested in befriending artists and learning from them the secrets of their craft.

Schlöndorff introduced Merkel to German actor Ulrich Matthes—best known for his much-praised role as Propaganda Minister Joseph Goebbels in the 2004 film about the final days of Nazi Germany, *Downfall.* The actor and the chancellor forged a close friendship, and Matthes has spent weekends at Merkel's country house. She often attends his Berlin theater performances and afterward lingers over drinks late into the night, absorbed in conversations that—though Matthes is resolutely silent regarding their contents—doubtless have little to do with her day job. (Former British prime minister Tony Blair expressed surprise to the author Martin Amis when he discovered this little-known side of Merkel, saying: "She likes to sit up late and have a lively time.")

When international opera star Renée Fleming was in Berlin to perform at the twentieth-anniversary commemoration of the fall of the Berlin Wall, she "received word that Chancellor Merkel was hosting a reception downstairs in the Adlon"—the storied hotel where Fleming and her husband were staying. "I assumed there would be a thousand people there," she said.

"I went down and discovered there were eight people in attendance. The reception was just for us: the soloists and our spouses. . . . It lasted two hours! I couldn't help but think how early the chancellor's day must have started, and all those meetings she had attended, and then in the evening an open-air concert at the Brandenburg Gate in the freezing cold! She didn't seem tired, and she didn't seem in a hurry to leave. Her energy is incredible. We were surprised and honored that she would unwind by spending time talking to us."

Regulars at the popular Bayreuth and Salzburg Music Festivals, Merkel and Sauer avoid the pandemonium that follows other celebrity couples. With a faint smile and a slight tip of her head, Merkel politely acknowledges those who recognize her. The audience understands that she and Joachim have come for one reason: to enjoy Wagner or Mozart. The couple's body language makes that plain.

Lest one assume her tastes are entirely highbrow, Angel Merkel has a strictly middlebrow passion for soccer. During Berlin's World Cup finals in 2006, newspapers featured interviews with the normally press-shy chancellor "confessing to" her passion for soccer, which she traced to the age of seven. She claimed to follow matches at a pub near her weekend home, as she and her husband did not have a television set. "I like being in company when I watch soccer," she told *Bild*, Germany's largest circulation tabloid. She even allowed a camera crew to film her visit to the German team at their hotel, where she grilled the players with questions that showed she'd applied herself to mastering offside rules with the same zeal she brought to unemployment statistics. She astonished reporters following her around by drawing diagrams of soccer maneuvers and would soon invite coach Jurgen Klinsmann to her office to explain why the Germans had lost so disastrously to the Italians in the semifinals. With statistics, graphs, and charts, the country's highest-ranking soccer fan proposed a training plan for the speechless coach.

In 2012 the chancellor attended the G8 summit at Camp David, the rustic presidential retreat located an hour north of Washington, DC, while the European Soccer Championship Finals were taking place in Munich, where Britain's Chelsea Football Club was playing Bayern Munich. Prior to the summit, Merkel had asked President Obama for a TV set to be installed near the conference room. "I kept the chancellor informed by text messages about the score," said her national security advisor, Christoph Heusgen. "When Bayern got a penalty shot, she could no longer stay in the conference room and joined me in front of the TV set." Gradually, the other leaders followed her (including British prime minister David Cameron, French president François Hollande, and Manuel Barroso, president of the European Commission).

Finally, President Obama appeared and asked, "Did we come here for the G8 or to watch soccer?" To which the chancellor answered, "To watch soccer." After Chelsea broke a 1–1 overtime deadlock with a dramatic penalty shot, Merkel hugged Cameron. Obama's German interpreter, Dorothee Kaltenbach, growled, "*Scheisse*" ("Shit"), to which Obama responded with a smile, "That's the only German word I know."

According to former EU foreign minister Catherine Ashton, the normally serious chancellor even "sometimes walked into EU meetings with her earphones on, listening to a soccer match."

If music, soccer, and stolen evenings and weekends with creative people are means of escape for Merkel, so too are books. "She loves to read," her former spokesperson Ulrich Wilhelm said.

We would recommend books for her: mostly biographies and history. Before state visits, she reads widely both about the inner structures of countries she visits and the character of the leaders. Is the leader a collaborative person? What is his style? How emotionally stable is he? Between meetings and on trips, she is always reading. In this regard, she and her husband seem very compatible. I spent eleven hours on a flight with the chancellor and her husband, and Dr. Sauer worked the whole time on his laptop, reading PhD dissertations and writing grant proposals.

Not everyone appreciates the chancellor's zeal for knowledge. In 2014, when Merkel turned sixty, the former physicist treated friends and colleagues to her idea of a good time: inviting historian Jürgen Osterhammel to deliver a forty-five-minute lecture on how Europe and Asia perceived each other during the nineteenth century. (Merkel, who had broken her pelvis while cross-country skiing the year before, had spent part of her recovery reading Osterhammel's 1,600-page tome on the subject.) Hundreds of CDU party faithful crowded the cavernous Konrad Adenauer Haus headquarters, listening patiently and awaiting cocktails. "You could see on their faces that they had trouble following what the academic was saying. The impact of expressions like 'temporal horizon,' 'speed of interdependence,' or 'composite analysis' was tough on them," *Der Spiegel* magazine reported.

Merkel also looks for ways to squeeze in conversation with other high-achieving women, even during tightly scheduled official trips. The pleasure she takes in their company was on display at a breakfast held in 2015 at Blair House, the president's official guesthouse, across Pennsylvania Avenue from the White House. At Merkel's request, the event included a wide array of women she wanted to meet, including Supreme Court Justices Sonia Sotomayor and Elena Kagan, Senators Susan Collins and Dianne Feinstein, and philanthropist Melinda Gates. "We had a very personal conversation around the table," said Karen Donfried, head of the German

Marshall Fund, driven by no agenda except the chancellor's curiosity. "She wanted to hear from all of us about how we combine leadership positions with personal lives and the 'only woman in the room syndrome.' She clearly enjoyed being with other women."

Merkel, however, bristles at comparisons to that other history-making female leader, the late Margaret Thatcher. "That comparison just doesn't hold up," Hillary Rodham Clinton agreed. "Merkel lets her actions speak for her. Thatcher was much more image conscious. Her public presentation was a big part of her persona. Angela Merkel is about the work. Thatcher approached every meeting as combat. For Merkel, it's more about finding a solution to the problem, usually by meeting halfway."

Nevertheless, Merkel and the small-town grocer's daughter, elected British prime minister three times, had a few things in common: scientists by training, both were very much their own creations and, as women in the male political world, had to forge every inch of their own path. Both Merkel and Thatcher were elected by parliamentary systems rather than picked by ordinary voters. Both were women with powerful intellects, able to master volumes of data, and both were unflinching in the presence of overbearing men. In appearance, Margaret Thatcher—with her decorative handbags, jewelry, feminine suits, and gleaming helmet of lacquered hair—stood in stark contrast to Merkel's deliberately plain aspect. Thatcher's security was known to carry not only sidearms but also the prime minister's stiletto heels in their pockets. Unlike Merkel's, Thatcher's closest aides were all men.

Merkel enjoys surrounding herself with other brilliant and powerful women. But remarkably, when asked to raise her hand at a public gathering to signify if she was a feminist, Merkel hesitated before doing so. When Schlöndorff approached a German women's group to support a full-page ad endorsing Merkel's 2017 reelection bid, they turned him down. The chancellor, they informed him, had not been sufficiently vocal in backing feminist causes. "They think she ought to be more public in her support of the women," he explained, "rather than frequently declaiming as she does that she is chancellor of all Germans."

As on many other issues, Merkel prefers attacking the patriarchy sideways, not frontally. While meeting with a group of young business leaders in Israel in 2018, she welcomed the all-male future tycoons, adding, "I would not be disappointed if next time there were women among the future leaders." Later, during the same visit, Merkel was accepting an honorary doctorate from Haifa University, when its president, Ron Robin, proclaimed proudly, "Sixty-five percent of our students are women." In response, the chancellor inquired what percentage of professors were women, to which Robin answered awkwardly, "Well, ah, we have some catching up to do there." With a light touch, Merkel had made—and won—her point.

Calling out men for sanctimonious behavior has been a source of quiet pleasure for Angela Merkel. "Part of her ego is to win against strong men, like Helmut Kohl and the others. She respects strong men—but only if they are strong in substance, not talk," Thomas de Maizière noted. In private, Merkel also expresses contempt for politicians who are ill-prepared and incurious. "Two-thirds of them, aren't really interested in the issues. They don't even read the papers in their dossiers. They don't know what we are talking about," she vented to Ambassador Wolfgang Ischinger, referring to the other heads of state who form the European Council, the EU's ruling body. She, of course, reads every briefing book and is especially strong on technical and legal details, something her colleagues and opponents find hard to match. In negotiations, she leaves them flat-footed with her grasp of minutiae. Where others might use charm and threats to get their way, Merkel uses logic and facts. When her opposite number is left fumbling, she suggests coolly that he do his homework.

After many hours with Merkel, former Australian prime minister Kevin Rudd noted:

She does not play "the woman's card." It's not that she isn't womanly, but there is none of that attempt at playing your cozy grandmother that Golda Meir was known for. No, with Angela, you feel you are dealing with a great leader, and not a gendered one. Once, as we stood on the terrace off her office in the chancellery, with glasses of Riesling, looking out at that amazing view of Berlin, from below, a group of middle-aged Germans spotted her and began chanting, "Mutti! Mutti!" I asked her if that meant "Mommy," and, slightly embarrassed, she said that it did. "Well, Angela," I told her, "there are many worse things for a politician to be called." But it was a sign that German society is still pretty conservative.

To have become chancellor of a country where some still refer to a powerful woman as "Mommy" is an achievement that speaks for itself.

In April 2013, Germans were shocked to see photographs of their famously private chancellor wearing a bathing suit. A photo spread of Merkel walking on a beach in Ischia, off the Italian coast, in khakis and a casual blue shirt, as well as in a bathing suit, and then in shorts, helping her stepgrandchildren climb a rock, were the sort of family-centered snapshots most politicians would exploit as proof that they were "regular people." Not Angela Merkel. The photos, published by the tabloid *Bild,* created such a furor that they soon vanished from the internet.

From across the Atlantic, Hillary Rodham Clinton admitted to envying Merkel's ability to control the media. "It's just amazing! Those pictures of her on the beach appeared online and then disappeared," she marvelled. The outrage that this breach of the chancellor's privacy provoked did not come from her, but from the public. In an age punctuated by intimate photos "accidentally" posted to social media, even her critics grudgingly respect Angela Merkel's scandal-free reign and cede her a right unavailable to most public figures: privacy.

Merkel won that fall's election with an intentionally ironic campaign slogan: "You know me!" In fact, even after nearly seven years, Germans really did *not* know their chancellor. (As an example, I, as her biographer, am sometimes asked by Germans if the chancellor has grandchildren.) Her family, her siblings, and her stepchildren are a no-go zone for the public. Nor do they know how funny she is in private, nor that she likes to have a good time with lively people after hours. Remarkably, her countrymen accept her need for privacy and even admire her for it. Merkel was winking at her fellow citizens with her winning slogan. Everyone was in on the joke.

And yet she does occasionally reveal her deepest emotions publicly. "This isn't a speech I ever wanted to give," a visibly stricken Angela Merkel told mourners at the 2016 funeral of her foreign minister, Guido Westerwelle—the first openly gay public servant to hold high German office—who died at age fifty-four of leukemia. (Two years before, at her sixtieth birthday party, Merkel had asked for donations to a leukemia foundation in lieu of gifts.) Merkel, who has often said that she plans to have a life after politics, was especially saddened that "Guido Westerwelle would not be allowed to live his second life," as she put it. In her eulogy, the chancellor revealed how much closer their relationship had been than one of simply colleagues. "Guido and I talked about life. We cared about each other," she said. She spoke about the last time they were supposed to see each other. "We wanted to meet in the early evening in the chancellery, but Guido had to cancel, to gather strength for his TV appearance in the evening. 'Another time,' we told each other. There would be no other time," she said barely above a whisper. Rarely has Merkel spoken so openly about the heavy toll public life has taken on her personal relationships. A television interview had prevented her from saying good-bye to her friend.

Trust, a gift she bestows sparingly, was key to the pair's intimacy. "We were always able to depend on each other," she told mourners. "This ability to keep silent when necessary, to be able to count on each other, is very rare." Merkel has no higher praise than this.

Yet the chancellor has also retained affection and gratitude for at least one person, once close to her, who lost her trust—and whose trust she lost in return. In July 2017 she and other leaders of the West came together to bury Helmut Kohl, the man who, more than anyone else, can be credited with Angela Merkel's political ascent. Now his onetime protégé followed Kohl's coffin, draped in the European Union's blue banner, into the EU Parliament in Strasbourg, France.

"He was a great German and a great European. He gave millions of men and women behind the wall a chance to live in freedom. Me, among them," she said, deeply moved. Indeed, it is virtually impossible to imagine Angela Merkel's astonishing career without Helmut Kohl's early support of his *Mädchen*.

"Thank you, Helmut, for the chance you gave me."

Merkel's relationship with Barack Obama (seen here chatting with the chancellor against the spectacular backdrop of the Bavarian Alps in 2015) was more complex than the world realized at the time. Though they were similar in many ways, she was suspicious of his rhetorical brilliance, and he was sometimes annoyed by what he saw as her stubborn side.

10

LIMITED PARTNERS

Love is not too strong a word to describe Barack Obama's feeling toward
Angela Merkel.

—Benjamin Rhodes, aide to President Barack Obama

"Ladies and gentlemen! Madame Speaker!" thundered the sergeant at arms
of the United States House of Representatives. "The chancellor of the Federal Republic of Germany!"

On November 3, 2009, Angela Merkel, beaming and blinking back
tears, strode to the podium to address a rare joint session of Congress.
Members of the House and the Senate sprung to their feet, applauding her
with shouts of "Hooray!" Generally embarrassed by excessive applause,
Merkel seemed to bask in the genuine warmth of her audience. The first
German chancellor to address a joint congressional session in more than
fifty years, Merkel delivered the sort of speech she would never give in her
own country: she talked about herself.

"Not even in my wildest dreams could I have imagined twenty years
ago, before the wall fell, that this would happen," she began. "I created my
own picture of the United States from films and books—some of which were
smuggled in from the West by relatives." It wasn't just Bruce Springsteen

or the Rockies she idolized. "I was passionate about the American dream. That dream is the opportunity of everyone to be successful, to make it in life through their own personal effort." However elusive achieving the American dream had become by the late twentieth century, Angela Merkel had shown, four thousand miles away, that it could still be done sometimes.

Allowing the wild applause to subside, she resumed.

> Today is the time to say thank you to the pilots who delivered food by airlift, and saved Berlin from starvation. . . . To the sixteen million Americans stationed in Germany over the past decades. Without their support as soldiers and diplomats . . . it would never have been possible to overcome the division of Europe. . . . Where once there was a dark wall, suddenly a door opened, and we all walked through into the streets, into the churches, across the borders. Everyone was given the chance to build something new, to make a difference, to venture a new beginning. I also started anew. . . . Yes, all things are possible.

In America, where emotional displays are not only acceptable but admired, Merkel felt freer to express herself—her gratitude, her optimism—than she ever had in Germany. But, never one to devote an entire speech to feelings, Merkel also wove two substantive themes into her heartfelt tribute. Presciently, she spoke of those on both sides of the Atlantic who feared globalization, saying, "We do not just brush these concerns aside. It is our duty to convince people that globalization is an immense global opportunity for each and every continent, because it forces us to act together with others. Alliances and partnerships . . . will take us into a good future," she continued, articulating the heart of her administration's foreign policy. While these lines may have seemed boilerplate in 2009, a decade later, they seemed almost utopian.

In closing, Merkel acknowledged two of her American heroes,

Presidents Ronald Reagan and George H. W. Bush, for enabling Germany's unification, commenting, "There is no better partner for Europe than America, and no better partner for America than Europe." Neither she nor those who applauded knew that Congress's roaring welcome would be the high-water mark in Merkel's—and perhaps Germany's—relationship with the United States.

Angela Merkel was slow to warm to Barack Obama. Observing the charismatic young politician during his campaign for the presidency, she was skeptical. Unsurprisingly for a Lutheran, Merkel's favorite virtue is humility—and among the qualities initially ascribed to Obama, humility did not feature. He seemed to her a young man in a hurry, as he channelled Martin Luther King Jr. and JFK and mesmerized the audience at the 2004 Democratic Convention—loaded with charisma, light on achievement.

"She was somewhat wary of him at first. She wanted to know, 'What's his agenda? What is he really like?'" Hillary Clinton recalled. In 2008 the popular magazine *Stern* featured Obama on its cover, with the headline "Savior—or Demagogue?," reflecting an ambivalence shared by the chancellor.

Presidential candidate Obama had already committed a major faux pas: to burnish his foreign policy credentials, he asked Merkel's permission to deliver a campaign address at the Brandenburg Gate, Berlin's most historic intersection and the former border between the Soviet and American sectors of the divided city. In Merkel's mind, he had not yet earned that privilege. In reply, the chancellor proposed less hallowed ground: the Victory Column in the Tiergarten. Obama accepted the demotion of venue with grace, blaming his staff for overreach.

Venue notwithstanding, Barack Obama's Berlin debut was more rock festival than political event. With hope and love shimmering in a Berlin park on a summer evening, a speech turned into a sort of well-organized

Woodstock festival, as two hundred thousand Berliners filled the wide avenue that links the Brandenburg Gate to the gold-topped column known as the Siegessäule—symbol of Prussian military victory in the nineteenth century. Seemingly floating to the raised podium on a blue carpeted runway, beaming the wide grin soon to become familiar to the world, Obama responded to the roar of the crowd with a wave that triggered another cheer. The candidate's speech may not have coined a phrase as memorable as JFK's *"Ich bin ein Berliner"* or Reagan's "Mr. Gorbachev, tear down this wall!" but the times had changed, and 2008 did not lend itself to simple exhortations. Obama summoned the image of a different wall than his predecessors had. "The walls between races and tribes, natives and immigrants, Christian and Muslim and Jew, cannot stand. These are now the walls we must tear down!" he urged. The crowd roared its approval. Obama's speech received the loudest cheers when he declared, "No one nation, no matter how large, or how powerful, can defeat such challenges alone." After George W. Bush's eight years of aggressive disregard for global norms—most notably, launching a ruinous war in Iraq without a UN mandate and based on unverified "evidence" of Saddam Hussein's "weapons of mass destruction." This was an implicit promise of a more collaborative America, "of allies who will listen to each other, who will learn from each other, who will above all trust each other."

Yet Merkel remained an Obama skeptic. "The idea that a person can touch other people so much with words that they change their minds is not one that I share," she noted dryly. "Still, it's a beautiful idea." Was there perhaps an element of envy behind her skepticism? As she watched Obama fire up the crowd on television, she knew that she could never rouse an audience to frenzy with words alone. Nobody shouts, "We love you!" when Merkel closes her remarks.

Merkel is an almost aggressively dull speaker. Her relationship to words is one of wariness: the fewer the better; it's results that matter. Thus, she sometimes fails to capture a distracted world's attention, however urgent her message. Such was the case when she addressed the UN General Assembly in September 2007 to call out Iran's nuclear weapons program. "Nobody should have the slightest doubt as to the danger of this program," she cautioned, even as the Iranian ambassador sat within her range of vision. "Let us not fool ourselves. The world does not have to prove to Iran that Iran is building a nuclear bomb. Iran has to convince the world that it is not striving toward such a bomb." Such a blunt warning delivered by a more forceful speaker might have captured the world's attention; from Merkel, it was barely a blip on the screen.

Merkel behind closed doors is far more forceful than Merkel at the podium. Even before she became chancellor, she had a meeting with an Iranian envoy who argued heatedly for Iran's need of nuclear weapons. The envoy concluded by asking Merkel why Germany did not trust his country. Merkel countered by asking him his views on the subject of Israel. When the Iranian finished railing about "the Zionists," Merkel answered calmly, "Now do you see why we are skeptical?"

Whatever Merkel's reservations regarding Barack Obama, by 2010, two years into his presidency, 80 percent of her countrymen approved of him, a historic record for an American president. It took Obama's passage of the Affordable Care Act that year for even the chancellor to acknowledge that the new US executive in chief could deliver.

With time, the East German Lutheran scientist and the son of a Kenyan father and a Midwestern American mother discovered they were very much alike, at least temperamentally. Both were cerebral, trusted facts over emotions, liked charts and thick briefing books (Merkel especially), and preferred to depersonalize politics—treating it more as a job to be done than an identity. Both were outsiders who had beaten astonishing odds. Merkel was surprised to observe, however, that in smaller groups, the radiantly charming Obama often came across as unsmiling, professorial, and even lawyerly—with a sharp edge. "She loves brilliant people," said Victoria Nuland, Obama's assistant secretary of state for European affairs from 2013 until 2017. "Merkel felt that Obama was her intellectual equal." Nuland, who was frequently in the room with the two heads of state, added, "She was flirtatious with Obama—almost giggly. Sometimes she also showed an earthy humor and told slightly off-color jokes re Putin's anatomy."

Obama's admiration for Merkel only grew over the years. According to his aide Ben Rhodes, "Angela Merkel is exactly the type of leader he models himself after; she is pragmatic but willing to take chances for principles." Another aide, future secretary of state Antony Blinken, recalled the president saying, "If I want to know something about almost anything, I'll ask Angela.'" She had been in office only three years longer than him, but it was her judgment that he admired and counted on. Their relationship was aided by the fact that Obama is a sincere feminist, who noted frequently that if you put women in charge, you'd solve half the world's problems. After all, it was the men who were causing all the trouble: Putin, Erdogan, Netanyahu, and, later, Trump. "Insofar as Obama developed a real relationship with a head of state, or politician, he did with her," Blinken observed.

After her husband awarded the chancellor the National Medal of Freedom in 2011, First Lady Michelle Obama whispered to Angela, "Barack treasures you, you know." Merkel was so pleased by this declaration that she shared the comment with her travelling press, asking them, a bit disingenuously, "What do you think Michelle meant by that?" To the amusement of the dignitaries at the dinner later that evening, James Taylor serenaded the chancellor with his popular ballad "You've Got a Friend." Later, Taylor said that the choice of the song was not his, but requested by the White House.

Another common bond between the two leaders is that neither relishes politics the way Bill Clinton or Helmut Kohl loved the game. Neither needs the affirmation of the crowd to feel fully alive. And neither Merkel nor Obama particularly enjoys the company of other politicians, preferring idiosyncratic outsiders. Both see themselves as problem solvers, with politics as a means to an end rather than an end itself. Both eschew theatrics: you won't catch either of them landing on an aircraft carrier in a flight suit, as George W. Bush did in 2003 as the warm-up act for his wildly premature declaration that the United States' mission in Iraq had been accomplished.

Both Merkel and Obama read Yuval Harari's somewhat ponderous *Sapiens: A Brief History of Humankind* for pleasure. And though their tastes are widely different, both find escape and relaxation in music. Merkel connects most powerfully with the traditional Lutheran hymns of her childhood, which she still enjoys singing in church, and, like so many of her countrymen, is moved by Bach's *Christmas Oratorio* and *St. Matthew Passion*. She likes to cook simple German dishes to the soaring sound of Russian soprano Anna Netrebko singing the part of Violetta in *La Traviata*; Obama prefers Aretha Franklin, Prince, and hip hop artists such as Chance the Rapper and Jay-Z. Both also possess dry, at times cutting humor, hers often expressed through facial expressions alone. When she toasted President Joachim Gauck on his seventieth birthday, Merkel commented that really the best person to give such a toast would be Mr. Gauck himself, a quip worthy of Barack Obama.

And yet over the course of their eight years working together as allies, Obama and Merkel's differences also emerged—drawn out especially by the many crises they faced side by side. Obama's somewhat laconic negotiating style did not match Merkel's tireless pursuit of even an inch of diplomatic terrain. "Cut it out," Obama reportedly scolded Putin regarding his cyber war against America; in particular Russia's brazen efforts to influence the 2016 presidential election in favor of the Republican candidate, Donald Trump. Offended by Putin's lies, the US president simply gave up trying to reason with him. This was not Merkel's way. She persisted in talking to him and pleaded with Obama to call Putin during various crises. "I can't do this alone," she flatly stated, according to those present. "Putin lives in a fantasy world surrounded by sycophants who tell him what he wants to hear," Merkel told Obama. "He boasts about getting a call from the White House." Despite her pleas that he engage with Putin, Obama soon wearied of the Russian's ploys and encouraged her to carry the ball for the West.

Nor did the American president find dealing with Merkel all smooth sailing. Though he regarded the German chancellor as "steady, honest, intellectually rigorous, and instinctually kind . . . she was also conservative by temperament," Obama wrote in his 2020 memoir. "Not to mention a savvy politician who knew her constituency. . . . Whenever I suggested to her that Germany needed to set an example by spending more on infrastructure or tax cuts, she politely but firmly pushed back. 'Ya, Barack, maybe that's not the best approach for us,' she would say, her face pulling into a slight frown, as if I had suggested something a little tawdry."

The two allies also disagreed on fundamental political principles. Angela Merkel's skepticism regarding the use of force to solve crises was on full display in March 2011, when the UN Security Council voted on a no-fly zone to stop Libyan ruler Mu'ammar Gaddafi from savagely bombarding his own people. Despite tremendous pressure from within her own government, as well as from allies in Paris, London, and—above all—Washington, to stand united against this vicious dictator, Merkel abstained. It was a hard call for the chancellor, who places great value on avoiding a clash with the United States. But in the end, her conviction that wars have unintended consequences, and rarely solve crises, won out. She understood that a no-fly zone was much more than its antiseptic name suggested. "No-fly" meant bombing Gaddafi's air defenses and patrolling Libya's skies indefinitely; for Merkel, this was war by another name.*

---

*Later, when President Trump betrayed America's allies the Kurds by withdrawing US forces from Syria, Merkel again vetoed Defense Minister Annegret

Hers was a lonely and much criticized decision, which isolated Merkel from Washington and put her in agreement with China and Russia. But in light of the anarchy that ensued in Libya despite the no-fly zone, it is hard to disagree with Merkel's decision.

Perhaps, too, she regretted her support of another catastrophic American war, in Iraq. In 2003, when she was not yet chancellor, she wrote an opinion piece in the *Washington Post* stating that Chancellor Schröder's opposition to it was "election tactics." Now, as chancellor, she felt differently: the disastrous outcome of the protracted war in Iraq had shaken her faith in America's ability to achieve its goals in the Middle East. She feared a repeat of Iraq in Libya more than she feared a clash with the White House.

It didn't help that Obama's call for a no-fly zone came as a surprise. Until the last minute, Merkel had been reassured that war could be avoided. Her defense minister, Thomas de Maizière, visiting the Pentagon shortly before the Security Council vote, told Merkel that Obama's generals were opposed to war, and so, the brass assured de Maizière, was the American president. But as Obama still wavered, anti-Gaddafi rebels in the city of Benghazi grew desperate, and Obama's secretary of state, Hillary Clinton, and UN ambassador, Susan Rice, predicted a massacre on "our watch." Deciding on war after all, Obama failed to call Merkel about his change of heart. (She learned of it only through her UN ambassador, Peter Wittig.) Nor did Merkel call Obama to say she would abstain in the UN vote calling for a no-fly zone in Libya. This time German participation in a potentially never-ending war in the Middle East struck Angela Merkel as riskier than "Germany alone."

Following its bombing campaign, the United States largely turned its

---

Kramp-Karrenbauer's proposal for a NATO no-fly zone to rescue Kurds trapped in Syria, expressing her general aversion to German involvement in military operations. Besides, she said, "The Russians would veto it anyway."

back on Libya, which—without a central government—has continued to founder in chaos, proving Angela Merkel's antiwar stand to have been tragically prescient.

The Obama-Merkel relationship, however, did not hit its lowest point until two years later, on June 23, 2013, when Vladimir Putin announced joyfully, "Christmas arrived early this year!" He referred to the arrival of an Aeroflot flight from Hong Kong to Moscow, which brought American whistle-blower Edward Snowden with the "gift" of thousands of classified documents. After years of scalding criticism from Obama (and Merkel) regarding his human rights violations, Putin was eager to offer Snowden political asylum.

Declaring self-righteously that he wanted to "inform the public" about what the American government was doing in its name, Snowden began releasing thousands of pages of classified documents to the *Washington Post* and the British newspaper the *Guardian*. These documents revealed, among other secrets, that President Obama's administration had been listening in on Chancellor Merkel's private cell phone—something intelligence agencies may do discreetly from time to time, even among allies, but generally aren't caught and exposed for doing so. For a large segment of the German public, this revelation catapulted the twenty-eight-year-old defense contractor gone rogue as their new hero—replacing Barack Obama.

For a victim of a surveillance state whose own lab partner and close friend had spied on her throughout their twenties, Snowden's revelation left Merkel furious. She called Obama at once and let lose an unrestrained tirade, made more forceful as she blasted him in German. "We are not in a Cold War anymore. Friends do not spy on friends," she reproached him. There was nothing the forty-fourth president could say to placate her—a trust had been breached. So frosty did relations between the two countries become that even Christoph Heusgen, known for his surreal calm, ceased speaking with his White House counterpart, Susan Rice, for a period of time. The silence between such close allies was unsustainable for too long, however. No one recalls precisely how long it went on—just long enough for the Germans to make their point.

For Obama, the embarrassment was both diplomatic and personal. Merkel was his closest friend among foreign leaders. "Rarely, if ever, did I see President Obama more frustrated," observed Rice. Charles Kupchan, Obama's advisor on Europe, told me, "Our attitude was that the Germans are in this weird time warp. As if they can just be the great economic engine of Europe . . . and not play by Big Power rules of the game, which means everybody is tapping everybody." But that cynical approach rankled the chancellor.

Victoria Nuland read the chancellor's telephone transcripts. "We didn't get anything from those taps. Merkel is too smart to say anything sensitive on her phone," she told me. "It was more stuff like, 'Where's the dinner?' and 'What's on the schedule tomorrow?'" To Nuland, Germany's outrage wasn't due to the privacy breach. "I think it was embarrassing for Merkel, as it was a sign that she wasn't part of Obama's innermost trusted circle," unlike countries such as the United Kingdom and Canada, with which the United States regularly shares intelligence. "With Germany . . . we share economic information, but not intelligence, as we consider the Bundestag to be a sieve," Nuland said candidly.

The German media—particularly the tabloids—had a field day playing to latent anti-Americanism. Particularly infuriating for Germans was Snowden's revelation that the United States had eavesdropped from a listening post near the historic Brandenburg Gate. "If they intercepted cellphones in Germany, they broke German law, on German soil, and those responsible must be held accountable," Merkel's interior minister thundered. Peter Altmaier, Merkel's chief of staff, told John Emerson, the American ambassador to Germany, that concrete action would be required to make things right. Emerson promptly sent the head of the CIA office in Berlin packing. ("Somebody had to take the hit," the ambassador reflected.) Meanwhile, Obama dispatched his chief of staff, Denis McDonough, to Berlin to try to sooth Merkel and her staff—to no avail.

Plans were already in place for a state visit from Obama later that June. "It was meant to be a feel-good thing, but it became something quite different," said Ben Rhodes. Germany's national broadcast network, ARD, reported that more than 60 percent of the population now regarded the United States as untrustworthy, while only 35 percent viewed America as a reliable ally—barely more than those who deemed Russia a good partner.

When Obama arrived at the chancellery, Merkel led him to her balcony and pointed to the S-Bahn train she used to take to the lab each day. She explained what should have been obvious to the president: "The reason the Germans are so upset, and why I'm so upset, is that we grew up in a surveillance state." This honest conversation seemed to accomplish what previous efforts at reconciliation had not. Each time Obama and Merkel appeared together in public over the next days, they were battered by questions about "spying on friends." But in the end, Chancellor Merkel's strategy was to let the grass grow over the breach of trust. Too much else was at stake. While Obama never took responsibility publicly for the surveillance, he nevertheless announced that, henceforth, "We are not going to tape our allies." Merkel was neither a grudge holder nor one to personalize matters of state. She got over the fact that Barack Obama approved the tapping of her private phone, because she had to. She got a new cell phone.

In just two months' time, Angela Merkel and Barack Obama were confronted by far more urgent matters. It was a crisis that would prove the chancellor's necessity to Obama and bring the two heads of state closer than ever before.

In Syria, a revolution that began with peaceful chanting and marches calling for an end to forty years under the brutal repression of the Assads had taken a dark turn. For the past two years, the Syrian army, backed by Putin, fired on marchers with live ammunition and deployed barbaric "barrel bombs"—shrapnel filled containers dropped from helicopters—on neighborhoods in Damascus and Aleppo, forcing hundreds of thousands to flee. Then, in August 2013, a devastating chemical weapons attack in the suburbs of Damascus killed more than 1,400 Syrian civilians as they slept. As a scientist—and perhaps as a German—who understands the devastating power of sarin gas, Merkel was shaken to the core. At the same time, she was determined not to counter violence with violence, weapons with weapons. That is just who she is—and who she is not.

Barack Obama, however, appeared to stake his presidency on the issue. "What message will we send if a dictator can gas hundreds of children to death in plain sight and pay no price?

. . . Assad must go!" he exhorted on August 31. For the outcome-oriented chancellor, this raised a crucial question: Just how far would the American president go to make that happen? Obama's was an unforced error she would never make.

Days earlier, Secretary of State John Kerry had already announced to the world that the United States intended to hold Syria accountable with bombs, not words. Having declared that the use of chemical weapons against civilians was a "red line" for him, Obama asked Merkel to support a military response to Assad's assault. "We needed her support, as she was the dominant leader in Europe," explained Rhodes. "I'd seen Obama and Merkel sit for hours with notepads, strategizing on how to get the global economy moving or keep Afghanistan from exploding." Now, however, it wasn't Merkel's strategic expertise Obama needed. "Obama needed the moral support of the leader he most admired and respected," said Rhodes. The French were ready to launch missiles against Damascus. Merkel was not.

"I say this to you as your friend: I don't want you to get into a situation where you are left out on a limb," she cautioned Obama. She offered to build European support for a joint answer to Assad's attack. "Then we will have a situation where you are not exposed to vague allegations," she said, ever mindful of the fiasco of America's war in Iraq. At a minimum, Merkel wanted to slow down America's headlong march into another Middle East war, pleading instead for all-out diplomacy. Obama, meanwhile, wavered. Merkel's cautionary words, as related to me by Rhodes, had a powerful impact on the president. "It was the first time I saw him look uneasy about bombing Syria."

"You're shitting me, right?" the famously profane Susan Rice demanded of Chief of Staff McDonough when he informed his colleague that Obama had decided against striking Syria. Instead, he would go to Congress for approval to retaliate with force. The Republican-controlled Congress was highly unlikely to approve the president's request for this strike, or much of anything else. It was an attempt to save face—to have an excuse for going back on his word—but it didn't work. America's flip-flopping damaged President Obama's global reputation, and the perception of the "unenforced threat" shadowed the administration's efforts to influence Assad. Angela Merkel had proven to be a loyal and forthright ally, but she could not undo the damage from Obama's early and unwise call for Assad's departure as a precondition for negotiation—thereby ensuring that this thuggish dictator would fight to the last Syrian to hold on to power.

Angela Merkel was shocked by this depiction of her making a Nazi salute, which was burned in effigy in Greece in anger over her imposing austerity on the ravaged economies of Europe's southern states during the global financial crisis.

11

EUROPE IS SPEAKING GERMAN NOW

In the course of a thousand years, the Germans have experienced everything except normality.

—A. J. P. Taylor, British historian

One of Angela Merkel's goals upon taking office was to make Germany a
normal nation—an odd wish, perhaps, to people from countries that seek
greatness. But after the devastation of two World Wars and forty years as
a nation divided, the opportunity to quietly enjoy the fruits of a thriving
economy seemed a welcome change. Peace was better than war, prosperity
better than poverty. And to be a respected member of the European community was far better than being a pariah nation. Those were the bitter
lessons of post–World War II generations, seeped in the knowledge that—
within memory—Germany had twice blown Europe apart. They have
even invented a word for the painful process of coming to terms with their
history: *Vergangenheitsbewältigung*, which translates roughly as "grap-
pling with the past." And work it is, beginning early with school trips to
one of the many concentration camps that dot the former Third Reich.
Another part of this process is not antagonizing other nations, former

victims of a different Germany, with showy displays of patriotism or German superiority.

And yet, ironically, Merkel herself revived the old anxieties about an overly assertive Germany. A strong, united Europe had long seemed to her a sort of guarantee against Germany ever reverting to its aggressive past—or suffering again from Russian aggression. But in 2008 that vision nearly crashed along with the global economy. That year's financial crisis sparked unprecedented discord within the EU over a fundamental question: Just how responsible should Europe's stronger members, Germany foremost among them, be in helping the harder hit, weaker member states?

Merkel's management of this crisis would expose her strengths as well as her shortcomings as a leader. She would eventually succeed in saving the euro (€)—the common currency, since 2002, for nineteen countries in the so-called eurozone—appeasing her own conservative constituency, and cementing her status as the all-but-official chancellor of Europe. As *New York Times* columnist Roger Cohen wrote: "Henry Kissinger famously asked what Europe's phone number is. Now he knows: Dial Angela Merkel." But this success would come at a price: to her own reputation and to Germany's.

For Angela Merkel, the European Union is a historic triumph: a borderless continent with nineteen members all using the same currency. Created in 1999 amid the optimism of the post–Cold War era, the eurozone was seen as more than a monetary union; it was a Europe "whole and free," in which future conflict would be impossible and unthinkable, a Europe where Europeans no longer had to show passports or change money each time they crossed a border. As such, the euro was much more than a mere symbol; it was a key part of maintaining this unity.

The euro, however, was born with several significant defects. There was no European Federal Reserve akin to America's Fed, no central banking system to alleviate financial crises or to regulate the individual nations involved, all of which maintained separate political cultures, budgets, and deficits. Moreover, there is limited mobility for labor inside the zone. A laid-off Greek carpenter won't find a job as easily in Germany as one in Texas might land in Minnesota. Americans may think little of moving from state to state in search of work; Europeans are frequently tied to their local economies by language, culture, and history—meaning that there is no easy way to reduce a member country's unemployment rate.

Merkel was enjoying a Haydn opera at the Salzburg Music Festival—a summer ritual she shares with her husband—when her phone pinged with the first warnings of problems in the American housing market. "The IKB is in trouble," read the text from Jens Weidmann, her chief economic advisor. "What's the IKB?" the chancellor texted back. As she soon learned, it was a regional German bank, Deutsche Industriebank, whose Delaware head-quarters was already reeling from the subprime mortgage crisis. The tentacles of the globalized economy and its many financial institutions reached into every corner of the planet—including the second smallest state in the union, Delaware. That minor bank in trouble in the United States would trigger an unforeseen cascade of events that would preoccupy Merkel for years and reveal how far her vision of a united Europe was from reality.

Such complex concepts as subprime mortgages, toxic assets, and sovereign debts were initially terra incognita for Merkel. During her campaign for chancellor in 2005, she had once confused gross and net. Now, as the world's interconnected economy crumbled around her, she had to decode Wall Street's reckless and often intentionally confusing new financial "products." The basics were easy enough to grasp: cheap loans and easy mortgages spurred a high-risk rush to build and sell real estate, with deregulated banks and other lenders eagerly providing money to hundreds of thousands of borrowers who were unlikely to ever be able to repay. The result was a global liquidity crisis—a cash flow problem, in plain English—and credit squeeze, resulting in the worst financial crisis in more than seventy-five years. (It is not within the scope of this narrative—nor this writer—to delve deeply into the arcane world of global finance, beyond what it revealed about Angela Merkel's leadership.) Suffice to say that 104 countries experienced a downturn in both imports and exports, as well as a steep decline in manufacturing, trade, and employment—a testament to just how globalized the economy had become. In Europe alone, five million people lost their jobs.

Germany fared better than other European countries partly as a result of long-ingrained habits having to do with culture, politics, business, and financial practices. Its population resisted the debt-fueled consumption boom prevalent elsewhere in Europe and the United States. As a result of a tradition known as *Kurzarbeit*, or "short-time work," companies were encouraged to give workers fewer hours rather than firing them. A nation that believes deeply in the virtues of hard work, thrift, and living within one's means, Germany outproduced its neighbors and kept its unemployment well below most others in the eurozone during the global recession. Resentment of both Merkel, who embodies those qualities, and her country inevitably followed. It turned out that such feelings had never really disappeared in parts of Europe.

The crisis eventually revealed what should have long been obvious: Europe is made up of economically dynamic, mostly northern countries, while countries on the so-called periphery, with more stagnant economies, were forced to operate under the same rules as their wealthier neighbors as members of the single-currency eurozone. The countries hit hardest across the globe were, as always, the most vulnerable. In Greece, Portugal, Spain, and Italy, unemployment soared above 20 percent, with up to half of Greek youths out of work. Such statistics rivaled Great Depression–era numbers and exposed a chasm between the haves and the have-nots.

Those seeking someone to blame found a convenient, all-purpose villain in the woman many had recently hailed as the chancellor of Europe. Angela Merkel was caught in a vise between the need to assist Greece—a member of the interconnected and interdependent eurozone trade block—and growing resentment in Germany against bailing out the "profligate South." Merkel's vision of a solidly united Europe, where the richest country (Germany) lends a hand to the struggling was on a collision course with her fear that a bailout would create a culture of dependency in Greece and set a dangerous precedent elsewhere. This was her dilemma and her toughest test as chancellor to date.

Everyone had a different solution. Her finance minister, Wolfgang Schäuble, urged that Greece be dropped from the eurozone until it cleaned up its finances. But the chancellor's goal was reform, not eviction. Germans supported her chancellor on this point, even as other wealthy northern Europeans did not.

In seemingly endless meetings with fellow EU members, she often pulled out a chart that showed how much less productive Europe was compared to China. Europeans must learn to compete in the new globalized economy, she would argue; we must bite the bullet and suffer pain now for the sake of the future. Proud of her country's rapid reconstruction of West Germany following World War II, an economic miracle known as the *Wirtschaftswunder,* she wanted others to follow the German model of austerity, cutbacks, and instilling sound habits of citizens paying their taxes—as they had rather flamboyantly *not* done in Greece, to say nothing of the need to purge a political class that lied to its people about the health of the country's economy and stole from them in the process. So she prescribed belt tightening. No bailouts until they were earned with responsible behavior. Conservative by nature, austerity was her answer to most financial problems. "If everyone just sweeps outside their door, the whole village will be clean," Merkel said sometimes, quoting Goethe. She had calmed Germans, who trusted her by now, with a few words pledging the security of their savings. But she would not do the same for countries that were really hurting, beyond Germany's borders.

Merkel seemed to downplay the fact that for every bad loan there is both a borrower and a lender, and that some responsibility should be borne by the banks—the institutions that are supposed to assess risk and act wisely but instead had enabled the gross excess of spending on infrastructure and projects well beyond their capacity to finance in the afflicted countries. Rather than punish the enablers, Merkel seemed to many to be punishing ordinary people for the wrongs of governments and the international financial systems. This view of austerity as punishment may not have been far off the mark. Tellingly, the German word for debt is the same as for guilt: *Schuld.*

The Nobel Prize–winning American economist Joseph Stiglitz met with the chancellor in Berlin and offered advice she did not follow. "She chose a narrow, German identity as opposed to a European, 'We the People' identity," he said. To outside observers, it seemed that while the chancellor may have professed to love Europe, she wasn't willing to hurt Germany to save it.

Germany offered a model of austerity but was unwilling to act as expansionary counterweight—that is to say, to spend—to help speed recovery, according to Stiglitz. The price of the globalized, tightly interconnected world, where the fate of one impacted the fate of all, had come due.

Not for the first time, Merkel failed to factor in the role that irrationality plays in human affairs. Anyone in Europe over the age of seventy-five could remember the horrors of World War II. In Greece, anti-German sentiment was kept alive by memories of Nazi soldiers raising the swastika over the ancient Athenian citadel, the Acropolis, in 1941. And so it was Angela Merkel, not politicians closer to home, who was now burned in effigy in Greek town squares, as the country sank deep into the misery of double-digit unemployment. Trash piled up around the capital's historic Syntagma Square, as all nonessential personnel were laid off by the cash-strapped government. All those banks that eagerly provided cheap loans were out of cash themselves. Enforced austerity drained life not only from Athens but also Rome, Dublin, Ireland, and Lisbon, Portugal. Protests clogged streets in many of the Continent's ancient capitals, with Merkel depicted as the prime instigator of painful government cutbacks.

A more deft politician, gifted in rhetoric, would have gone to Athens and told its suffering population, "I will stand by you, but we cannot save you without some sacrifice"—a tough, Churchillian "blood, sweat, and tears" speech. Churchillian was, of course, not a natural mode for Merkel. When she finally did travel to Athens in October 2012, she experienced something new in her political life: public rage. Greeks lined the streets as her motorcade passed, jeering and waving banners that said, "Merkel, you are not welcome here!" A group burned a swastika flag as her car sped by, while another car, filled with people dressed in Nazi-style uniforms, broke through a police cordon. Merkel was shaken. In Germany, displaying the swastika is a criminal offense.

Pressure from President Obama added to her stress. "You need to act and be more decisive," he urged her. "Spend more of Germany's surplus on loans to the neediest countries." At the 2011 G20 Conference in Cannes, France, he prodded her, "C'mon Angela, You are the queen of Europe! You can do it!" To which she replied bitterly, "They call me the queen of Austerity." For perhaps the first time since the nineties, she shed tears of frustration in public. *"Das ist nicht fair. Ich bringe mich nicht selbst um."* "I'm not going to commit [political] suicide. . . . Our central bank is independent. You Americans wrote our constitution. You are asking me to violate restrictions on my office"—in other words, override her central bank—"which your country insisted on," she reminded him, referring to Washington's role in drafting Germany's postwar constitution.

But her emotions weren't public enough. In speeches, her stern mien and her pieties sent exactly the wrong signal to Europe's hardest-hit countries.

It is difficult to imagine two more dissimilar figures than Merkel and her chief European partner during these years, the hyperactive French president Nicolas Sarkozy, nicknamed "Bling Bling" for his showy antics and fondness for millionaire's yachts. An impulsive publicity hound, Sarkozy seemed to embody everything Merkel scorned. (It is difficult to imagine Carla Bruni, Sarkozy's glamorous singer-model wife shopping for fish, as Merkel's husband was observed doing in preparation for a dinner the chancellor hosted in honor of the French president.) Thrown together by circumstance, however, Merkel, as always, made the best of it. "Standing next to you, Nicolas, I feel like an energy-saving lamp," she once quipped.

Acknowledging their intertwined fates during the euro crisis, Sarkozy celebrated Merkel winning the prestigious Charlemagne Prize in 2008, in the historic German city of Aix-la-Chapelle, near the borders separating Germany, Belgium, and the Netherlands. "I have so much admiration for this woman of the East," the effusive Frenchman declared. "What a journey for a young woman from behind the Iron Curtain, at the head of twenty-seven countries and a reunited Germany!" Then, turning to the astonished Dr. Sauer, Sarkozy said, "Angela and I are a harmonious couple, and she is a woman of courage whom I have learned to respect in the last year, Monsieur Merkel." Dr. Sauer did not look amused.

Sarkozy's gaffe notwithstanding, this was a historic ceremony between two longtime rivals, and Merkel seized the moment to articulate why saving the euro and keeping Greece in the fold was more than a matter of economics. "Why spend countless days and nights to achieve a common goal after difficult negotiations? Because if the euro fails, it is not just the currency that fails," she said. "Europe fails." The common currency, after all, was as essential to a unified Europe as open borders.

"Merkozy," as French media dubbed the two leaders, ultimately forged an awkward but united front. Germany was too rich, too stable, and too vital to the health of the rest of the Continent—even France—to ignore. They gave an ultimatum to both the Greek prime minister, George Papandreou, and to Silvio Berlusconi of Italy, which was looking increasingly at risk: accept EU monitors to supervise their countries' finances in return for bailouts. They had no options left.

So, a deal was struck, but at a price. When the head of the Christian Democratic Union's parliamentary bloc, Volker Kauder, declared, "Now, all of a sudden, Europe is speaking German," in proud reference to Germany's role in the rescue of the euro, Merkel winced. The image of Germany dictating to Europe was among her nightmares, and yet she was partly to blame. She dawdled as millions suffered and took too long to appreciate the human cost of the global recession. She lost the public relations war. As the richest European country—and the lynchpin of the union she cherishes—she had no choice but to rescue the less fortunate, regardless of how shamefully their economies had been managed and regardless of the role played by Wall Street's reckless bankers in inciting this global financial crises. It happened on Angela Merkel's watch, and solving it was the unavoidable price exacted from the chancellor of Europe's wealthiest and best-managed economy.

Though Merkel would agree to several bailouts for Greece over the years, her sluggish response prolonged the pain. Her methodical approach to problems simply did not work when so many lives were directly impacted. For many, Merkel's excess caution also gave the impression that she was impervious to human suffering.

Angela Merkel explained once that she is able to sustain herself on stored energy during a crisis with very little sleep, then collapse once it has passed. For her, performing in public is more exhausting than unknotting complex problems. Avoiding drama helps economize energy; her description of herself as an "energy-saving lamp" is apt. A sturdy ego that doesn't need daily or hourly massaging is also an advantage. Seemingly immune to humiliation herself, she does not humiliate others. All of which frees her energies to deal with the problem at hand. If complexity annoyed her, she would have exhausted both herself and Germany long ago.

In 2015, in a decision that seemed to be a rebuke of Merkel's harsh austerity measures, Greeks elected Alexis Tsipras, a charismatic young socialist, as their leader. One of his campaign promises had been to escape the harsh regime Berlin had imposed as a condition for its third bailout. Before long, however, the newly elected Greek firebrand succumbed to the full Merkel treatment.

Tsipras's finance minister, Yanis Varoufakis, recounted how his boss was won over by Merkel through her "psychological manipulation and remarkable diligence."

> Angela Merkel suggested that after the formal EU dinner, the two of them get together so that Tsipras could present his document [regarding ending EU-imposed austerity on Greece], and they could discuss it. The formal dinner dragged on almost to midnight, and Alexis thought the chance for their tête-à-tête had disappeared. Not so. Angela led him to an adjacent conference room and proceeded to spend hours going over every sentence of the agreement with Tsipras. . . . When at last they had finished [four hours later, according to records], she congratulated him on the text. . . . Her congratulations, her diligence, and her mastery of the Greek plan in incredible detail made quite an impression on Alexis.

The all-night session between the two leaders resulted not in the loosening of Germany's budget reins, as Tsipras had hoped, but in his agreeing to Merkel's conditions—including higher taxes and spending cuts in exchange for that third bailout.

On the morning of July 13, 2015, after negotiating all night, Merkel faced television cameras at the Brussels headquarters of the European Union and announced that "Grexit" had been averted. Greece was staying in the EU. "The advantages outweigh the disadvantages,"* the visibly exhausted chancellor said in her typically succinct style. Journalist Bernd Ulrich, who was present, interpreted that statement as: "My dear people, it was really tough, and I have been working like a dog these past months (years!) to keep Greece in the EU. . . . This is very important for Europe. . . . But I don't want to make a big deal out of it. You know me! Anyway, I need to get to bed."

And with that, Merkel flew back to Berlin for a few hours' sleep in her own bed.

Germans may well have interpreted Merkel's comments as Ulrich suggested, but the chancellor was speaking to a far larger audience, one that was hoping for a different message: a message with heart. Merkel would never get the credit she deserved for supporting Greece's ultimate rescue from the brink.

The most dangerous by-product of this period, however, wasn't the blow to Merkel's image. It was the birth of the first successful post–World War II German far-right political party, the Alternative für Deutschland (AfD), which was founded in opposition to the EU's bailout of Greece. The rise of modern populism in Germany and elsewhere can be traced back to those first bank failures in 2008. But the significance of this new movement wouldn't reach the chancellor's notice until 2016; other crises would shield it from view until then.

---

*Merkel rarely explains her decisions, but the "disadvantages"of her agreement with Tsipras included a period of enforced austerity in Greece, followed by more responsible governing and higher growth until Covid-19 slammed the country in 2020, and derailed the positive trajectory it was embarked on—as the pandemic did elsewhere.

Daniel Baer ✓
@danbbaer

Wow. Chancellor Merkel is indefatigable. Week's travel looks like fictional airline route map from inflight mag. @dpa

Die diplomatische Woche der Bundeskanzlerin

	Donnerstag, 5.2.	Freitag, 6.2.	Freitag, 6.2.
Ottawa ⑥	❶ **Kiew** Friedensinitiative mit Präs. Hollande	❷ **Berlin** Empfang des irak. Ministerpräsidenten	❸ **Moskau** Zweiter Teil der Friedensinitiative
Washington D.C. ⑤		Berlin ②⑦	Samstag, 7.2. ❹ **München** Sicherheitskonferenz

So., 8.2./Mo., 9.2.
⑤ **Washington D.C.**
Gespräche mit Präsident Obama, Vertretern von Weltbanken etc.

Montag, 9.2.
⑥ **Ottawa**
Gespräch mit Premierminister St. Harper

Brüssel ⑤   ❶ Minsk Kiew ❶
München ④   Moskau ③

dpa-22223

Mittwoch, 11.2.	Mittwoch, 11.2.	Donnerstag, 12.2.
❼ **Berlin** Kabinettssitzung	❽ **Minsk** Ukraine-Gipfel	❾ **Brüssel** EU-Gipfel

10:13 PM · 2/10/15 · Twitter for iPad

A map of the chancellor's exhausting travel schedule during her shuttle diplomacy in search of a peaceful solution to Putin's war on Ukraine in 2014. She negotiated on the West's behalf, as she was the only leader who could get through to the autocrat.

12

THE WAR IN UKRAINE—"GET ME ANGELA ON THE PHONE"

War is only a cowardly escape from the problems of peace.

Thomas Mann, German-American author (1875–1955)

If the eurozone crisis forced Angela Merkel to assume responsibility for Europe's financial stability, Russia's war in Ukraine forced her to take on a role she wanted even less for Germany or herself: that of political leader of the West. The role would be exhausting and nerve wracking. In Ukraine, Merkel would exhibit her superior skills as negotiator but also expose the limitations of her brand of dogged diplomacy in an increasingly lawless, authoritarian era. The playing field pitting the revanchist Kremlin autocrat against the principled, cautious Merkel—confined by the German constitution's weak executive powers—was far from level. Nevertheless, Merkel proved she could stand up to Putin when others would not (or could not). As the crisis escalated, Merkel would emerge as the most determined defender of established democratic norms, which—with the notable exception of the bloody wars in the Balkans in the 1990s—faced their gravest challenge since the end of the Cold War.

Ukraine, the second largest country in all of Europe, has long been the tragic victim of geography. Both Hitler and Stalin aimed to subdue and exploit this region on the Continent's periphery for its fertile farmlands; rich natural resources, including iron ore, natural gas, and petroleum; and strategic significance straddling East and West. Indeed, more died in Ukraine when Hitler and Stalin were in power than anywhere else in Europe. For Hitler, Ukraine's large Jewish population made the region an ideal target for mass murder. Before him, Stalin aimed to bring the second most populous part of the Soviet Union to heel by imposing collectivization and industrialization, robbing peasants of their own produce and turning them into beggars—and then cadavers—in the twentieth century's second-worst man-made famine. (The worst came later in Maoist China.) Rafael Lemkin, a Polish lawyer who coined the word *genocide*, called Ukraine "the classic example of Soviet genocide."

After the fall of the Soviet Empire in 1991, Ukraine, its land and population bled dry by Hitler and Stalin, and with virtually no democratic traditions to fall back on, struggled for decades under various corrupt or semicorrupt mostly former Communist leaders until 2014, when it seemed that at last its fortunes might improve. But that was when Putin began to aggressively assert old Russian claims over this long-suffering country, causing Ukraine to capture the world's attention, and sucking Merkel, Putin, and, so far, three American presidents into its vortex. At the root of the crisis was Putin's goal of restoring Russia to its historic place among the world's powers. To achieve this, he needed first to restore its old empire. He needed Ukraine, its immediate neighbor to the east and northeast, inside Russia's orbit, loyal not to Washington or Brussels but to Moscow.

The trouble began in February, when Ukraine was on the brink of signing a wide-ranging political and economic agreement with the European Union that would open up favorable trade with the rest of the Continent, and pull Ukraine closer westward politically—while holding out the prospect of eventual EU membership. Determined to block the deal, Putin pressed Ukraine's corrupt president, Viktor Yanukovych, to instead join Russia's own Eurasia Economic Union—a political, military, and economic alliance he'd established as a countermeasure to both the EU and China. Assuming he would be able to buy off the restive population with a $15 billion check, Putin promised to bail out Ukraine's faltering economy. In return, the country was to withdraw from the EU trade deal.

But events took an unexpected turn. Fearless, youthful demonstrators flooded the ancient streets of Kiev, demanding, "Yanukovych must go!" Over the next days, the crowds swelled and grew bolder, and their calls to end the corruption that had long sapped their country's future grew louder. They demanded that Yanukovych sign the pro–European Union treaty, as he had promised. Putin observed these protests, reminiscent of the traumatic events he'd witnessed in Dresden in 1989, with alarm; mob rule was spreading within a territory he deemed Russia's "sphere of interest." His worst nightmare seemed to have jolted him awake.

On February 18 Yanukovych's troops opened fire on a demonstration in Kiev's Maidan square, killing a hundred protestors and turning a peaceful protest into an uprising. Three days later, unable to control the crowds and fearing that his fate would be akin to those of other despised dictators, Yanukovych fled to sanctuary in Russia. Hearing this news, the Maidan demonstrators erupted in wild cheers.

Two observers from outside the country—both personally familiar with the mechanics of authoritarianism—understood the significance of the power vacuum that Yanukovych's departure had created in Ukraine. Angela Merkel recognized its peril; Vladimir Putin grasped the opportunity.

Putin moved first.

Maskirovka (masquerade) is a technique developed by the Russian military in the early part of the last century that can be summarized by three words: deception, denial, and disinformation. On February 27, not quite a week after Yanukovych's flight, a motley crew of Soviet veterans of the war in Afghanistan, Russian intelligence agents, pro-Russian Ukrainians, and mercenaries, all wearing unmarked uniforms, seized public buildings in the Crimean capital of Simferopol, as well as in the major Black Sea port of Sevastopol (where Russia maintains a naval base) and in the southeastern cities of Donetsk, Luhansk, and Kharkiv, declaring Ukraine's independence from Kiev.

The weak Ukrainian armed forces were caught flatfooted. Years of neglect and corruption had stripped down the military to a poorly equipped force of thirty thousand—no match for a modern Russian military invasion; the Yanukovych government had even put the building that housed the Defense Ministry up for sale. In Washington, DC—at the Pentagon and in the White House—alarm spread quickly. "We feared the Russians would continue their advance to Mariupol, Ukraine's only major port on the Sea of Azov," said Evelyn Farkas, a Pentagon official charged with Russian and Ukrainian affairs during the Obama presidency.

Psychologically, the United States was almost as unprepared as Ukraine for this Cold War scenario. "We had been getting intelligence reports of the Russian military modernizing, upgrading the threat of action to high," Farkas admitted. But while Russia had invaded neighboring Georgia in 2008, that had been assumed to be "a unique event. The Cold War was over. Armies were not supposed to march on their neighbors in twenty-first-century Europe. The policy people in the administration were not that concerned," recalled Farkas. Now Washington advised the Ukrainian military to stay in its garrisons to avoid a bloodbath.

Merkel was somewhat less surprised than her American counterparts were. She had never been under the illusion that Putin would turn into a freedom-loving democrat. She had hoped, however, that his love of wealth and the West's example of the riches to be won through innovation would prod him toward more open and EU-friendly policies. Until 2014, Merkel had optimistically let the EU manage Ukraine policy—what there was to manage. Ukraine was not a major concern of hers. Putin's invasion shattered a vision of European security that had been enshrined in countless treaties and documents promising to respect one another's borders and sovereignty—all signed by Russia. By invading Ukraine and claiming Crimea,* Putin was now defining Russia's future not as a part of the West but in opposition to it.

Even as the West reeled, Putin continued to move, spewing a cloud of lies and shifting versions of events that were straight from a dusted-off Soviet-era script. "Illegal Fascist Junta Threatens Kiev and Russians in Crimea," the Kremlin claimed, while deploying social media and all other available means of communication to fuel local mobs. Given a large Russian population in Crimea, the lies fell on susceptible ears. In Donetsk, a major industrial center, pro-Russian militia in camouflage and ersatz military gear stormed the local legislature, brandishing Soviet and czarist-era banners (with even a Confederate flag for added nostalgia). Putin claimed the population of Crimea had requested Russian intervention—the same Kremlin-hatched fantasies peddled in 1956 to justify crushing the Hungarian Revolution and reprised in 1968 to validate sending tanks to extinguish the Prague Spring in Czechoslovakia. Even as far back as 1948, Moscow had justified the Soviet blockade of West Berlin with the same script in the opening confrontation of the Cold War. But the Cold War was supposed to be over.

The West was divided over how to respond. President Obama had neither patience nor the credibility to deal with the Russian leader, whom he had derided publicly. "If Putin were that self-confident, he wouldn't keep

---

*Crimea, a peninsula on the northern coast of the Black Sea, had changed hands between Ukraine and Russia many times in its history, but it has been officially part of Ukraine since 1954.

taking his shirt off all the time," he had been quoted as saying. Referring to Russia as a "regional power" didn't help their relationship, either. Unlike Obama, Merkel did not have the luxury of publicly venting her views about the Russian autocrat. Kiev was 5,000 miles from Washington, DC; Ukraine's capitol was a mere 750 miles from Berlin. Giving Putin the back of her hand was not an option.

The chancellor, unsurprisingly, advocated diplomacy as the way out. "Merkel had enormous confidence in her ability to talk and even reason with Putin," said Victoria Nauland. "She would say, 'Let me soften him up a bit.' She frequently reminded us, 'I'm a scientist. I like to break down problems to their smallest and most manageable parts. And I don't let emotions get in the way. What counts is finding solutions." While he remained skeptical, Obama had no better idea for responding and left her to take charge of the situation and work with Putin on the West's behalf. His decision was based on a combination of his personal distaste for engaging with the Russian leader and his respect for Merkel's ability to get the job done.

Putin rarely engages at length with foreign leaders who are not in some way beholden to him. Merkel was the exception. It's not that she was eager to mediate between Putin and the West. Nor did she have her sights set on a Nobel Peace Prize—awards are not a validation she seeks, not even that lofty one. She simply understood that she was best qualified for the task. The president of the European Council, Herman Van Rompuy, was intimidated by Putin and unenthusiastic about the prospect of negotiating with him. Merkel alone seemed immune to the menace of Putin's silences—as well as his other KGB stratagems.

Putin was as determined as Merkel to win this showdown, but, unlike her, he was willing to use weapons to get his way. Russian troops, whether uniformed or not, were on the move in the Donbas, Donetsk, and Luhansk regions of Ukraine, driving people from their homes with bombs and tanks and mowing down Ukrainians for defending their own country, even as a beaming Putin attended the magnificent closing ceremony of the Sochi Olympics.

Seething quietly, Merkel would nonetheless speak to Putin thirty-eight times during Russia's offensive in Ukraine. "They were in daily contact. She tried to get him to climb down from his aggressive, bombastic behavior through patient talk," said Wolfgang Ischinger, a member of the chancellor's negotiating team. Merkel was determined to provide Putin with an off-ramp from what she saw as a fundamentally nefarious and unprovoked war. Whatever her private views—and disgust is not too strong a word—Merkel felt that by talking, she might eventually bring Putin back to reality. "She is such a rational being, she felt that at some point he would understand that his position—in overt violation of a nation's borders—made no sense in 2014," Ischinger explained. Though she desperately hoped to get Putin to give up the territory he had seized already, she was also stalling for time. After years of terrible neglect, the Ukrainian army needed to rebuild—if not to defeat the vastly better equipped Russian army, then at least to block its advance.

Putin and Merkel would generally begin their conversations in Russian, but when the chancellor aimed for absolute precision, she switched to her native tongue. First, she tried reason. "You are in defiance of international law," she told him, using the informal *"Du,"* as she always does with Putin. But he continued to lie to her, denying that the offending troops were his. "Anybody can buy our uniforms," was his shameless explanation.

To demonstrate that his lies had consequences, Merkel cancelled their next calls. Russia, she knew, could ill afford a total rupture with its most important trading partner on the Continent. Nevertheless, for six weeks, Putin kept up the fiction that the troops dismembering Ukraine were not Russian—even as his commandos seized the Crimean regional parliament and two airfields. "He is living in his own world, out of touch with reality," Merkel told Obama bitterly.

"She would call Obama after talking to Putin," Antony Blinken, then a White House aide, recalled. " 'I don't know what to do with a man who just lies constantly to me,' she told Obama, who laughed and said, 'Makes two of us.'" Putin did not necessarily expect to be believed. His lies were a taunt; it's impossible to negotiate with someone who won't even admit to his or her position. Trained by the KGB to spread confusion and doubt, actual diplomacy was not part of the Russian's repertoire.

His bravado, however, Merkel was better equipped to deal with. Germany's ambassador to Washington, Emily Haber, observed Merkel negotiate and noted, "She drains the drama out of her interlocutor's posturing by restating what he just said in the simplest—almost childlike—language. When Putin blusters about his 'national interest' or 'historic grievances,' Merkel boils it down to a few simple phrases, making him sound less than brilliant." Her goal was always to make her opponent spell out what exactly he was trying to achieve, free from the clouds of verbiage, so that serious negotiation might take place.

Those who saw her during those tense weeks agree that Merkel kept her emotions under tight control. "I kept thinking, she must be so pissed off at this unholy and unprovoked crisis," said Daniel Baer, former US ambassador to the Organization for Security and Co-operation in Europe (OSCE). "But I never saw her angry. She had this look that said, 'I can't afford to be angry. People with smaller problems can afford anger. I can't.'" Years before, Merkel shed light on what happens to her in such moments. "I am as focused and as concentrated as a tightrope walker, only thinking about the next step," she said. Without tanks or stealth militia to match Putin's, her weapons in this fight were mostly focus and steely determination.

The chancellor opposed sending heavy arms—advocated by some in London, Paris, and Washington—to help the desperate Ukrainian forces. Beyond a deeply held conviction that arms fail to end most conflicts, and frequently escalate them, Merkel was also mindful of her countrymen's

Nineteen-year-old Angela Kasner (second row center) at a New Year's Eve party with Templin friends. She was the first in her class to wear blue jeans, which resulted in a lecture from her school principal about "inappropriate Western attire."

In 1989 Angela Merkel and her future husband, Joachim Sauer, attended a summer course in chemistry in the Polish city of Bachotek. They are shown here with Malgorzata Jeziorska, a Polish professor of quantum chemistry.

A very rare, undated picture of Angela and her two younger siblings, Irene and Marcus. Marcus followed his older sister to a career in physics. Irene is a physical therapist. Though both are close to their famous sister, they never give interviews regarding Angela.

In 1990 Angela Merkel campaigned for a seat in the Bundestag for the first time, seeking to represent the district of Mecklenburg Vorpommern. She is shown here in a fisherman's hut on the island of Rügen in the Baltic Sea. A low-key but empathetic campaigner, she was elected that year and in every subsequent election until her retirement.

Angela and her parents, Herlind and Horst Kasner, in 2005, the year their daughter became Germany's first woman chancellor. Angela was closer to her mother than to her rather aloof and demanding pastor father, but, as lifelong socialists, neither parent ever voted for her.

On January 21, 2007, Russian president Vladimir Putin, aware of Merkel's fear of dogs, unleashed his black Labrador, Konni, to test her mettle during her visit to his palatial residence in Sochi. She did not flinch but told her staff later, "He has to do this to show his manhood." Their relationship would be among her most vexing and longest lasting with any head of state.

Angela Merkel spent her fifty-sixth birthday in Xi'an, China, admiring the famous Terracotta Army of the First Emperor. Merkel was fascinated by China's long, rich, and turbulent history, and invested great effort and time—including annual trips—to cultivating close relationships with Beijing's leaders. By the end of her time as chancellor, she would be deeply disappointed by Xi Jinping's hard authoritarian turn.

President Barack and Michelle Obama welcomed Angela Merkel and Joachim Sauer to the White House on June 7, 2011. At that evening's state dinner held in the chancellor's honor, Obama presented Merkel with America's highest civilian honor: the Medal of Freedom. Their relationship was not always smooth, but Obama considered Merkel his role model as head of state.

Angela Merkel is a soccer fanatic. Here she interrupts a G8 conference at Camp David on May 19, 2012, to watch Germany's Bayern-Munich play against Britain's Chelsea. She is joined by Obama and a jubilant British prime minister David Cameron, as well as José Manuel Barroso, president of the European Commission; French president François Hollande (seated); and the chancellor's national security advisor, Christoph Heusgen.

The selfie that went viral: the Chancellor posed with Iraqi refugee Shaker Kedida at a refugee reception area in Berlin on October 9, 2015, the year she allowed close to a million Middle Eastern refugees to enter Germany.

The chancellor shows Queen Elizabeth the view of the rebuilt Reichstag from her chancellery terrace on June 24, 2015.

Europe's two most powerful women: president of the European Commission Ursula von der Leyen, and her mentor, Angela Merkel. Von der Leyen, a doctor who is also the mother of seven, was formerly Merkel's defense minister. The chancellor has quietly supported other women as they follow in her footsteps.

Angela Merkel enjoyed a brief taste of freedom during a walk on the beach in Biarritz, Spain, breaking away from the G7 summit meeting in August 2019, accompanied by her security detail and her press speaker, Steffen Seibert.

Shortly after her heartfelt warning to the nation regarding the looming Covid pandemic, the chancellor was seen shopping in her neighborhood grocery store. Note that there are more bottles of wine in her cart than rolls of toilet paper. Merkel beseeched her country-men not to hoard.

strong pacifist streak. (A 2015 poll showed that six out of ten Germans oppose the use of force, even if an ally is attacked.) Moreover, under the German constitution, the German armed forces are not under the chancellor's direct command.[*]

Some would argue that the Federal Republic and its chancellor have overlearned their own history. Such critics missed a crucial distinction: "history," to many in the West, means World War I and World War II. Merkel's formation was the Cold War. The West ultimately defeated the Soviet Empire through containment, patience, and strategy. NATO forces did not liberate Hungary, Czechoslovakia, or West Berlin when Soviet tanks rumbled into their capitals, with no plans to leave. When pressed about why the West should withhold lethal weapons in Ukraine's fight to survive Putin's aggression, Merkel explained:

"As a seven-year-old child, I saw the wall being erected. Although it was a stark violation of international law, no one believed at the time that one ought to intervene militarily in order to protect the citizens of East Germany. I'm one hundred percent convinced that our principles will in the end prevail. No one knew that the Cold War would end when it did—but it did."

Angela Merkel lived to experience liberation—her own, as well as her country's—without bloodshed. Now the cautious realist in her prevailed over the indignant idealist.

By March 2014, Putin ordered a referendum in Crimea, which—under Russian armed presence and with a large ethnic Russian population—unsurprisingly voted to join the now reconstituted Russian Empire. On March 18 a triumphant Putin announced, "In people's hearts and minds,

---

[*]A two-thirds majority of the Bundestag must approve war if the country is under direct threat.

Crimea has always been an inseparable part of Russia." A month later, he finally admitted that the so-called little green men—militia without signifying badges—were Russian servicemen in disguise.

By now, the Republican foreign policy establishment in Washington supported arms deliveries to Ukraine, but those in the Obama administration pushing for this were outvoted. The White House feared the conflict turning into a proxy war between Russia and the West. Given Obama's respect for her judgment, Merkel figured prominently in this decision.

According to historian Timothy Snyder, this was a mistake. "Merkel and Obama should have provided missiles and other lethal weapons to the Ukrainians, who were fighting for their survival," he told me. "It would have shown the world that they considered Russia's invasion sufficiently serious." The West's chief negotiator, however, remained adamant. Merkel had observed the unintended consequences of "winnable" conflicts in Iraq and Libya, and she saw no way that Ukraine could ever compete with Russia in a military confrontation. She also understood before most did that tanks and artillery were not the most dangerous weapons of war in the twenty-first century. "I fear nonmilitary, hybrid warfare which *undermines our democracies, infiltrates our media, and shapes our public opinion*," she would say at the Munich Security Conference in 2015. Hers was an early warning of the approaching battlefields of cyber war, social media, and disinformation campaigns—warfare at which Putin was already proving to be more nimble than the West.

"We had plans to push back against social media as a platform for disinformation," Blinken said. "We went to Silicon Valley to discuss ways to curb Russian disinformation. But we just didn't get the giant role of social media's impact." In 2016 the Obama administration and the candidate running to succeed him, Hillary Clinton, confronted Putin's powerful new weapon, but, by then, it was too late.

Weaponizing information has been one of Russia' low-cost techniques to sow dissent among democratic states. It's not as though states don't routinely listen in on one another's phone calls, but there is an unwritten rule that nations do not then make public the information they've gleaned. In February 2014, however, while Putin's militia attacked vulnerable Ukrainian targets, he diverted the world's attention with one of his "shiny baubles," in Snyder's words, leaking a conversation between Victoria Nuland and George Pyatt, America's ambassador to Ukraine, wherein the two discuss various Ukrainian politicians. Pyatt is heard complaining about how slow the EU was to act decisively. Nuland cuts him off with "Fuck the EU!" The tape went viral and briefly made Washington, not Moscow, seem like the arrogant bully in Ukraine.

Merkel was offended by Nuland's carelessness on the phone. Though the chancellor occasionally lets rip with profanity, it's usually in reaction to a missed goal. (Though the English *shitstorm* is a term she has used a number of times to describe political and media turbulence.) But given her East German–bred paranoia about surveillance, Merkel would never be caught saying anything potentially compromising in a phone conversation. Christoph Heusgen asked Nuland to send the chancellor a note of apology for this breach of diplomatic protocol, which she duly did.

During negotiations, Merkel had her own *maskirovka* moment. Knowing of Putin's need for the international community's affirmation and his desire for membership in the most exclusive club of European and North American powers, the G8, the chancellor delivered a double blow. Putin had expended enormous effort and millions of rubles in staging the 2014 Winter Olympics in Sochi, soon to be followed by a G8 summit in the newly constructed Olympic city, a perfect backdrop to display that Russia was back in all its czarist splendor. But Merkel spoiled his party. Not only did she announce that there would be no G8 summit in Sochi, but also she shared that Russia was no longer a member of the club. Exercising soft power was Merkel's way—but she showed that soft power could deliver a blow Putin would feel.

• • •

During the spring and summer of 2014, Russian troops were still on the move in eastern Ukraine, inflicting thousands of casualties on both civilians and soldiers, and taking prisoners. Negotiations between Putin and Merkel had reached a standstill. Then, with a single terrible event, Putin inadvertently revived Obama's interest in ending the conflict—and in backing up Merkel to do so.

During a rare telephone conversation with Obama on July 17, Putin broke in to say, "Mr. President, I am getting reports of an airplane crash over Ukraine . . ." Obama signalled aides to check with the intelligence services as he continued talking to the Russian president. By the time he hung up, Obama's computer showed images of bodies and body parts drifting over eastern Ukraine, where Russian forces were still fighting locals. Flying from Amsterdam to Kuala Lumpur, Malaysia Airlines Flight 17 had been blown out of the sky by a Russian separatist antiaircraft missile. All 298 passengers, many en route to an AIDS conference, were killed.

The next day, the White House concluded that the plane was shot down by a Russian-made surface-to-air missile that had been launched from Russian separatist territory in eastern Ukraine. Typically, Putin responded with feigned indignation, followed by heated denials and the usual countercharges of fake news reports, Western official, and media bias. Despite his blizzard of lies, international outrage erupted against what amounted to state-sponsored terrorism. Five countries were directly affected by the tragedy: Australia, Belgium, Malaysia, Ukraine, and the Netherlands, the last of which lost the greatest number of citizens.*

The shooting down of a plane carrying civilians created a firestorm in

*In March 2020, after six years of investigation, the trial of four men with ties to Russian security services, charged with 298 counts of murder (each punishable with up to a life sentence in prison), finally began. Among those cited for "daily contact" between the accused and the Kremlin was Putin's close advisor Vladislav Surkov.

the Obama administration and a shift in relations between Washington and Berlin. Denis McDonough, Obama's chief of staff, set up a hotline between himself and Peter Altmaier, his German counterpart. Having concluded earlier that engaging with Putin was a waste of time, Obama henceforth was all in—as long as Angela led the effort. From here on, the pair would be in lockstep. Obama routinely instructed aides, "Get me Angela on the phone."

That September, at a NATO meeting in Wales, the Western alliance committed to "reinvigorate" its military and defense capacities and pledged to establish a rapid reaction force that would be permanently stationed in Eastern Europe. President Obama, back in the traditional Atlanticist mode he once shunned in favor of the pivot to Asia, pounded on the table and called on all NATO members to spend more on defense, grumbling to aides that members were "all hat and no cattle" when it came to military spending. (In her sixteen years as chancellor, Merkel did not give a single speech about Germany's weak defenses. She understood that the topic remains unpopular, and her heart was obviously not in persuading her countrymen otherwise.)

Meanwhile, confident in her own powers of persuasion, the chancellor, with the aid of other European leaders, kept talking to Putin. That same month, in the ornate ceremonial hall of the Palace of Independence in Minsk, Belarus, Merkel and Putin hunched over a map of the contested region, locked in negotiations over the fate of Ukraine, sometimes for fifteen hours at a stretch. Merkel spent so many hours at that table, she said she realized the time of day only by whether roast meat or bread and jam were being served.

Equipped with aerial photographs, battlefield maps, and up-to-the-minute intelligence on the progress of Russian troops, Merkel asserted her forensic familiarity with every detail of Russia's invasion: the militia's daily movements, the outposts it had seized, and the casualties for which it would be held accountable. "I think I know every tree in Donbas," she once claimed. These facts, rather than actual arms, were her weapons. With facts, she could try to hold Putin to account. She pushed hard for an immediate cease-fire and the withdrawal of heavy artillery from the front lines, pointing to Lohvynove, a tiny village of thirty families in eastern Ukraine, which Russian-backed separatists had just stormed. Putin's grand vision of restoring the Russian Empire boiled down to this: a village of no particular significance, threatening no one, that might not survive the night.

At times during their negotiations, Putin left the table, and—in a version of good cop, bad cop—sent in his aide, Vladislav Surkov. Putin knew Surkov exuded just the sort of machismo that got under the chancellor's skin. Surly and brusque, he didn't bother to disguise his role as Putin's attack dog. Merkel had a tougher time maintaining her iron self-control with this Kremlin operative than with Putin. Slavishly loyal to his boss, whom he called "Russia's Charles de Gaulle," Surkov proclaimed, "It's up to the Russian people to decide if Russia becomes a loner or an alpha male surging over other nations." There was no question as to either Surkov's or his boss's preference.

When the door to the Minsk negotiating chamber opened a crack, journalists caught a glimpse of Merkel still leaning over a map of Ukraine. "Many of the officials inside were falling asleep, including the French foreign minister, Laurent Fabius," said an eyewitness. Merkel's and Putin's concentration never flagged.

During the final stretch, Putin and the new Ukrainian president, Petro Poroshenko, presented a strange portrait of the occupier and the occupied, sitting side by side. French president François Hollande sat beside Merkel. "Angela never negotiated alone. . . . She never wants to be *seen* as the leader of Europe—even if that is who she is," said her one-time boss, Lothar de Maizière. Reward for the long days and nights finally arrived at eleven o'clock the following morning, September 4. "We are hopeful," said the weary chancellor, as she announced the cease-fire to waiting media.

Though she had no illusions regarding how long it would be honored—if at all—she had Putin's signature on a document with which to try to hold him to account. Lives could be saved. Ducking into her waiting black sedan, the chancellor headed to the airport and a few hours of well-deserved sleep at home in Berlin.

The armed portion of the war in Ukraine was now over—in theory if not in reality—but the Russian occupation of Crimea continued. Still, Merkel had one other powerful weapon to deploy: economic sanctions. The chancellor, a firm believer in the free market, was generally reluctant to pressure German businesses. She knew sanctions would have a big impact on the country's economy, and thus on her support from industry leaders, but she also understood that German sanctions against Russia would be key in showing Putin he couldn't expect to get away with this sort of behavior again. She didn't see any other way to bring him to heel than through his—and his cronies'—bottom lines.

Putin felt confident that German business interests would block Merkel's proposal. Her plan would shrink the annual German-Russian trade of six thousand German firms employing three hundred thousand workers by more than a quarter. Nevertheless, she convinced key executives to subordinate profit for the sake of Europe's long-term security. None of them—not the car manufacturers or the pharmaceutical giants—were enthusiastic about a sanction regime that would cost billions of dollars and thousands of jobs, but they all fell in line. German banks also retreated from Russia, making it much harder for Putin's oligarchs to finance new ventures.

Merkel rallied the twenty-six other European Union member states to stay solidly united behind these same sanctions. Hungary and Italy were late holdouts, putting their trade and other relations with Russia ahead of European solidarity, and France agreed only reluctantly to suspend its lucrative Russian arms deals. But over the next eighteen months, all EU members consented to three rounds of sanctions on Russia, punishing Putin and his cronies with travel bans, frozen bank loans, and no trade for as long as the aggression in Ukraine lasted. This coordination between the United States and the European Union was a technical feat, involving hundreds of people managing many moving parts. But breaking down complexity into manageable parts is something Merkel excels at—as is building consensus. Without her, the EU would not have held together. But it has. For seven years now, Russia has been hurting. And Putin seems to have learned his lesson, so for now, at least, the other countries that made up the former Russian Empire are safe. It's an imperfect peace, but for Merkel, that's better than all-out war.*

Witnesses of Merkel's shuttle diplomacy in 2014 and 2015 speak of it as if describing an unforgettable tennis match that just kept going, broken serve after broken serve, indifferent to time and weather. Dan Baer, part of the group monitoring the Ukraine cease-fire agreement, tweeted the chancellor's travel schedule during the week of February 10, 2015: "Monday Kiev, Tuesday Berlin, Wednesday Moscow, then Munich, Washington, DC, on to Ottawa, Brussels, and, finally, home to Berlin. Chancellor Merkel is indefatigable. Her week's travel looks like a fictional airline map from an in-flight magazine." But it was not fictional, and she was a woman in her sixties.

Perhaps because she was bone tired—she had started her day in Moscow and Minsk the day before—Merkel's remarks to a global gathering of policy makers in Munich that Wednesday were tinged with emotion. She began by speaking of history. "The Shoah, that utter betrayal of all civilized values unleashed by Germany, ended seventy years ago. After this horror, after decades and centuries of bloodshed, a new international order was

---

*The Minsk Accords and Minsk Two, which established the restoration of Ukraine's territorial integrity as its goal, were the result of those long days and nights.

created to secure the peaceful coexistence of peoples," she said, referring to organizations such as NATO and the European Union—organizations that had worked together to bring an end to the war in Ukraine. "It's unclear if our discussion in Kiev and Moscow yesterday will succeed. Nevertheless, it is worth trying. We owe it to the people of Ukraine," she concluded. To her, the war Putin had unleashed was not about spheres of interest or historic grudges; it was about *people*. Whether she succeeded or not, Merkel said, she was pursuing peace for *them*.

At a quarter after two in the afternoon, the chancellor departed Munich for Washington, DC. She spent most of her eight and a half hours in flight preparing for her meeting with President Obama and his team. Also on her schedule was the upcoming G7 summit in Bavaria, and ISIS was also showing disturbing signs of renewed life. Merkel had no time to enjoy the balmy fifty-seven degree weather when she landed in Washington, DC; she headed straight for the White House, where, without ceremony, she was led to the Oval Office. Biden, Secretary of State John Kerry, and her advisors, Heusgen, and spokesman Steffen Seibert huddled for several hours. Ukraine was the dominant subject. Facing the press afterward, Merkel repeated that this war would not be won with arms. Asked if she saw risk in her negotiating strategy, she answered, "Of course. But it would be worse if we did nothing." President Obama, standing beside his visibly exhausted friend, added, "If it is successful, it will be the result of the extraordinary efforts of Chancellor Merkel."

Four years later, ignorant or altogether indifferent to the chancellor's superhuman tenacity, Obama's successor goaded Ukraine's new president, Volodymyr Zelensky, "You know, Germany does almost nothing for you." Zelensky, who knew better, was in no position to argue with Donald Trump.

Sporadic fighting in Ukraine, which Russia dials up or down as it chooses, has not let up since 2014. As of 2019, some thirteen thousand Ukrainians have died, a quarter of them civilians. Roughly ten Ukrainian citizens a month still die defending their country. Nevertheless, Ukraine is more unified now than before Putin's aggression. In a sense, the Russian leader lost Ukraine when he resorted to an army to keep it in his sphere of interest.

But in other ways, Putin is closer to achieving his goals. The euphoria of the early days when thousands of Ukrainians demonstrated in Maidan square, proudly waving the blue-and-gold European Union banner, has long since faded. Putin is well aware that as long as he keeps his war simmering, NATO will not offer Ukraine membership, as per a stipulation in the organization's bylaws. The Russian Empire may not be expanding, but neither is its rival. For now, the war remains cold. But for Merkel, a frozen conflict with a chance for future progress is always better than all-out war.

There is another way in which the war in Ukraine was a success for Putin. The conflict enabled him to test more than his lethal new missiles and armored tanks. His brazen fabrications, cyber warfare, and daily distractions to divert and confuse were the same weapons with which Russia would disrupt the next American presidential election. Newly empowered, Putin was ready to move from the relatively low stakes of a regional conflict to the global stage.

Before then, Merkel would have challenges to face much closer to home.

Merkel's emotional encounter with a Palestinian girl in Rostock in July 2015 would have long-term consequences, leading to her most dramatic decision as chancellor: to open Germany's borders to a million Middle Eastern refugees.

13

THE SUMMER OF REEM

Here I stand, I can do no other, so help me God.
—Martin Luther, German Reformation leader (1483–1546)

We should all learn from the Germans about how to treat refugees.
—Tom Segev, Israeli historian and son of
German Holocaust survivors

In 2015 Angela Merkel's decision to address Europe's growing refugee crisis would transform Germany into the moral center of the world. With nations around the globe increasingly succumbing to xenophobia, she turned Germany into an immigrant nation with a breathtakingly bold decision—one out of character for a leader known for caution—that would seal her own legacy.

The fourteen-year-old girl spoke careful German, inflected with a trace of her Lebanese Palestinian origins—and by a slight tremble. Reem Sahwil's nervousness was understandable; she was addressing the chancellor of Germany. "I don't know what my future looks like. It would be horrible to be uprooted again," she said. "We are happy here. I have goals. I'd like to go to university here."

It was July 15, 2015, and Merkel was holding a routine town hall meeting in Rostock, near her home district in northeastern Germany. There was nothing particularly unusual about the setting, the cameras, or the bright, carefully selected girl with the microphone. Politicians do hundreds of these meetings with constituents, and the chancellor was on automatic pilot. "Politics is a tough business," she told the girl, somewhat impatiently. "There are thousands of people who have come here, and those who are not fleeing wars must leave Germany. If we say everyone can come, we simply will not be able to manage."

The girl began to weep. And suddenly, everything changed. The chancellor breathed a single, unplanned word into her microphone: *"Gott."* "God." Her lips pressed tightly, her eyes softening with emotion, Merkel took a step toward the girl.

The alarmed moderator, microphone in hand and clearly startled by this unscripted turn of events, blurted, "Madame Chancellor, this is a sensitive matter for—"

Merkel spun toward the hapless fellow and snapped, "I know it's sensitive!" Reaching out with one hand to stroke Reem's back, she mumbled, "Oh, come, come. You seem like such a nice girl. And you've done very well today." It was hard to tell who was more moved: the fourteen-year-old refugee or the sixty-one-year-old leader of Europe.

There had been a dramatic spike in refugees arriving in Germany in recent years, from 77,000 in 2012, to 475,000 in 2015. The human flood had begun in earnest in 2014, when Syrians and sub-Saharan Africans fleeing wars and collapsing countries began transforming tiny tourist destinations on the Aegean Sea into overflowing refugee camps. Rumors of impending cutbacks in the UN's overstretched World Food Program's lifesaving aid to refugee camps also helped swell the growing human tide toward Europe. Western European leaders, who generally did not see this as their problem, averted their gaze—or worse, scorned the refugees. British prime minister David Cameron called them a "swarm," while populist prime minister Viktor Orban of Hungary ordered billboards erected in the countryside warning refugees, "You will not take our jobs!" Turkey offered temporary shelter, but—without work permits—settling there was not a solution for people whose hopes for a quick return to their homelands were evaporating.

Those who survived the perilous journey from Syria, to Turkey, to Greece, and across the Balkans—many with children hoisted on their fathers' shoulders and nursing infants in their mothers' arms—now faced the least friendly country yet. Though a member of the EU, Hungary openly flouted the union's (admittedly vaguely stated) humanitarian values of basic decency toward those in need. During the summer of 2015, Orban ordered barbed wire unspooled along Hungary's border with Serbia. Cameras caught Hungarian border guards brandishing rifles to block men, women, and children from squeezing under it. "Nothing justifies violence against those who seek asylum," said Merkel, horrified by images of armed guards herding exhausted refugees into cage-like containers on the Hungarian-Serbian border.

Following Merkel's emotional encounter with Reem, the chancellor kept thinking about the young refugee. She twice invited the girl to Berlin, where Reem told Merkel about her life in Rostock for the past four years and how much the German city felt like home. "My friends, my room, and my doctors are all here," she said. She could finally get treatment for her cerebral palsy. The meetings were poignant for both the young girl and the chancellor. Reem felt for her, commenting later that Merkel "was as helpless as we were."

Horrifying photographs kept coming that summer from a place Merkel knew well: Budapest's Keleti train station, where a young Angela Kasner had visited the once-grand gateway to the former Austro-Hungarian Empire during her student days when she roamed the Eastern bloc. That familiar landmark had become a microcosm of Europe's indifference to the plight of strangers. Beneath the station's soaring arches, Syrian refugees had erected ragged tents. This makeshift refugee camp soon overflowed with thousands of people, trapped by a government that neither granted them asylum nor allowed them to continue on their way. Orban proclaimed himself the defender of European Christianity against a Muslim "invasion," and state-controlled television was ordered not to broadcast images of refugee children for fear that some Hungarians might question his describing them as potential terrorists. Despairing at the thought of never being allowed to board trains to Austria or Germany, many refugees set off for the Austrian border on foot. That August, seventy-one of them suffocated to death while locked inside a refrigerator truck abandoned by human traffickers on an Austrian highway. Even some detached observers were beginning to stir. Angela Merkel was no longer a detached observer.

The images from Hungary—a member of the European Union with its own history of abetting Nazi genocide—shook Merkel. The EU's system for dealing with refugees, the so-called Dublin Regulation, wherein migrants were supposed to register and be processed in the country where they first landed,* was broken—made irrelevant by the sheer numbers of refugees (more than common "gateway" countries such as Greece and Italy could process) and by members' defiance of the rules. Adding to the chaos, the refugees themselves resisted registering in a country as openly hostile toward them as Hungary. To be done with the whole situation, Orban finally waived through thousands of migrants, allowing trainfuls to escape the stench and chaos of Keleti station. But that was not a solution; just another eviction.

And so, in late August 2015 Merkel announced—without warning—a

---

*Their fate—whether categorized as political refugees or economic migrants, whether granted permanent or temporary asylum—was to be determined *locally* but in accordance with a bureaucracy set up under EU regulations. All these meticulously agreed-upon regulations were now swamped by the reality of Europe's largest postwar migration, for which neither Brussels, the EU's capital, nor any other country, had prepared.

change of policy. "Germany will not turn away refugees," she said, defying the EU's Dublin Regulation and her usual caution. "If Europe fails on the question of refugees, then it won't be the Europe we wished for," she continued, calling on the twenty-six other EU members to offer asylum to greater numbers of refugees, each according to its capacity. "I don't want to get into a competition in Europe of who can treat these people the worst," she announced. As the number of people crossing the Mediterranean in rickety vessels or trekking across the Balkans toward Germany grew, the burden, she made plain, was not on the refugees who were seeking help but on *us*. No other leader in Europe or elsewhere spoke with such moral clarity about the West's obligation toward the casualties of its never-ending wars.

As an avid student of history, Merkel was surely familiar with the events of another sparkling summer, 1938, when thirty-two nations, including the United States, had gathered in the glorious French spa town of Évian on Lake Geneva to discuss what to do about German and Austrian Jews desperate to escape Hitler's tightening noose. Ultimately, they decided to do nothing, allowing millions of Jews to perish in the hands of the Nazis. Merkel was determined not to allow history to repeat itself.

In retrospect, what's surprising isn't that Merkel felt compelled to speak out on the issue but that she did so seemingly without discussing the matter with her European allies. Partly, it was summer, so she had trouble getting hold of some of her own vacationing ministers, though most were eventually consulted and persuaded by their chancellor. As we see, however, one was not: Horst Seehofer, the head of her sister party, the Bavarian Christian Social Union (CSU), who, for whatever reason, did not answer his cell phone when the chancellor tried to reach him and then claimed later that she had not made the effort. Seehofer wasn't the only politician to disapprove. Some more conservative members of her own party charged Merkel with acting out of thoughtless emotion. Yet it is difficult to imagine Angela Merkel doing anything from emotion or impulse alone. Still, many certainly felt there would have been better ways to go about changing Germany's and the EU's policy on refugees.

"She should have tried for an EU solution," said the ever-Machiavellian Henry Kissinger. "That way, if they turned her down, she would have been seen to be acting as a result of the EU's failure to do so." Others criticized the chancellor for taking too narrow an outlook. As Helmut Kohl noted piously, "Lone decisions and national solo acts, however justified they might appear to the individual, must become a thing of the past. . . . There must be a better understanding again among the peoples of Europe as to what is feasible"—in effect, suggesting that the woman opening her country's doors to thousands of refugees was the selfish one in this scenario. Kissinger agreed. "To shelter one refugee is a humanitarian act," he admonished his onetime protégé, "but to allow one million strangers in is to endanger German civilization." To which Merkel replied, "I had no choice."

Perhaps she didn't. "At that moment, she wasn't thinking about the political consequences. It was a moment different from all others in her life," commented Ellen Ueberschär, a German Protestant theologian who has known the chancellor for decades (and who learned English from Angela's mother). "Christ is always on duty. This is part of her Christian background. It was her Martin Luther moment." Given Merkel's Lutheran values, her grounding in Germany's darkest history, and her more recent experience of causing human suffering by imposing austerity on Greece, it's possible that the chancellor truly felt she had no alternative. But it's also clear that she expected her European allies to see the situation as she did and support her decision.

Those watching from afar found that outcome unlikely. "I observed this with a deep sense of foreboding," said Hank Paulson, former US secretary of the Treasury. "She has such a powerful sense of right and wrong. But, in other situations, she walked a tightrope masterfully. With refugees . . ." Paulson shook his head, "Of course, she did the right thing. But I was afraid it would be her political undoing."

•   •   •

Reminiscent of the night the Berlin Wall came down without fanfare or preparation, Germany suddenly allowed thousands of migrants into the country. They came mostly from the Middle East, the majority fleeing the savage Syrian civil war, but also many from Iraq and Afghanistan—fleeing wars the United States had started and largely abandoned. Germany's border was open, and the usual sorting out of migrants versus political refugees was—like the rules regarding numbers allowed in—overwhelmed by their numbers. Unlike in 1989, when Angela went to the sauna, this time Merkel was in charge. She did not order Germany's borders to close when up to seven thousand refugees arrived each night during September and October. By late fall, two hundred thousand refugees had applied for German asylum, and some eight hundred thousand more were to come by year's end. Nor did the chancellor sugarcoat to her countrymen the situation they faced collectively, calling this "our greatest challenge since reunification."

And yet, Angela Merkel was by no means alone in welcoming the refugees to Germany. When their trains pulled into the gleaming Munich station, exhausted men, women, and children were greeted by a sea of signs that read "Welcome to Germany" held aloft by cheering citizens lining the platforms. Volunteers offered warm drinks and flowers. Soon they would help convert schools and stores into dormitories, while others put up posters with offers to mentor young refugees or organize language or music classes.

Other German towns followed Munich's example. Tempelhof Airport, which had been used for the US-led airlift that saved Berlin from the Soviet blockade in 1948 and 1949, was quickly converted into a vast refugee center. Villages in Bavaria found hundreds of beds at three o'clock in the morning. Germany's extraordinary generosity surprised most of the world—and often even the German people themselves.

"Everybody pitched in, including my Porsche-driving, golf-playing dentist," said Steffen Seibert, Merkel's spokesman, who himself hired three young Syrians as interns in the chancellor's press office. Similarly, National Security Advisor Christoph Heusgen recounted, "I had a doctor friend in Munich who said they were treating hundreds of cases of kidney stones, because the refugees didn't get enough water on their journey."

The country felt pride in a quality not traditionally associated with Germany—humanitarianism—at a time when the United States, the historic sanctuary for refugees, was retreating from that role. Germans enjoyed being on the right side of history for a change. But Germany is a conservative society, unaccustomed to rapid change. And while Merkel made her position clear, declaring, "If we can't put on a happy face for refugees, then this is not my country!" not all of her countrymen agreed.

Crisis can bring out the best in a leader, as it often has for Angela Merkel. But this particular crisis also brought two of her worst leadership characteristics to the fore. She failed to articulate forcefully why her policy was in Germany's interest. And when the usually measured chancellor feels convinced about an issue, she assumes others must surely agree with her.

Both qualities had previously caused trouble in her political life, but never so much as they would now. Perhaps because she viewed welcoming refugees as primarily a moral concern, Merkel failed to explain why accepting refugees would ultimately serve German national interests, as well as burnish the country's global image. For instance, since well over half of the refugees were under twenty-five years old, and Germany faces an aging population, many employers benefitted from this infusion of a young workforce eager to learn new skills. Nor did she ever explain the difference between economic migrants and refugees literally running for their lives, something that might have helped Germans see the issue from the same moral lens she did. At times, Merkel would brush off her constituents' concerns almost flippantly, saying simply, "Anyone who fears refugees should get to know one." Her own party, however, largely supported their chancellor, and many among the rival Social Democratic Party not only supported her but also deeply admired her *Willkommenskultur*, as Germany's new policy of welcoming refugees was named.

Merkel would remind Germans that her refugee policy was dictated by the country's proud postwar constitution: the *Grundgesetz*. "If the message is that people simply don't want to take in any foreigners—especially not Muslims—then it is *they* who are in opposition to the German constitution [and] our international legal obligations," she would say, dryly dismissing opposition to her policy as xenophobia. But the chancellor's claim that she was merely acting in accordance with the constitution ignored the fact that other German politicians had revered the constitution for decades without doing anything close to what she'd done.

Bad luck also played its part. It did not help that the man in charge of much of the nation's human infrastructure, Minister of the Interior Thomas de Maizière, was stricken with pneumonia and forced to work from his hospital bed part of that summer, contributing to the initial chaos. It was a massive effort for the government to organize on the fly: transforming vacant hangars, school gymnasiums, and abandoned factories into shelters and then transporting thousands to their new "homes" throughout the land, all the while keeping a meticulous record of who was sent where and their particular circumstances. And they kept coming. De Maizière, Merkel's longest-serving minister, along with Ursula von der Leyen, left the Cabinet in 2018 but still serves in the Bundestag. "No one had to sleep on a park bench," he told me proudly from his spartan office near the chancellery, decorated only by a simple wooden cross on the wall.

But that wasn't good enough for the chancellor. Emily Haber, de Maizière's deputy during the refugee crisis and currently ambassador to the United States, recalled a tense meeting when Merkel challenged de Maizière's somewhat tentative decision-making. "Don't you think things through to the end and work your way back from the outcome?" Merkel asked de Maizière impatiently. Dissatisfaction with the interior minister's leadership, which most agree ended his decades of service for the chancellor, was perhaps a bit unfair. This seemed to be one occasion when Merkel herself had started at the end without thinking enough about the path to and from that destination.

At the same time, she was more astute than others about the stepping stones. "The chancellor was advised to announce that it was a single emergency-related policy," Ambassador Haber said. "But she refused to do that. 'If we do that, there will be a run on our border,' she told us. 'It would be like announcing that your bank is guaranteed only until Saturday. Panic would ensue; a sense that the border is open today, so let's go!'

"Of course, she was right," Haber continued, "since you can't just close borders with guards. You need a legal framework, transit facilities, legal measures. It took us six months to put it all in place." Merkel had to a great extent created the pressure to move quickly, but her ability to resist impulse and think things through paid off. The image of German armed guards barring a desperate human rush at its border would have reversed a half century of goodwill toward the former Third Reich.

After the initial scenes of euphoric welcome, newscasts soon relayed images of disorder at the border—a condition Germans find particularly disturbing. But thousands of volunteers stepped up to help a vast new bureaucracy that adapted with relative speed. Hundreds of thousands of refugees, including Reem Sahwil and her family, were granted permanent asylum. By late 2018, three years into Germany's new refugee policy, fully half of the eight hundred thousand new arrivals were either employed or in job training programs. All newcomers were required to learn German, attend schools if they were of school age, and could not choose their place to settle in Germany. Merkel was determined to avoid the dense concentrations of immigrants that ring cities in France and Great Britain.

"*Wir schaffen das*," the chancellor repeated throughout the fall of 2015 whenever asked how she'd make it work. "We can handle it." Such a bland formulation is pure Merkel in its undramatic, calming tone. She hoped the words would have the same effect as when, at the height of the euro crisis, she had used a similarly even tone to assure Germans that their savings were safe. But this time Merkel's flat assertion was weaponized by the anti-immigrant Far Right and transformed into a battle cry against her.

The Alternative für Deutschland had formed in 2010 during the euro crisis to protest Germany's bailout of Greece. A party based on Euroscepticism, one of the AfD's salient features is that it is largely a party of men, with women making up a mere 17 percent of its voters. Some of its members had previously belonged to the CDU but had grown disenchanted with Merkel's social and economic liberalism. From the start, however, the Alternative für Deutschland was by far the most overtly nationalist and anti-immigrant political party in postwar Germany.

Two years later, the AfD, struggling for relevance as the bailout retreated further into the past, found a new cause and switched its mission to the much more emotionally charged battle against Merkel's refugee policy. Its name a sly distortion of the chancellor's own frequent assertion that "There is no alternative" (which she first used during the financial crisis), the party found rich soil for its anti-immigrant crusade in the former East Germany. West Germans continue to pay a so-called Solidarity Tax, or *Soli,* based on their income levels, to shore up the East, leading populists in Merkel's region to fear that aid to Syrians would mean less for them. "*What about us?*" they demanded.

Merkel's strategy for dealing with the AfD was to deprive it of the oxygen of attention. "There will be zero tolerance for those who call into question the dignity of other people," she stated flatly, urging her countrymen to show a quality not generally associated with Germans. German thoroughness is great, she said, but what we need now is German flexibility.

Angela Merkel is patient. From Helmut Kohl, she learned that some-times the best policy is to wait things out. But as the months wore on, the backlash accelerated and sometimes erupted into street violence in towns such as Chemnitz and Heidenau in the former East Germany. And still she did nothing. Again and again, Merkel missed the opportunity to make a stronger case for her policy—beyond asserting its moral correctness. Win-ning over hearts and minds is a role she never mastered, not a trivial deficit for a politician.

The performative aspect of leadership—persuading, inspiring, and *sell-ing*—is a fundamental skill. As a scientist, trained to ferret out facts and ana-lyze data, Angela Merkel has often assumed others to be equally rational, an attitude that blinds her at times. Her rhetoric never matched the zeal of those who demonized her. In a country exhausted by fire-breathing dema-gogues, that deficiency had long been an advantage. But the times were in-creasingly intemperate, and Merkel seemed unable or unwilling to change with them.

In the small town of Heidenau, close to the Czech border, in late Au-gust 2015, Merkel confronted the fact that she had become a figure of hate to some of the very people who shared her history. "*Wir sind das Volk!*" ("We are the people!") cried an angry mob, holding signs appropriating the slogan associated with the downfall of the Stasi state in 1989. Only now the enemy was Merkel, not the secret police. "*Verräter!*" ("Traitor!"), they bellowed at their chancellor, hissing and booing as she passed by, her head down, pretending not see or hear them. "C—t!" Some hurled the ugly word at her.

Convinced that engaging with a mob only provokes it, the distraught chancellor uttered only a single word—"repulsive"—before she ducked into a former hardware store that had been converted into a refugee shelter.

Another group, consisting of more peaceful protestors, had lined up on the other side of the same road in Heidenau, hoping for their chancellor's attention. In her rush to escape the mob, Merkel ignored them. This group now watched a live telecast on their iPhones as the chancellor addressed four hundred refugees inside the shelter. "She is telling them that she will protect them," one of the protestors cried, "and she didn't even look at us! What about us?"

By the time Merkel emerged from the shelter, the formerly peaceful protestors had merged with the angry mob. A politician with a keener antenna for the public's mood might have held two events in Heidenau that day: one for refugees and one to address the concerns of the locals, who were also anxious. Although the majority of Germans approved of Merkel's refugee policy, many of them did not live in places like Heidenau, which, following unification, saw its businesses shuttered and its children and grandchildren moving west, where the better jobs were. Even where the economy was stable, many felt their way of life and social status threatened. They needed their chancellor's reassurance. But on this late summer day in Heidenau, Merkel did not attempt to listen to those demonstrators who were genuinely fearful of the future. Distaste for their cause and indignation at their manner of expression blocked Merkel. It was an instance of her moral superiority preventing her from reaching out to a disgruntled subset of her population—and they were not going away.

When Merkel said that asylum "knows no upper limits" during the refugee crisis of the fall of 2015, she meant that the *human right* to asylum has no limits. But that is not what thousands of refugees in squalid camps in Jordan, Lebanon, and Turkey heard. They heard what they wanted to hear: the chancellor of Germany will take us all. When a Syrian refugee, Anas Modamani, snapped a selfie of himself and a smiling Merkel, refugees in camps throughout the region turned her into a patron saint. Whereas during the euro crisis Merkel was painted with a Hitler mustache, now her crumpled portrait was carried in the backpacks of desperate refugees in crowded camps around the Mediterranean, who chanted the name of their newly anointed savior.

Merkel also underestimated the lightning speed with which social media circles the globe. On Facebook, thousands of refugees not only gasped at the selfie of the chancellor and one of *them* but also downloaded directions on how to get from Syria to Germany, aided by GPS on their phones. Thousands of refugees installed the Safe and Free Route to Asylum for Syrians app daily, getting advice on everything from how to buy train tickets to what to wear ("nice clothes, hair gel, and deodorant")—a veritable *Rough Guide* for the twenty-first-century refugee.

Merkel has never expressed regret for the most dramatic act of her life. When, six months later, she was asked if she had second thoughts about her open border policy, she replied with a single word: "No." But even as the German legislature passed its first Asylum Package, doubling the country's budget for refugees, the chancellor was forced to fine-tune her expansive refugee policy. In what eventually amounted to a controversial €6 billion payoff, Merkel negotiated with President Recep Tayyip Erdogan of Turkey—not a natural ally for her—to agree to admit all asylum seekers landing in Greece to his country without permitting them to continue on to Germany. The borders were starting to close.

Though she never retreated from her "*Wir schaffen das*" policy on refugees, by December 2015, Merkel had retooled her political message. Gone were the days of saying that anyone who didn't welcome refugees with a smile wasn't part of her country. Gone were the days of putting the onus of welcoming refugees on ordinary Germans. The time had come to make clear what she expected of these newcomers. "Refugees have a responsibility to adapt to German ways," she said, eliciting thunderous applause from the 2015 CDU Party Congress. "Multiculturalism is a sham." Ever distrustful of words, she failed to elaborate on this harsh-sounding statement. What she meant was that she didn't want Germany to devolve into a nation of separate ethnic groups coexisting side by side. At any rate, the audience liked what it heard. After a nine-minute ovation, she brusquely thanked them, adding, "We have work to do." Indeed, she did.

When she'd opened Germany's borders to refugees, Merkel had dreamed of reawakening what the European Community professed to stand for: solidarity among a values-based community of nations. But rather than being inspired by her example, no other country matched Germany's expansive *Willkommenskultur.* Sweden and Austria were more generous than the other European nations, but they too were closing their doors.

In November 2015, terrorists affiliated with the Islamic State of Iraq and Syria, or ISIS, launched coordinated attacks in Paris, killing 130 people. The following month, a young Muslim married couple who'd become radicalized barged into a holiday party in an office building in San Bernardino, California, and opened fire with semiautomatic weapons, killing fourteen and wounding twenty-two. In a subsequent police chase and shootout, both assailants were killed. The husband turned out to be a US citizen, born and raised in Chicago, while his Pakistani-born wife was a legal resident, making this an act of domestic terrorism. The tragic incident fueled easily exploitable anti-immigrant fears. Thirty Republican governors issued statements opposing the resettlement of Syrian refugees, and the GOP-controlled House passed a bill virtually stopping Syrian refugees from entering the country.

The White House, in response, "increased the cap on refugees from Syria from seventeen thousand to one hundred ten thousand," Obama's aide Ben Rhodes told me. "I'm doing this for Angela. So she won't be alone in this," Obama said. While Merkel understood that the US president's hands were tied by Congress, she wondered why Obama, still the leader of the West, did not vigorously urge other European nations to accept more refugees and thus ease Merkel's burden. And why hadn't he engaged personally with Putin—spent his own capital—to contain the war in Syria, the source of the refugee crisis?

• • •

The fact that one million refugees had been allowed into Germany was, of course, the headline of 2015. However, an equally startling figure received far less media attention: an estimated six million to seven million Germans helped them.

Angela Merkel may not be a powerful speaker, but one of her strengths as a leader is that she is a forceful listener. This skill was on display in the spring of 2017, when the chancellor gathered volunteer foot soldiers of her refugee policy from all over Germany. Seated in a semicircle around Merkel in the chancellery's atrium were students with backpacks and women in conservative suits. If her image were less well known, the chancellor would have been indistinguishable from this audience. Sometimes derisively called "*Gutmenschen*," "good people," they are among her most supportive citizens.

"Yes, it's a hard road, but it's about Germany. It's about Europe," Merkel told them, "It's about our reputation, our standing in the world. This is a very important chapter in our history. That's why I say, 'Thank you.'" But she wasn't just there to talk. On this early spring morning, the chancellor was having an actual conversation with her citizens. Periodically jotting down something in a small notebook, her focus seemed absolute— even her eyes seemed to be listening. Merkel seemed to be searching for answers just as they were.

"How can you send refugees back to Afghanistan when Afghanistan is not safe?" asked a young man with a mop of curly hair. Lately, Merkel had begun doing so. She did not deny that Afghanistan was unsafe but explained that the Afghan president had requested that she not categorize his country as a war zone. "It was a political decision," she answered. A young man who identified himself as Syrian piped up and, in near-perfect German, said, "I am unable to qualify for a course on banking because I don't have the technical vocabulary in German." The chancellor took down his name.

While she clearly enjoyed speaking with these volunteers and refugees, she also had her duty in mind. "Our country is very divided," she acknowledged. "I can't remember when Germany was so divided—not since the wall fell. Then, I was part of the group that wanted to be let in." The volunteers seemed amused by this image of their chancellor as a refugee. "But I am chancellor of all Germans, those who are for and those who are opposed to refugees," she reminded them.

The turbulent year 2015 ended in the worst way imaginable for Angela Merkel. As the chancellor sat down to a simple, quiet New Year's Eve dinner with her husband in their Uckermark cottage, a terrible scene unfolded in Germany's fourth largest city.

The piazza between Cologne's great cathedral and the train station along the Rhine is a traditional magnet for New Year's Eve revelers. The streets were crowded well before midnight, and police were scarce—expecting no more than minor trouble from rowdy kids with firecrackers or the usual drunken misbehavior for which the night is known. Instead, groups of men, identified later as "North African or Arab in appearance" and "non-German," surrounded groups of women, grabbing, molesting, and even, in some cases, raping them.

"They grabbed our arms, pushed our clothes away, and tried to get between our legs," one victim reported. Two hundred people filed criminal complaints. The first list of suspects included nine Algerians, eight Moroccans, five Iranians, four Syrians, three Germans, one Iraqi, one Serb, and one American. Twenty-two of the thirty-two suspects were found to be in some stage of the asylum process. Aggravating this already toxic situation was the media's apparent reluctance to cover the incident and the police's hesitance to report it.[*]

---

[*]It must be noted that there is no German equivalent to Fox News. In general, German media are far more moderate in tone and substance, more skeptical, with more

Among the first to seize on the shattering story was a reality-TV star turned American presidential candidate. Still largely unknown to most of the world, Donald Trump tweeted, "Germany is going through massive attacks to its people by the migrants allowed to enter the country."

Three months after the euphoric welcome in Munich, German public opinion shifted. "From then on, everything we did was seen as wrong," Thomas de Maizière said of the media coverage and the public mood. " 'What kind of idiots could accept so many people at the border? They're all criminals!' "

Merkel herself soon sat for a widely watched television interview to address the issue, striking a somber note. "The state has a responsibility to ensure that our laws are obeyed by everyone," she emphasized. "This country is based on the equality of sexes, on the freedom of religion, freedom of expression, on tolerance. Everyone must adhere to these principles."

Nor would she reverse a policy that remained among her proudest achievements. As always, the chancellor tracked carefully her countrymen's reactions and was soon reassured by what her polling revealed. De Maizière's fears proved to be an overreaction. Even in the aftermath of the Cologne attacks, 90 percent of Germans favored granting refuge to those fleeing war—a tribute not only to the new, democratic, and tolerant Germany but also to its leader of more than a decade. Yet when it came to her larger dream of European solidarity in the face of what she called its gravest crisis since the Second World War, that vision remained elusive. By 2020, as the brutal Syrian war ground on, the EU still had not forged a unified policy toward the migration crisis.

Had even a few of the other twenty-six EU countries joined Germany, the matter could have been resolved long ago. Lebanon, with a population

---

fact-checking, than their American counterparts, though a thriving tabloid press exists side by side with the more serious news culture.

of less than 5 million, provides refuge to 1.5 million Syrians—the same number that entered Europe in 2015. The EU's population is 550 million. Even if every last person in Syria sought refuge there, they would make up just 0.03 percent of the population of the EU.

Throughout the refugee crisis, Angela Merkel seemed composed, showing no sign of either sleepless nights or of second-guessing herself. She had chosen a risky option in line with her moral principles and seemed at peace with her decision. Nevertheless, the prophets of Merkel's demise went to work. In a *New York Times* opinion article entitled "Germany on the Brink," conservative columnist Ross Douthat wrote:

> "If you believe that an aging, secularized heretofore mostly homogeneous society is likely to peacefully absorb a migration of that size and scale of cultural difference, then you have a bright future as a spokesman for the current German government. You are also a fool. . . . Angela Merkel must go—so that her country, and the continent it bestrides, can avoid paying too high a price for her high-minded folly."

The AfD's leader, a woman named Frauke Petry, agreed.

But the chancellor received support from an unexpected source: her ex-husband. In his first and last public statement regarding his former wife, Ulrich Merkel endorsed her refugee policy. The recently retired Dresden-based chemist said, "Her refugee policy was the first time she actually conducted values-based policy. It was the right thing to do, to show humanity and compassion." He also admitted that he had never voted for his ex-wife. Compassion, however, was not a popular political theme in 2016. And the chorus of people who thought it was time for Merkel to step down was growing louder.

Merkel deliberately averts her gaze as she passes the newly elected leaders of the Far Right AfD—Alexander Gauland and Alice Weidel—in the Bundestag on October 24, 2017. To Merkel's chagrin, their presence in the parliament and in public life has turned German politics more combative and sometimes even violent.

14

THE WORST OF TIMES

The only thing worse than fighting with allies is fighting without them.

—Winston Churchill

The year 2016 would be the most challenging of Angela Merkel's tenure as chancellor. Her cherished European Union foundered; a wave of terrorist attacks traumatized German society, threatening her refugee policy; and on November 8, America, the country she admired above all others, elected a new president who endorsed the autocrats that she so reviled.

Merkel had long been conscious of overstaying her political welcome. She was well aware of the example set by Helmut Kohl, who, after sixteen years as chancellor, was voted out and disgraced; she had been the one who'd insisted it was time for him to let his younger colleagues lead the Christian Democratic Union. Merkel had declared publicly already that she wanted "to find the right moment to get out of politics, so I don't end up a half-dead political wreck." As the end of her third term approached, she was getting ready to move on to her own second—actually third life—until the events of 2016 closed the door on her escape.

It is fascinating to note that Antigone is Merkel's favorite classical heroine. Antigone was all passion, all righteous outrage, and thus, in the end, unfit for life. Angela Merkel's leadership leaned mightily on her willingness to compromise to get the job done. In her view, a state is a system that must deliver for *all* its citizens—hence her repeated claim "I'm chancellor of all Germans." But in the ill-tempered new era, many faulted the chancellor for lacking the passion that had ultimately doomed Antigone. Merkel, however, proved both fit to lead and fit for life.

Yet in 2016, the joy, it seemed, had gone from politics. After eleven years as Germany's leader, the strain and the loneliness of her position seeped through her self-possession. "I would be happy if you at least wished me luck," she plaintively told her CSU coalition partners after a stormy meeting. But 2016 would be the year when Merkel would make the leap from de facto leader of Europe—economic, political, and moral—to assume the mantle of leader of the Free World.

In May 2016 Angela Merkel marked the centenary of the First World War's most savage clash: the Battle of Verdun. Head bowed, she walked among the sea of white crosses, the burial ground of three hundred thousand French and German soldiers. The Great War was meant to be the war to end all wars. Yet a mere two decades later, following America's retreat into isolationism, Chancellor Adolf Hitler methodically and malevolently engineered the next conflict, bringing the Holocaust in its wake. As a group of children waving kitelike white streamers bounded across the fresh green field where their forefathers had once spilled their blood for a scrap of territory, Merkel wept.

Europe hadn't been able to come together to prevent a Second World War. But three years after World War II's end, Winston Churchill proclaimed, "We hope to see a Europe where men of every country will think as much of being a *European* as belonging to their native land. We hope that wherever they go in the European Continent, they will truly feel 'Here, I am at home.'" Much to Merkel's dismay, by 2016, many Britons seemed indifferent to that history and to a sense of Europe as their home.

The British have always had a somewhat ambivalent view of the EU. During the first British referendum on remaining in the union, in 1975, German chancellor Helmut Schmidt was warned to stay clear of the British campaign. But the headstrong Schmidt believed the situation's urgency called for breaking protocol. Addressing the British Labour Party, he declared, "All I really want to say—even at the risk of a walkout—is this: your comrades on the Continent want you to stay." Schmidt received a standing ovation, and Britain voted to remain.

In 2016's highly polarized environment, it is unlikely that words from a German chancellor—especially one who rejects the power of words to change minds—would have convinced enough pro-Brexit Britons to vote against departure. Still, it was a bitter outcome for Merkel when Great Britain voted to leave the European Union on June 23. The blow felt both personal and bewildering. She had kept Greece in the fold but was helpless against Brexit—a far more damaging departure. She feared other exits might follow. Adding to her unease was the fact that, with London's withdrawal from the EU, Berlin became all but officially the capital of Europe—never Angela Merkel's ambition, for herself or for her country.

Merkel characterized Britain's historic decision with a single word: "regrettable." Once again, her self-control and sense that speaking out after the fact would be fruitless muted her genuine distress. She was well aware that such a rupture in the Western alliance was nothing but good news for Vladimir Putin, for with Brexit, the EU would be losing 40 percent of the bloc's military capacity. But there was little she could do.

Even as her enemies on both the Far Right and the Far Left mobilized, pointing fingers at her refugee policy for provoking Brexit by fueling British anti-Muslim racism, the majority of her countrymen approved of her. Between February and July 2016, the chancellor's approval rating rose 14 points to 59 percent. But the year was far from over.

•   •   •

A month after Brexit, while France celebrated Bastille Day, a Tunisian terrorist shocked the world by plowing a rented bus into a crowd of celebrants on a seaside promenade in Nice, killing 86 people, including children, and injuring 458. Four days later, an axe-wielding seventeen-year-old Afghan refugee attacked passengers on a train in the German city of Würzburg, wounding five before he was overpowered. A deadly shooting in a crowded Munich shopping mall, which claimed nine lives and sent the Bavarian city into lockdown, followed four days later. The teenage gunman, though German-Iranian, self-identified as Aryan and was inspired not by ISIS but by Anders Breivik, a Far Right anti-immigration Norwegian mass shooter who slaughtered seventy-nine people in 2011. The Munich massacre left Germans feeling more vulnerable than at any time since Merkel had announced her refugee policy the summer before.

A grim chancellor interrupted her Alpine vacation to face a country on edge. Making no attempt to disguise her own anxiety, she called the attacks "an ordeal for all of us as taboos of civilian life are being shattered. Any one of us can be a victim now," and promised an early warning system to monitor online social networks. But, the unsmiling chancellor, her eyes ringed by dark circles, insisted, "Our need for security must be balanced with our values. We are facing a huge challenge. We must maintain our values and our constitution, which spells out the right of refugees."

The summer's storms had not yet passed. That same month, rogue elements in the Turkish military launched a coup against Recep Tayyip Erdogan's government. The Turkish president barely escaped arrest, and, using his cell phone, directed his supporters to launch a counterattack in the streets of Istanbul and Ankara. With air force jets strafing from the skies, the rebels were crushed within hours. Counterrevolution followed revolution: Erdogan ordered the arrest of thirty-seven thousand, while a hundred thousand others who had been deemed "collaborators" were fired from their jobs. Independent media were virtually eliminated in the aftermath of the failed coup. The Turkish strongman was relentless in avenging the uprising and continued to tighten his grip on a country that Angela Merkel had hoped would become a model, secular Islamic republic.

By the fall of 2016, Merkel was being blamed for her party's four successive defeats in regional elections—following gains by the newly empowered AfD. After eleven years under the same chancellor, Merkel fatigue played a role in the CDU's less than stellar numbers.

Merkel finally buried her most overused and much derided slogan, "*Wir schaffen das*," acknowledging ruefully that "We can handle this" was an inadequate answer to the rolling crises of 2016. "I used the phrase to encourage people, I will not use it anymore. . . . God knows, we didn't get everything right in the past years," she admitted. Remorse, rarely expressed from such a high office, did not mean a retreat from her policies, however.

The worst news, however, came not from within Germany but from outside. In a brief telephone conversation, outgoing US president Obama informed the chancellor that Republican Donald Trump had won the presidential election, defeating Democrat Hillary Clinton, a former secretary of state, senator, and First Lady. Though stunned, Merkel wasted no energy on hand-wringing. The country she most admired had made its choice.

For Angela Merkel, America was the land of beginnings, the nation that enabled her to restart life in midstream. Since 1945, the United States had undergirded German security. Without Washington's steady leadership of the West during the Cold War, the Soviet Empire would not have fallen. In the Russian parliament, when a lawmaker rushed in with the news that Donald Trump had won, the entire hall jumped to its feet, erupting with wild cheers and applause.

Now Merkel had to reconsider her own political future: whether to run for a fourth term in 2017 or, as she had long planned, to leave before she became what she feared—a spent force. If she wanted to stay in office, she would have to put up a fight. Her so-called grand coalition, consisting of the CDU-CSU and the SPD, which brought her to power in 2005,* was wobbling. The Social Democratic Party was in crisis, weakened by Merkel's appropriation of many of its key programs: on women's rights (in 2014 she adapted a binding 30 percent gender quota for German corporate boards); on marriage equality (by instructing her party to vote its conscience on the matter, which it then passed); on climate change (always near her heart, though she made only modest gains, compared to what the Green Party was advocating); and, most dramatically, on eliminating nuclear power. The pro-business, center right Free Liberals, also part of her government, were ready to quit after having performed very poorly in the polls. And, most critically, the Bavarian Christian Social Union threatened to reverse the chancellor's refugee policy. (It could not, and did not, but the CSU's demagogic leader, Horst Seehofer, was making Merkel's life miserable.)

When she sat down to her final dinner with President Obama in mid-November—two months before the end of his second and final term—Merkel, who had once taken forty-five minutes to jump off the high dive, still had not made up her mind.

She chose the location of their dinner with great care. It would not be in the chancellery's official dining room but in Berlin's iconic Adlon Hotel. Located on the history-drenched intersection of Unter den Linden and the Brandenburg Gate, from its opulent dining room Obama could see both the rebuilt Reichstag and the recently unveiled Memorial to the Murdered Jews of Europe. The fabled hotel had inspired the classic 1932 film *Grand Hotel,* in which the Swedish American motion picture star Greta Garbo

---

*Between 2009 and 2013, the Free Democratic Party (FDP), a liberal, Center-Right party, not the SPD, was the CDU-CSU's junior coalition partner; the SPD reentered Merkel's coalition for her third term.

uttered her most famous line: "I want to be alone." The Adlon was the capital's showpiece and a living museum.

In a small private dining room, the dinner would be just the two leaders, with their closest aides dining in a separate room nearby. For three hours, they spoke freely and without the usual note taker—this was a dinner between two friends. They spoke of the significance of Brexit and Trump's election and the new reality the chancellor would face without her American ally. "You must run," Obama urged her. In his eight years as president, this was his longest private dinner.

When Obama and Merkel emerged to greet their respective staffs, "They both looked drained," Ben Rhodes recalled. The chancellor spoke with contained emotion: "We have worked so closely together. We now have an outcome we did not want. But we have reason to be proud." Rhodes raised his glass and toasted, "To the new leader of the Free World." Angela Merkel barely smiled. That was a role she neither sought nor relished.

Still, two weeks after Trump's election, on November 20, Merkel announced that she would run for a nearly unprecedented fourth term as chancellor in 2017. If elected, and she completed the term, she would have served as chancellor for sixteen years, longer than any other except for Helmut Kohl (also sixteen years) and Otto von Bismarck (nineteen years, from 1871 to 1890). "I have thought long and hard about this," a somber Merkel told hundreds of CDU members gathered at their Berlin headquarters. "This election will be more difficult than ever before—or at least since German unification. We will be challenged from all sides, from the Right, as never before. . . . Our values, our interests, and, simply put, our way of life are challenged . . . especially after the elections in the US." She was clear eyed about what she thought she could accomplish in a fourth term, saying, "No person alone can change the situation in Germany, in Europe, and the world, especially not the chancellor of the Federal Republic of Germany."

But others had seemed to have more faith in her abilities. Confident in their candidate, 89.5 percent of Merkel's party approved her run.

It was a rational decision but nonetheless a tough personal one. Merkel had seen faces distorted by hate and heard their obscenity-laced rage—all directed at her. She knew how contentious her fourth term would be, at home and abroad. But with the global rise of authoritarianism and populism, she ran because she saw no *alternative*. If she left the field, Trump, Putin, and Xi would have it to themselves.

With the departure of Barack Obama, Angela Merkel would be the reluctant leader of a liberal world order in crisis.

The year 2016 had one final blow to deliver. Christmas markets are a cherished and long-standing German tradition. With their picturesque wooden cottages displaying handicrafts, jewelry, and regional foods, such open-air markets spring up all over Germany in December, drawing thousands of shoppers and tourists. The aroma of spiced wine and bratwurst filled the air of the bustling Christmas market by the Kaiser Wilhelm Memorial Church, deliberately left a half ruin as a reminder of World War II, on West Berlin's busiest avenue, the Kurfürstendamm. Just after eight o'clock at night on December 19, 2016, a large truck plowed into the festive crowd, killing twelve people and injuring fifty-six others. The driver, Anis Amri, was a Tunisian immigrant whose asylum application had been turned down. He fled the scene, precipitating a manhunt throughout Europe. Four days later, Amri was gunned down by police in Milan, Italy. The terrorist organization ISIS soon claimed credit for this attack, the deadliest to occur in Germany in decades.

The day following the Christmas market attack, the US ambassador to Germany paid his farewell call on the chancellor. "I walked into her office and said, 'I'm so sorry,' and Merkel cut me off with 'I'm sorry you are leaving too," John Emerson recalled. "She did not want to react to the attack before she had all the details, who was behind it, how many people were involved, how badly hurt were the wounded people, and so forth. At that point, she did not have all the facts.

"It was so typical of Merkel: she would not want to express herself without having full command of the facts."

What the chancellor was eager to learn from the ambassador was how she should prepare for her first meeting with Donald Trump. "She had watched his rallies," Emerson said. "She understood that she would face an American demagogue, a type familiar to Germans, but new to Americans. I suggested she get on a plane and start building a personal relationship with Trump. I told her, 'With Trump, it's all personal.'"

This iconic photograph of the chancellor shows her seemingly standing up on behalf of the entire Western alliance against an unruly and disruptive Donald Trump at the G7 summit in Charlevoix, Canada, in June 2018.

15

ENTER TRUMP

He who can make you believe absurdities can make you commit atrocities.

—Voltaire (1694–1778)

God has a special providence for fools, drunkards, and the United States of America.

—German chancellor Otto von Bismarck

Trump seemed unfamiliar with history's strongmen, but they were all too familiar to Germans, particularly those of Merkel's generation. From Napoléon I, to Hitler, to Stalin, authoritarian campaigns to make France or Germany or the Soviet Union "great" had ravaged Europe and filled its cemeteries. In her final years as chancellor, Merkel would often express concern regarding what happens when those with personal memories of war disappear.

"Grab some high ground and hold on to it," Obama advised Merkel after Trump's election—advice that proved much tougher to follow than the president implied. Merkel was not naïve enough to think she could convert such a man to democratic norms, but as long as she had a platform, she would give voice to her values and fight with all she had to stop the slide into global disorder. She did not realize then that merely "holding on" would require the dogged optimism and perseverance of Sisyphus.

During the Republican primaries, Trump had picked off his foes one at a time by insulting and demeaning them. Bullying a group of nations who largely agree with one another proved more difficult than throwing his weight at one target at a time. Keeping the Western alliance united became Merkel's primary goal. She would try to inspire the citizens of the world to act globally, not nationally. Inspiration wasn't a natural mode for someone as suspicious of—and often stiff with—words as she was. But democracy was in need of a champion, and Angela Merkel rose to the occasion.

To prepare for her first encounter with Donald Trump, Angela Merkel read his 1990 interview in *Playboy* magazine. All of Trump's bluster, contempt for "losers," and self-adoration, which, in the years since, had become familiar to the world, were on full display even then. Needless to say, humility—Merkel's favorite virtue—was not. The interview nonetheless offered sobering early signs of his Darwinian approach to the world. "I'm an untrusting guy [who enjoys] crushing adversaries," he boasted.

Already evident from this old interview was his bizarre resentment of Germany. (Oddly, for many years, he claimed to be of Swedish, not German heritage.) When asked the then comically hypothetical question "What's the first thing President Trump would do upon entering the Oval Office?" he answered, "I'd throw a tax on every Mercedes-Benz rolling into this country."

Merkel pressed on with her research, reading *Trump: The Art of the Deal*, his ghostwritten 1987 autobiography. Although intended to showcase the real estate tycoon's negotiating brilliance, the book paints a portrait of a man unconcerned with outcome and entirely focused on claiming victory. To familiarize herself with Trump's personal mannerisms—gestures, body language, scowls, and the calculated speed with which his bonhomie turns ferocious—Merkel even endured watching a season of TV's *The Apprentice.*

For Merkel, familiar with Hitler's use of mass rallies, most shocking were Trump's campaign rallies in the American heartland. Such scenes became particularly disturbing when he directed his audience's angry energy toward Democratic nominee Hillary Clinton in a menacing chorus of "Lock her up! Lock her up!" He will change once he gets to the White House, her national security advisor assured her. "He will *not* change," she replied. "He's going to deliver on his promises to the people who elected him."

Merkel understood that she would need to summon qualities well beyond *Demut*—humility—to survive in the Age of Trump. For starters, she would need every ounce of her self-control. Trump had already revealed his all-consuming neediness and capacity for envy in December 2015, when Merkel was chosen as *Time* magazine's "Person of the Year"—a baby boomers' print equivalent of an Oscar. This was particularly true for Trump, who displayed framed copies of fake *Time* covers bearing his own image on the walls of all four of his golf club offices, until the magazine threatened legal action. "*Time* would never pick me," Trump tweeted, following Merkel's selection, "despite me being the big favorite. They picked a person who is *ruining* Germany."

Nevertheless, the chancellor had to find a way to work with the new president. Clinging to her respect for the United States, as if to a life raft, she blamed the outcome in 2016 not on the American people but on their Byzantine electoral college system—which had given Trump a clear victory despite his having lost the popular vote to Hillary Clinton by nearly three million votes. Proceeding with her usual caution, Merkel called Trump to congratulate him and to remind him of "our common values, including democracy, liberty, respect of the law, and of human dignity." Among the thousands of congratulatory messages showered upon the new president,

Merkel's was surely one of the least effusive. She would not flatter him; she would not be the first to request a White House meeting; let British prime minister Theresa May and Japanese prime minister Shinzo Abe rush to Trump Tower and the Oval Office. She bided her time and made studied adjustments to suit the new era. To get a handle on a personality as unfiltered and volatile as Trump's, Merkel recognized that she would need to follow his tweets. "I don't tweet; I simply enter 'Twitter Donald Trump' in my search engine, and then I've got everything," she said.

Her old friends from the pre-Trump GOP, including Robert Kimmitt, ambassador to Germany during her early years in Helmut Kohl's Cabinet, tried to reframe her approach. "Angela, brush aside all his tweets and outbursts, and deal with Trump the businessman. He's a deal maker, so make deals with him," Kimmitt suggested. George W. Bush's national security advisor, Stephen Hadley, advised, "Practice strategic patience." There will be "adults in the room," the Republican elders assured her, arguing that once it was explained to Trump that Ukraine had given up its nuclear arsenal in exchange for the West's guarantee of protecting its borders, the new president would recognize the need to stand up to Vladimir Putin's aggression. Besides, GOP advisors told her confidently, there were still Congress, the State Department, and the Pentagon to rein in Trump's worst instincts.

When General Michael Flynn, one of Trump's wild card picks, was fired after twenty-four days as national security advisor for having lied to the FBI about his interactions with the Russian ambassador—hope surged in the chancellery. Other Trump Cabinet choices were already familiar to Merkel and her team from countless international gatherings, including Secretary of State Rex Tillerson, the former chairman of Exxon; Secretary of Defense General James Mattis; and Flynn's replacement, Lieutenant General H. R. McMaster. All were NATO and EU supporters. In the early months of Trump's presidency, there was still hope regarding the possibility of continuity in the transatlantic relationship.

But if you were paying close attention—as Merkel surely was—Trump soured those hopes even before he was sworn in. "People don't want to have other people coming in and destroying their country. . . . I don't want to do what Germany did," he declared in a January 16 interview. Perhaps most distressing for Merkel was Trump's casual dismissal of NATO. "It's obsolete," he said of the organization whose policies had kept Europe safe for seven decades, adding, "Countries aren't paying what they're supposed to, which I think is very unfair to the United States." Turning to the European Union, the incoming president was equally dismissive, commenting, "The EU was formed, partially, to beat the United States on trade." When asked who he would trust more, Merkel or Putin, the American president claimed to be neutral. "I start off trusting both, but let's see how long that lasts." The answer was, not long at all. The safeguards painstakingly erected by the postwar generation of leaders on both sides of the Atlantic against a future Stalin or Hitler were wobbling.

Former German foreign minister Joschka Fischer articulated the shock that Merkel and her team were reluctant to express publicly at the time. "I never thought that it would be possible to destroy the West from *inside*," he said. Trump's behavior was troubling for all of Europe, but especially for Germany, given the two countries' entwined histories. "Germany was essentially founded by the United States in 1949. It was the American spirit and vision, as well as its massive infusion of capital, that enabled Germany to rebuild after utter physical and moral destruction," Fischer explained. "Now an American president has questioned the future of NATO—the model of a postwar success story—whose greatest achievement is Germany." For many Germans there was an almost Freudian sense of loss at the end of the postwar alliance. "We feel like children abandoned by a parent, a 'Where is Papa?' feeling," said Wolfgang Ischinger, who had served as ambassador to the United States during George W. Bush's presidency.

Angela Merkel encountered many an ignorant head of state—that was not the great shock of Trump. What confounded her was the cavalier way he attacked the pillars of the Western alliance. That, and his utterly ambiguous relationship with Putin. Would Trump have cared that the Russian had been among the mourners at the 1988 Berlin funeral of Klaus Fuchs, the German atomic spy who did the greatest damage in the history of the United States? That was all ancient history to Trump—if it registered at all.

Trump's aides had advised Merkel's team, Don't lecture him. He's a half-page man with a very low attention span. No details, no background, nor too many facts. "We prepared harder for the first meeting with Trump than for any other in her years as chancellor," said Christoph Heusgen.

"We reached out to Canadian prime minister Justin Trudeau, who had recently met with Trump one on one. . . . We also spoke with Vice President Mike Pence, and to Ivanka Trump and Jared Kushner for their advice. We rallied German CEOs from Daimler, VW, and BMW to join our White House meeting, which they did. We prepared charts to show how many jobs German companies provide in America, showing that Germany has ten times the level of investment in the US as the other way around."

Trump's preparation for meeting the German chancellor in March 2017 was somewhat more casual. True to his reputation for winging it, the forty-fifth president of the United States received his briefing from McMaster on the morning of his first meeting with Merkel—in the bathroom adjoining the Oval Office, with the door ajar.

Trump greeted the chancellor in the White House Portico, leading her into the Oval Office with customary courtesy. From there, the optics soon deteriorated. Trump seemed to ignore Merkel's offered handshake. "We reporters heard the chancellor say, 'Let's shake hands,' so he must have heard too," said Kerstin Kohlenberg of the German weekly *Die Zeit*. "He did not wear his earpiece when she spoke German. When she leaned in, he leaned away."

Once the reporters and their cameras had left, Trump reverted to his fa-vorite reality show gambit: attempting to throw the contestant (in this case the visiting head of state) off her game. "Angela, you owe me one trillion dollars," he growled. Steve Bannon, Trump's then chief strategist, is cred-ited with having dreamed up that figure, intended to drive home Germany's supposed back dues for NATO.

"That's not how it works," Merkel replied coolly, noting that NATO is not a dues-paying club.* Besides, the United States owed Germany too. The sprawling American military bases still in Germany were staging grounds for US operations in the Middle East and Afghanistan, she ex-plained. Mostly, however, she held her fire. It would have required more than Trump's available bandwidth to convey Germany's strong pacifist streak. A recent poll showed that 55 percent of Britons and 41 percent of the French population were ready to use military force to counter a Russian attack against a NATO ally, while only 34 percent of Germans declared themselves ready to do so. In reply to the president's charge that allow-ing so many refugees into Germany was "insane," Merkel cited rules re-garding refugees' rights, enshrined in both the American-inspired German constitution and the Geneva Conventions. Trump cut off Merkel, abruptly switching to a topic he found more pleasant: his recent poll numbers.

Trump's habit of veering wildly from one issue to the next rattled less composed, less prepared heads of state. "You could get whiplash from the way he switched subjects and his mood swings," observed Fiona Hill, a member of Trump's National Security Council. "One minute, he was al-most gallant—'Angela, you are amazing!'—then, suddenly, 'Angela, you're ripping us off, and it's gotta stop!'" Merkel's carefully calibrated approach

---

*The North Atlantic Treaty Organization is based on the notion of collective de-fense, with all twenty-nine member states contributing—though only nine have met the guideline of 2 percent of their own gross domestic product. But that 2 percent is merely a guideline, not a "bill," as Trump characterized it.

with Trump seemed to work—up to a point. She never lectured and avoided inundating him with facts, explaining things in a low-key way. She stayed calm, limiting her overt signs of irritation to the occasional eye roll. Used to bombastic men, she spoke in a lion tamer's low, even tone, first in English and then in German.

"He actually listened to her," marveled Hill. "After all, it was better than all those briefing books. Style and swagger count for him, and Merkel has quiet command. Her low-pitched voice is disarming when she speaks English." While Trump found British prime minister Theresa May "annoying"—guilty of trying too hard to ingratiate herself with him—he said that he "could listen to Merkel all day."

The chancellor tried to make the best of the situation. In a meeting between German and American business leaders the following day, she found herself seated next to Ivanka Trump, the president's daughter, who was occupying the place generally reserved for the vice president. So, this White House, she noted, was a family business, and Ivanka was clearly the favorite. On the spot, Merkel invited the first daughter to Berlin to attend the upcoming Women20 summit, an offshoot of the G20. "Wooing Ivanka was smart," noted Hill. "Ivanka likes [Merkel], and that counts with Trump."

Switching back to gracious host mode, the president led Merkel upstairs to the White House private quarters and showed her the historic Lincoln Bedroom. The chancellor took the opportunity to again emphasize that Trump should avoid using trade as a weapon against his allies, noting that the world was too interconnected for unilateral tariffs and trade barriers to work. If one country raises tariffs, the others will follow suit, setting off a trade war. When Trump hailed the easy potential wins from a trade war, Merkel replied, "Well, it's your call, Mr. President." She hoped that reminding him that he was responsible might encourage him to act responsibly.

The ritual press briefing that concluded their first diplomatic encounter provided its own useful lessons—for both leaders. While all eyes were fixed on the chancellor, a sneering Trump told the White House press corps, "At least we have something in common. We have perhaps both been wiretapped by the prior administration"—a snide reference to his false charge that the Obama administration had spied on him during the 2016 campaign. Yet while a handful of reporters snickered, the chancellor's face remained perfectly expressionless; only her head cocked in disbelief and raised eyebrows gave her away. She would neither indulge his delusions nor smile on command.

The chancellor was en route back to Berlin when Trump tweeted, "Despite what you have heard from the FAKE NEWS, I had a GREAT meeting with German chancellor Angela Merkel. "Merkel hates it when he goes after the press like that," said an aide, noting, "She knew that it would give other strongmen the idea that the press is fair game." But then, in all too typical schizoid fashion, he went on to tweet: "Germany owes vast sums of money to NATO, and the United States must be paid more for the powerful and very expensive defense it provides to Germany!"

Upon her return from her trip, Merkel was forced to accept the new reality. The logical next step would have been to shore up Germany's military capacity—not because Trump wanted the country to, but as a pro-German policy. In fact, since 2015, Merkel had prodded her reluctant coalition partners, the Social Democrats, to expand the military budget by 40 percent. Yet how could she explain to Trump that for the fourth largest economy in the world to increase its military spending to the 2 percent of total GDP he demanded would require an increase of tens of billions of dollars, making Germany's the third largest defense budget in the world behind only the United States and China? In the end, the unintended consequence of Trump's bullying made Merkel's attempt to boost Germany's defense budget impossible. "Pay more to this guy?" Ischinger asked rhetorically. "No way."

•   •   •

Just four months into the Trump presidency, Merkel chose an almost comically German setting to answer his defiant challenge to the Western world order. Inside a beer tent in Munich, in the company of ruddy-faced men in traditional lederhosen hoisting mugs of the local brew served by women in girlish dirndl, the chancellor let it rip. The United States, she announced to those gathered for serious beer drinking—but with a global audience in mind—was no longer a reliable partner.

She made a similar statement following a depressing G7 summit in Sicily that same month: "The times in which we could fully count on others are somewhat over." That "somewhat" is typical of her aversion to absolute statements, always leaving the door ajar for a better outcome. But for Merkel, this was an unusually strong statement. "It is clear to me that we Europeans must take our destiny into our own hands," she added later. "Of course, we need to have friendly relations with the US and the UK and with other neighbors, including Russia. But we have to fight for our own future ourselves." That the United States was now just one among a list of Germany's "friends," alongside Russia, made this a bitter watershed. "There is now a president who clearly believes America First," said the chancellor, who would never boast of putting Germany first. Merkel has a visceral distaste for even minor manifestations of nationalism. Asked what she liked about her country, Merkel's typically droll answer was: "We have nice, draught-proof windows." Once, at a CDU banquet, she'd requested that the small German flags that decorated each table be removed.

But Trump forced her hand. "For us, this means we must defend our own principles and values in Europe," she announced. How the European Union could do so, even as Brexit yanked another cornerstone from the alliance, remained to be seen. Still, Merkel's forceful words carried more weight than those of any other European leader. Germany, and this chancellor in particular, had been America's staunchest European ally, perhaps second only to Great Britain. (The irony of the two most globalized countries—the United States and Great Britain—opting for nationalism—was striking.) Merkel was now charting a different, more Europe-centered, course. She was far too cautious, however—and too sharply aware of Germany's continued need for the US security umbrella in a dangerous world to ever contemplate breaking with Washington. The radical change was in her tone, which, in diplomacy and statecraft, is paramount.

And so it was with diminished expectations that Merkel entered the White House in May 2018 for her second Oval Office meeting with Trump. It lasted for fifteen minutes, just long enough for him to declare, "The EU is worse than China, except smaller," adding that the European Union was set up to take advantage of the United States. When she was asked by the press if Trump would carry out the tariffs he had threatened to impose on European steel and aluminum, Merkel could answer only, "The president will decide." This was her attempt to once again force Trump to take responsibility for his actions, though it didn't seem to be working. Her steely self-control slipped when Trump abruptly began riffing on veterans' affairs. "When someone treats our veterans badly, we can fire them so fast! Almost as fast as they do in Germany!" he said, turning to Merkel, whose eyebrows—at times her most expressive feature—shot up in astonishment.

"The next decade will show if we have learned from the past," Merkel said after lunch with Trump. "Or not." That was all this woman of few words said, and it said it all.

Trump's brand of insult "diplomacy" was on full display in Charlevoix, Canada, at the next annual G7 summit, in June 2018. Traditionally, the summit is a relaxed gathering of old friends and familiar faces in a picturesque setting, where members commit once again to the West's democratic principles and economic partnerships. That year was a chance for the youthful Prime Minister Justin Trudeau to highlight the natural beauty of Quebec's Laurentian Mountains. Trump had other plans. A now iconic photograph from the dismal gathering captured the mood. Merkel stands, arms stiff, leaning toward a scowling Trump, his arms crossed, his jutting jaw expressing a "See if you can make me" taunt, while Trudeau, Shinzo Abe, and Emmanuel Macron, France's new president, dolefully observe the scene, letting Merkel confront the bully. Trump chafed at such multilateral gatherings, where he was always outnumbered. He even resisted signing a bland confirmation of the "rules-based international order" communi-qué—a boilerplate affirmation of democratic values and the solidarity of the free-market Western democracies—until the last minute, when, under pressure from Merkel, he sullenly relented. Leaning back, Trump then re-trieved a couple of Starburst candies from his pocket and tossed them in the chancellor's direction.

"Don't say I never gave you anything, Angela!" he said with a smirk. The childish gambit landed with a thud, as Merkel neither smiled nor frowned. She pretended she hadn't noticed—the least satisfying response for a bully. President Harry S. Truman's second secretary of state, Dean Acheson, once said of him, "He was free of the greatest vice in a leader: his ego never came between him and his job." In her refusal to take Trump's bait, Merkel exhibited the same quality—and it drove Trump crazy.

Dealing with a woman against whom his usual techniques of insult and intimidation fizzled was frustrating. Practiced at evasion, Merkel's tech-nique is to feign incomprehension, dodging and answering a question with one of her own. Unaccustomed to such an elusive foe, Trump made her his favorite target for verbal abuse. But, bizarrely, at times, Trump also ex-pressed grudging admiration for Merkel. Upon meeting Germany's new ambassador to the United States, Emily Haber, in the spring of 2018, he asked her, "Are you as intelligent as your boss?" In like fashion, as Trump retreated from the NATO conference he had just disrupted, he commented to bystanders in the press, "Isn't she great?" referring to Merkel, then gushed, "Love this woman!" Naturally, he was soon tweeting, "Crime in

Germany is way up!"—when, in fact, it was at its lowest rate since 1992. Facts, as Merkel knew by now, would never get in the US president's way.

The members of Merkel's team were able to claim some progress with their American counterparts on issues that did not interest Trump, such as the Balkans and Afghanistan—perennial trouble spots where normal statecraft and diplomacy continued. (When Trump, speaking to a group of Baltic leaders, confused their region with the Bal*kans,* the chancellor no longer raised even an eyebrow.) But with affairs related to NATO, Iran, Russia, China, and climate change—the issues Merkel cared about most— relations were frozen—and worse. Trump delivered on his threat to pull out of the painstakingly negotiated nuclear deal with Iran and withdrew from the 2015 Paris Agreement on climate change. These struck at the very heart of Merkel's core convictions: Iran, because it threatened Israel's security, and the Paris Agreement, because it harked back to her role in laying the groundwork for the Kyoto Protocol during her early days as minister of environment.

"It's not pretty. I speak of *disillusionment,* which is quite a lot by my standards," an exasperated Merkel told Germans. Boiling down what was perhaps the crucial difference between Trump and herself, she said, "I believe in win-win situations. He believes only one person can win, while the other loses."

From that point forward, the chancellor left routine interactions between Washington and Berlin to foreign ministers, Treasury secretaries, trade representatives, and ambassadors. "She does not have a 'relationship' with Trump," said Christoph Heusgen, her then national security advisor. "They talk. He hears her. He gets excited, and then he forgets, and the next time, he raises the same issues and arguments. But there is no real forward movement," Heusgen grimly declared, "The jungle really has grown back." By 2018, the chancellery and the Foreign Ministry were, in the words of one of Merkel's top aides, dealing with obscure "weirdos" in the White

House. She was done attempting to salvage the transatlantic partnership; invigorating Europe would become her primary objective. Her instruments to achieve that were largely symbolic, as she was not actually the chancellor of Europe—however much the media enjoyed bestowing that title on her. She led by persuasion and by example, and by signalling her growing alarm at the foul winds blowing from Washington. Merkel had not chosen the intemperate times in which she served, nor would she abandon her core beliefs to suit them. Above all, she wanted Europe and Germany to ride out the Trump years—hewing to their values—and ready to fight (with ideas, not arms) another day.

Midway through the Trump presidency, Merkel's world looked very different from when she had assumed the chancellorship in 2005. She now confronted an angry and aggressive Russia, an increasingly authoritarian and expansionist China, and "illiberal democrats" in the EU's East, while Turkey's Erdogan dashed Merkel's hopes for a moderate Islamic republic at Europe's doorstep. In the Middle East, the seemingly progressive young Saudi Arabian crown prince Mohammed bin Salman proved to be little more than a cold-blooded murderer.

A poignant alarm had been recently raised for Merkel in a newly published, nearly thousand-page tome, *The Thirty Years War: European Catastrophe, German Trauma, 1618–1648,* by German historian Herfried Münkler. The work, which she devoured, reconstructs the savage seventeenth-century war that eventually engulfed most of Europe, from Spain to Sweden, and decimated the continent's population. Merkel invited its author to the chancellery, where, for two hours, she and the historian discussed how war again erupted seventy years after the Peace of Augsburg had ended Europe's bloody religious wars in 1555. After seventy years of peace, few people with personal memories of the atrocities of the earlier war survived. Thus, Europe stumbled blindly into another round of mindless and savage fighting.

Merkel increasingly noted the dangerous similarities between those four-hundred-year-old events and today, "because it is now roughly seventy years since the end of World War II, and those who experienced the war themselves will soon no longer be among us," she remarked sadly in a speech in May 2018. Looking around her, Merkel saw frightening portents of another global unraveling. "They feel they can do whatever they like. One more demand here . . . another there . . . and be a little more aggressive, and suddenly all order is in ruins," she said—without needing to name names.

The times called for stronger words—words Angela Merkel did not have. She simply would not, or could not, answer bombast with passionate intensity. Silence, understatement, and dry wit were her preferred weapons. Asked about Trump's continued threat to tax German cars, she said, "If our cars suddenly pose a threat to US national security, then this comes as a shock to us," pointing out, "In fact, the largest BMW factory is not in Bavaria but in South Carolina! If anyone has a grievance, we need to talk about it. That is how things work in the world," she concluded sharply at an international security conference in Munich in February 2019. No one needed to be reminded that the man who felt threatened by BMWs and Mercedes wasn't much for talking—not when a tweet would do the job.

In the spring of 2019, Merkel's mother, Herlind Kasner, died at the age of ninety. (Her father, Horst Kasner, had died at eighty-five eight years before.) Typically, Merkel suffered this loss entirely in private, without even taking the day off to grieve. Yet the mother who never gave interviews, nor spoke in public about her daughter, had played a significant role in Angela's formation. Herlind, who gave up so much to accompany her husband to the East, who was banned from teaching English in the Soviet zone, was the one to whom the young Angela vented after school about her growing discomfort with the East German regime. Though they never got around to having the oysters at the Kempinski Hotel, as they had promised each other when the wall fell, Herlind Kasner lived long enough to see her firstborn sworn in as chancellor of a united Germany four times. Despite the fact that her mother was an active member of the local Social Democratic Party in Templin and never voted for her daughter, the two had been very close. With her death, Angela lost one of a very small handful of people whom she trusted absolutely.

Two months later, on a trip to Cambridge, Massachusetts, to deliver the commencement address at Harvard University, Merkel was seated next to the university's president, Lawrence Bacow, and spoke about her loss. "It was obvious that she was still deeply affected by her mother's death," he said. Of course she was. What is notable is that Angela Merkel felt freer to share her grief with a stranger, in a foreign setting, than at home, where she knew all eyes were on her.

On that cloudless day in Cambridge, Merkel experienced her most idealized version of America. "When the chancellor arrived at Harvard, the atmosphere in the Yard was reminiscent of when Nelson Mandela was our commencement speaker," Shakespeare scholar and historian Stephen Greenblatt said. "Her visit created a sense of the presence of a historic figure of great moral courage; our last best hope for a way of life whose survival seems no longer ensured. The students seemed to understand that they have a stake in what Chancellor Merkel is trying to preserve."

Transported by the almost medieval pageantry of a Harvard commencement—the faculty in their colorful robes, thousands of students, parents, and generations of alumni gathered in cheerful fellowship—Merkel appeared uncharacteristically resplendent in a red-and-black silk robe. Scanning the sea of boisterous, fresh-faced students at the threshold of life, she beamed her fullest smile. Margaret M. Wang, daughter of Chinese immigrants and the youngest-ever president of the Harvard Alumni Association, introduced the chancellor as the leader of Europe, crediting her with promoting marriage equality, passing Germany's first minimum wage law, and opening her country to more than a million refugees. The audience jumped to its feet before Merkel even began speaking. "Let's start!" she said briskly, never comfortable with overlong ovations.

Speaking from the same podium from where, in 1947, Secretary of State George C. Marshall had proclaimed a $17 billion grant to bolster Western Europe's decimated economies and stabilize its democracies against Moscow's spreading empire, she was mindful of the historical resonance. The chancellor gave her strongest answer yet to the dangerous divisiveness flowing from the White House. "What seemed fixed and unchanging can change," she warned. "We have to think and act globally, not nationally. Together, instead of alone. . . . Take nothing for granted. Our individual freedoms are not guaranteed. Democracy, peace, and prosperity aren't, either."

Turning directly to the graduating class, she urged them, "Stand firmly by your values, not your impulses. . . . Stop for a moment. Keep quiet. Think," she said, revealing her own approach to decision-making.

Aware that from this platform she had Washington's attention, she plunged into actual policy: "Protectionism and trade conflicts endanger free world trade, and the foundations of our prosperity. . . . Climate change and the resulting rises in temperature are caused by humans. Going it alone, we will not succeed. Don't build walls. Break down walls. Lies should not be called truth, nor truth, lies," she concluded, and for the umpteenth time, the audience sprang to its feet and applauded a statement that, in ordinary times, would have seemed self-evident, demonstrating that these were not ordinary times.

Merkel may be the anti-demagogue, but she could not fail to delight in the exuberant admiration of the audience at Harvard Yard. Hyperanalytical, supremely distrustful, and often frustratingly cautious, she is also human. After the sneers and jeers hurled at her by some of her own aggrieved citizens, the whoops of cheer surely lifted her spirits. Nor had she magically become a dazzling public speaker on a par with Obama. For this audience, however, she embodied the values they aspired to emulate. For Angela Merkel, the students' reaction was affirmation of the best kind. They applauded her plea to respect others and her call to distinguish fact from fantasy—at a time when both were under threat. And yes, they applauded the woman who addressed them, for upholding those endangered values.

"She would never give a speech like that in Germany" said Eva Christiansen afterward. "Germans would find it too emotional, too sentimental"— the very qualities, along with her unadorned, direct style, that the Harvard students applauded.

The exhilaration of that perfect day in Cambridge did not survive summer. Later that month, in Osaka, Japan, Merkel confronted the American president at one of their final meetings. At the gathering of the twenty most advanced nations, the so-called G20, Trump once again trampled on democratic values and traditions. Joking with Putin, Trump made light of Russian interference in American politics. Grinning broadly, index finger wagging, Trump "warned" the Russian, "Don't meddle in our elections!" A bemused Putin shook his head in mock horror at the very notion that he would do such a thing. He had reason for his self-satisfied smirk. Only days before, Putin had made headlines worldwide when he announced the "death of liberal democracy."

"The liberal idea has outlived its purpose," Putin argued in a headline-grabbing interview in the *Financial Times*, pointing to global disillusionment with open borders. The issues that Putin pronounced obsolete were at the core of the German chancellor's leadership.

Merkel continued to strike a precarious balance between her values and the world's undeniable tilt toward authoritarianism. No country needed the Chinese market, Russian energy, and American security guarantees more than Germany. No country had less appetite for the world to devolve into great power rivalries than Germany. The EU, for Merkel, was meant to curb destructive nationalism. But for how long could it do so without Britain? Without America?

Increasingly, the chancellor focused her attention on Europe and the ties that bound twenty-seven nations into a tenuous union. Merkel seized the five hundredth anniversary of Leonardo da Vinci's death as an opportunity to remind the West, "For the past five centuries, the most important inventions originated in Europe. This has not been the case for some time." "Wake up, Europe! Wake up, America!" was her message.

In June 2019 Merkel summarized all the unexpected hurdles faced by Western democracies, since those triumphant days in 1989, when the wall fell, and she crossed from East to West. "Soon after, conflicts broke out in the Balkans, then in the Islamic world, China rose as a major economic power, showing that an undemocratic state can be economically successful, and major challenge for liberal democracies. Then came the challenge of Islamic terrorism and, particularly, the attack on the United States on September 11, 2001," she concluded, in her scientist's turn of phrase. "We do not yet have absolute proof that the liberal system is going to win the day," the chancellor said, with typical understatement. "That worries me."

That summer, the relentless stress finally caught up with Merkel. Her body—remarkably robust for a sixty-five-year-old woman who for decades has maintained a schedule that few people half her age could endure—seemed to be betraying her. Twice within ten days, she was seen trembling at public events, gripping her arms to keep them from shaking. While a military band played the German and Ukrainian national anthems during a ceremony welcoming Ukrainian president Volodymyr Zelensky, the chancellor appeared unable to prevent her whole body from shaking. The one thing Germans took for granted about Merkel was her remarkable constitution. Did their Iron Chancellor, known for heading straight to the office after flying all the way from Beijing,—have an underlying health condition? During this season of multiple crises, some observers interpreted her trembling as a sign of growing weakness. (Aides attributed it to unprocessed grief following her mother's death.)

"I would simply say, you have known me for quite a while and know that I am able to fulfill my office," Merkel told German media. "As a human being, I also have a personal interest in my health, especially as my political career is ending in 2021, and I would like to lead a healthy life after this one." With this simple and very human explanation, Merkel closed the discussion as to whether she was physically fit to carry on with her life's work.

By American standards, German media's reluctance to pursue the story of the chancellor's health seems remarkable. "Our press association held a meeting," said Anna Sauerbrey, a Berlin-based columnist, "and we decided to stick to our tradition of not covering the chancellor's health unless it prevents her from doing her job. She is obviously doing her job. We consider this a private matter." In this unsettling new world, this collective decision by the media to respect the chancellor's privacy seemed downright quaint.

Angela Merkel did more than merely sound the alarm about the West's threatened values. When Trump criticized four minority Democratic congresswomen (three of whom were born in the United States, and the fourth, a naturalized American, was a Somali refugee), suggesting they "should go back and help fix the totally broken and crime-infested places from which they came," Merkel announced, "I firmly distance myself from Trump's attacks," adding, "I feel solidarity with the women who have been attacked. . . .

"The strength of the United States is that people from all different nationalities have contributed to making it great," she reminded Trump.

Mostly, however, her efforts to bolster the values she cherished were invisible to the public. A German chancellor's scope for *action*, particularly in the domestic realm, is deliberately circumscribed, as befits the nation's dark history. Unlike Putin, Xi, Erdogan, and Prime Minister Narendra Modi of India, Merkel lacked the power to impose her will—nor would that ever be her style. She works the system incrementally but persistently through relationships she built over the decades. Her people—loyal CDU colleagues—are on the ground throughout the Federal Republic, keeping her informed. With her powerful Cabinet representing the major political parties and her coalition's dominance of the Bundestag, where laws are mostly politely debated and passed, she is the conductor of a well-rehearsed orchestra.

Yet the hard truth is that her time as chancellor was defined less by issues that she cares about (climate and digitization for example) than by rolling crises that never let up: from the global financial crisis, to the Fukushima nuclear disaster, to the war in Ukraine, to the greatest humanitarian crisis in postwar Europe: the arrival of a million refugees. That event, the resolution of which is her proudest achievement, also led to Angela Merkel's next crisis: the sudden rise of the Alternative für Deutschland (AfD).

Police patrol a protest against the AfD in the city of Frankfurt in September 2017.

16

"SOMETHING HAS CHANGED IN OUR COUNTRY . . ."

It happened. Therefore it can happen again.

> —Primo Levi, Italian Jewish Holocaust survivor and author

Hatred is not a crime.

> —Alexander Gauland, coleader of the
> Alternative für Deutschland (AfD)

Angela Merkel appeared to sleepwalk through her fourth campaign for chancellor, as if the times had not radically changed.

On September 24, 2017, Germans let Merkel know that she was out of touch. Fewer of her countrymen voted for her party than at any time since World War II. The Christian Democratic Union's support plunged from 41.5 percent to 33 percent—losing 65 seats in the 598-seat Bundestag. All parties, save one, lost in these elections taking place in a country bored and uninspired by its politicians—including its chancellor of twelve years.

Merkel managed to retain the chancellorship, but it hardly felt like a victory. Once again, she would govern in coalition with the Christian Social Union, with the Social Democratic Party as her junior partner—the so-called grand coalition—which did not feel so grand now. It took Merkel six months to form her coalition government. The protracted process can be blamed largely on the SPD, which suffered its own worst election result ever and was deeply divided and deadlocked between its more radical wing—fed up with having Merkel appropriate so many of its issues—and the more amenable (older) members. Merkel tried alternate routes to forming a coalition government, with the liberal Free Democratic Party and the environmental Green Party, but they weren't interested in operating in her shadow, however much it had just been eclipsed by the alarming real winners of this election: the AfD.

The shock of the 2017 election was the greatest success of a Far Right party in Germany since 1945. After an overtly xenophobic campaign, ninety-four members of the AfD now filed into the staid Bundestag, filling more than 15 percent of the chamber's seats. With the arrival of the AfD, a brutal new tone entered Germany's formerly polite politics of consensus; among the party's founders, seventy-six-year-old Alexander Gauland, pledged to "hunt" Merkel down. While few took that ugly threat literally, the word itself was jarring. Most upsetting for the chancellor was that her own region appeared to be the most receptive to the AfD's message of hate and fear. Almost 20 percent of voters in the East backed the right-wing nationalist party; across Germany as a whole, support averaged 12.6 percent.

Merkel's first reaction to the election's outcome was true to her character: to drain the drama from the situation. "I'm not disappointed; we are not changing our approach," she said—neither a credible nor perceptive answer to Germany's new political reality. "Fear is not a good driver," Merkel likes to say. But neither is denial. By insisting she didn't need to change her approach to governance, Merkel missed a chance to connect with people whose grievances—imagined and real—made them ripe for populist exploitation. After twelve years as chancellor, she seemed cut off from a segment of her population and unwilling or incapable of dealing with the emotional content of their dissatisfaction.

The Alternative for Germany posed a new challenge for a woman who built her career on her ability to find common ground with her opponents and then implement just enough of their policies to steal away their support. The AfD is a one-issue party, and that issue is a hatred of Angela Merkel and all that she stands for: refugees, women's empowerment, marriage equality, the EU, and NATO. "She reflects a zeitgeist which is no longer current," Angela's friend Shimon Stein noted when we met in his favorite Berlin café the morning after the elections. As a former Israeli ambassador who chose to retire in Germany, he was genuinely concerned regarding his new country's future. "We assumed Germany to be unique because of its terrible history. Now, in the process of 'normalization,' it has joined its neighbors where populists are either in opposition or as member of existing governments. It's a test for Angela, and she has to move fast," Stein said, "which is really not her way."

When the AfD first emerged in opposition to the EU's bailout of Greece in 2013, Merkel tried ignoring it—not even mentioning it by name—in hopes of robbing it of the oxygen of attention. Collaborating, even indirectly, with the Far Right, even if her own party needed the AfD's support to defeat another party, was a red line Angela Merkel would not cross. But the AfD did not vanish just because she refused to acknowledge its presence. So Merkel eventually returned to her usual practice: patient dialogue—not with the Far Right's hate-spewing leaders, but with citizens susceptible to their message. When she finally did reach out to the AfD's constituents, it was late in the day.

East Germany does not have a string of dead cities or Appalachia's poverty. But when people in the East compare themselves to those in the West, they feel they are losers. It is more than a perception problem. Thirty years after unification, which has benefitted the East immensely, it still lags behind the West in income, employment, and optimism. People in the East, with a population of sixteen million, compared to sixty-seven million in the West, earn 86 percent of what their West German counterparts make, and there are no major companies headquartered in the East.* The 2015 arrival of roughly one million mostly Middle Eastern refugees tipped resentment of the West into something more toxic. For all these reasons, the AfD found fertile ground for its message of hate and exclusion among the discontented in the East.

The fact that some of the more prosperous regions in the East voted for the AfD underscores that their choice was not simply a case of "It's the economy, stupid." It was also fueled by the East's need to be acknowledged for its contributions to German society as more than the West's needy relatives, and for having suffered for fifty years under the Stasi regime.† One of *theirs* was the most powerful woman in the world, and what had she done for *them*? Some in Merkel's circle compared the people of East Germany to the many African Americans who were disappointed by Barack Obama's presidency. Whatever Obama may have done to advance their situation, it was never going to be enough, ran this line of thought.

Statistics do not reveal the hollow heart of many East German cities. One must take the eastbound train from Berlin to Frankfurt an der Oder to appreciate the sense of having been left behind that pervades parts of this region. Only an hour from the capital's multiethnic brew, this is the poor

---

*Average annual income in the East is $22,5000, versus $26,300 in the West. Unemployment in the East was 10 percent higher than in the West, though this trend is improving rapidly.

†Thanks to the Marshall Plan, the US program that provided $15 billion to finance its rebuilding, West Germany got an early start after the devastation of World War II and was flourishing by the 1970s. But in East Germany, the Soviets not only imposed a dictatorship modelled after their own, but also stripped its wealth and left the region in ruins—even hauling railroad tracks back to Russia with them.

cousin of that other Frankfurt, Germany's financial hub, on another river, the Main. The only bearded Muslim faces or veiled women most here have seen are those on Alternative für Deutschland posters bearing the threatening message "Islam doesn't belong here." Such xenophobic propaganda was unfurled before the 2017 election and succeeded in scaring one-fifth of the townspeople into voting for the AfD, whose founder, Alexander Gauland, grew up in Frankfurt an der Oder. But on the streets, one rarely finds a non-white resident. In fact, these streets are eerily empty, especially after sunset.

An immaculately restored train station, well-groomed parks, and a sense of emptiness—a virtual ghost town—greet the visitor. A gleaming new shopping mall stands nearly empty of customers, its shops full of discount housewares, clothes, and toys—made mostly in China. Here globalization is synonymous with a plague, not progress. The Communist era's once lively recreation center and movie house is boarded up and covered with graffiti. After 1989, one-third of the town's population left, as the local economy—based on manufacturing and inefficiently run factories that were not coming back—was gutted. The best jobs often went to professionals who arrived from the West to run things, even as some of the town's blue-collar workers crossed the brown Oder River to Stubice, Poland, on the other bank. There one finds noisy, smoke-filled pubs, a lively street scene, and a booming local business selling black-market cigarettes. With its crumbling, graffiti-covered buildings and potholed streets, Stubice has not benefitted from West Germany's generous Solidarity Tax and still looks Cold War poor. But then, Stubice does not compare itself to Stuttgart or Hamburg. Somehow the atmosphere on the Polish side of the Oder River feels lighter, less resentful.

The AfD pours oil on Frankfurt an der Oder's sense of victimization. From the newspaper kiosks, local right-wing papers proclaim pro-AfD headlines such as "Das Vergessene Land" ("The Forgotten Land," referring to East Germany), and "Dexit" (a call for Germany to exit from the EU).

The fact that there were no cuts in Germany's generous social welfare system as a result of the influx of refugees seemed to be almost beside the point. East Germans wanted attention to be paid to them—60 percent of AfD voters said their vote was a protest against inattention—and now there was a political party ready to do so. "There are not two Germanys," Thomas Mann, perhaps the most distinguished chronicler of twentieth-century Germany, once noted, "but only one whose best turned into evil through devilish cunning." Angela Merkel feared another wave of such cunning but seemed ill-equipped to prevent it.

"We need fearful people," the AfD's Frauke Petry admitted. In Berlin, there were schools where 80 percent to 90 percent of the students spoke a first language other than German. That was very frightening for East Germans used to an all-white, Christian—if no longer in practice, then historically—population. The capital's clamorous melting pot can seem hostile—*foreign*—to people from Frankfurt an der Oder. For many, it is as if the new post-*Wende* era (as Germans call the time after the fall of the wall) was part of a continuum: following the Nazis, and then the Communists, they were now experiencing a third oppression, this time by the *Wessi* and their leader, Angela Merkel.

Fear is among the most easily exploitable human emotions. When a middle-aged East German woman rose during a town hall meeting to ask what Merkel planned to do to prevent the "Islamization" of Germany, the chancellor replied calmly, "Fear has never been a good advisor, neither in our personal lives, nor in our society. Cultures and societies that are shaped by fear will not get a grip on the future." Her words were true enough. They also did little to change the woman's mind—or the minds of any other AfD supporters who read about the interaction afterward.

A visit to the AfD's headquarters in the gorgeously restored city of Dresden, clarifies how the Far Right exploits that fear of the "Other"—and how little facts actually matter. The walls are plastered with campaign posters: "New Germans? We can do it ourselves," reads one, showing a young, blonde, very pregnant German woman, intended as a retort to the chancellor's claim that immigration will boost Germany's plummeting birthrate. Another shows two women in swimwear, photographed from the back, with the tag line "Burkas? We prefer bikinis." Though in two days in Dresden I encountered no one who might be described as Middle Eastern, Reinhard Günzel, one of the local AfD leaders* insisted, "Crime is up in Dresden. I will not allow my wife or daughter out at night because of *these people*." He arrived at our meeting on an old-fashioned bicycle, and—when he removed his helmet and smiled a crinkly smile—he reminded me not of a neo-Nazi but of my high school science teacher.

When presented with statistics revealing that crime in Dresden is actually *down*, Günzel replied with a shrug, "Well, there may not be a lot of crimes, but you don't want it to happen to *you*." Like the chancellor, Günzel is also a trained physicist and once worked in the East German Academy of Sciences. There the similarity between them ends. A former member of the East German Communist Party, he joined the AfD when Merkel left the border open to hundreds of thousands. Günzel does not believe that today's Germany has a special responsibility to atone for the Holocaust. *Vergangenheitsbewältigung*, the processing of the past, is not a concept familiar to him. Nor is it to many East Germans. And this is a particular dilemma for Angela Merkel in bridging the chasm that still divides East Germany from West Germany. The two sides do not share the narrative of guilt, redemption, and atonement, which she embodies.

Because anti-Semitism remains largely taboo in Germany, the AfD masks its racism behind somewhat more acceptable anti-Islam bigotry. "Everyone is welcome, provided they learn our language, our history, what

---

*Born in 1944 and formerly an army general of Germany's elite Special Forces unit. Günzel was fired in 2003 for supporting the right to make anti-Semitic remarks by a conservative German politician.

makes us tick, and support our *Grundgesetz*—our constitution," Günzel asserted. But this purported respect for the constitution is a red herring. Earlier, he commented that the AfD would attempt to amend the part of the constitution regarding the right to asylum for those fleeing wars.

"In my childhood, everybody had an *Opa* [Grandpa] who looked like these guys," said the former foreign minister Joschka Fischer, referring to Günzel and Alexander Gauland. "They were survivors of the prior era. We have to fight against them and call them by their name. If they think and talk like Nazis, and use expressions like the 'Thousand-Year Reich' and refer to the Holocaust as 'birdshit,' we have to call them Nazis. . . . Angela Merkel, in her heart, despises these guys as much as I do."

And yet "these guys" were offering East Germans something she was not. Privileged by her exceptional intelligence and having had her path smoothed by a series of influential mentors, Merkel underestimated how rocky the road since unification has been for many other East Germans. Her former patron Lothar de Maizière offered a grim biblical analogy: "In the Old Testament, there is the story of Moses wandering in the desert with his people for forty years. After twenty years, half the people said, 'We're going back. We were better off in captivity!' Moses prays to God and asks, 'Why are my people so fainthearted? How long will this take?' God answers, 'Until the last one who was born in servitude dies.'"

Though intimately familiar with the Old Testament, Merkel failed to heed the lesson of Moses's struggle. Until late in her tenure, she seemed blind to her fellow East Germans' sense of being history's victims. "That is ridiculous," she said once in an interview, dismissing complaints of post-unification hardship. "We in the East decided voluntarily to join the Federal Republic of Germany. The reasons were simple and convincing: the economic and political order in the West was more successful, efficient, and reasonable, and, on top of that, freer. No ands, ifs, or buts. We wanted to join this system," she insisted, even as she chided the *Ossis* for avoiding "the mental effort" to change. Merkel's was the overly pragmatic view of someone who denied that the "inner wall" would take longer to demolish than the concrete one. The supremely rational scientist didn't appreciate the irrational, emotional elements behind human behavior.

There was also a gendered element to the AfD's success. The party tapped in to a phenomenon sometimes referred to as "Eastern Man"—a term used to describe working-class males who feel disadvantaged, as women in the East have fared better than men since the fall of the wall; many moved West at the first opportunity. (Only 9 percent of women cast their ballots for the AfD in 2017, while 28 percent of men did.) The town of Chemnitz, for instance, currently has only eight women for every ten men. Such demographics provided an ideal breeding ground for a male-dominated party. As the ultimate avatar of the successful "Eastern Woman," Angela Merkel daily reminds many Eastern Men of their failures.

After the fall of the wall, the East did away with its own elite by purging Communists—and rightly so. (We observed the fallen East German politicians during Merkel's own rise in her early political career. The shadow cast by even a hint of Stasi collaboration took many down.) There was, in fact, a more thorough purge after the wall fell than in the post-Nazi period. This meant however, that the new elite *had* to come from the West. In retrospect, more might have been done to train a new generation of East German elite for public and private service, but it did not happen. Only the most ambitious, focused, and nimble at self-reinvention flourished in the West's highly competitive environment—for which Communism had ill-prepared them. Among them, Angela Merkel was the most successful. She became chancellor.

Those overseeing unification—notably President H. W. Bush and Secretary of State James Baker of the United States, and German chancellor Helmut Kohl, among others—missed an opportunity to give the newly unified country a different name to signify a fresh start. Instead, East Germany joined the Federal Republic of Germany, making many East Germans feel to this day as if they are an appendix. For too long, Merkel seemed oblivious to this sense of grievance, which is alien to her character. She is an activist and an optimist with tremendous self-confidence—qualities that have powered her rise but sometimes blinded her to the needs of those less well equipped to cope in a harsh new environment.

Since the 2017 election, the AfD became the main opposition party in the Bundestag, occupying the chamber's front row—although with just 15 percent of seats, the party remains, for the meantime, more of a warning than an actual threat. In her final years in office, Merkel still refused to engage with them, however, feeling that would "normalize" their presence in German political life. But AfD members would often deliberately loiter in the corridor leading to the chancellor's parliamentary office. While others in parliament avoided this route to the chamber, the chancellor could not.

March 14, 2018: Entering the light-filled Bundestag chamber, the chancellor strides forward, gazing straight ahead as she passes Alexander Gauland, seated in the front row, and moves quickly to friendlier territory, exchanging greetings, shaking hands, patting friends on the back. You would scarcely know from the calm she projects that Angela Merkel is about to be sworn in as chancellor for the fourth and final time—a big enough deal that Joachim Sauer has finally decided to attend his wife's swearing-in ceremony, unobtrusively taking his seat in the balcony beside Merkel's mother. Joining them as the chancellor's guest is Charlotte Knobloch.

For the head of Munich's Jewish community, such proximity to Gauland is disturbing. Following his election, the head of the AfD declared: "Hitler and the Nazis are just a speck of birdshit in more than a thousand years of successful German history." The arrival of roughly one million Muslim refugees from the Middle East since 2015 also presents German Jews with uncertainty. Many refugees come from countries where hatred of Jews is part of their formation; some Jews fear that the chancellor's refugee policy may upset Germany's delicate social balance. There are places where wearing the *kippa*, the Jewish skullcap, is no longer considered safe. But Knobloch is present in the Bundestag on this day to show her support. "Merkel has made a vow to us: no compromise in the fight against anti-Semitism, even Muslim anti-Semitism," she tells me.

As their names are called, Bundestag members line up to cast their votes for the chancellor in what is a pro forma ritual. Ushers make sure the curtains in the small voting booths set up on the rim of the chamber are fully dawn. Twenty minutes later, Bundestag president Wolfgang Schäuble announces the unsurprising result: Angela Merkel has been reelected chancellor. Many MPs cheer and leap to their feet in sustained applause. Members of rival parties—Social Democrats, Free Democrats, and Greens—present the smiling chancellor with bouquets of flowers. This image of the triumph of German democracy is marred only by Gauland and his governing partner, Alice Weidel, who remain seated with their arms folded; twin pillars of passive aggression. Then a member of the Free Democrats walks over to them and whispers something inaudible—doubtless about customs and the importance of following rules and maintaining civility. The AfD members stand reluctantly and join the line to congratulate the newly reelected chancellor, who accepts their proffered words and handshakes with the faintest nod and her best poker face.

In somber tones, Wolfgang Shäuble declares, "I wish you all the best on this difficult path," before lowering his gavel to close the session. As if to make that point, Shäuble imposes a fine on one member of the AfD who had taken a picture of his secret ballot and posted it immediately on social media. This may have been a small act of defiance to the Bundestag's principle of secret voting, but the new member of parliament used the gesture to make a larger point: *We are not playing by your rules.* It was a fitting and disturbing start to Merkel's final term.

In her sober, almost funereal, inaugural address, Angela Merkel acknowledges that "Something has changed in our country. The tone of arguments has become rougher, the respect for different opinions has eroded, as has cohesion between old and young, between East and West, city and countryside, between people who have been living here for generations and new arrivals. The question is: Does the rule of law still work?"

For the first time in a long time, she seemed not to have an answer.

Merkel may have survived politically, but her most important legacy, her refugee policy, had been under attack for some time—and not only from the AfD. From within her own coalition, Bavaria's president, Horst Seehofer, the charismatic head of the CSU, Merkel's sister party, had been blasting the chancellor's policy in the lead-up to the 2017 elections. "Islam does not belong to Germany," he proclaimed, echoing the AfD. A beer hall populist who preferred the company of Hungarian president Viktor Orban to that of Merkel, Seehofer worried that the Alternative for Germany Party would siphon votes from his center-right Christian Social Union. Lifting a line from the AfD, he began referring to Merkel's policy as "asylum tourism."

"Merkel had her *selfies* with refugees; now we need images of refugees being put on a bus," he said. Never mind that the arrival of refugees had already slowed significantly—for Seehofer the demagogue, facts and figures were secondary to riling up his base.* He also advocated putting crosses in all public buildings and touted an "axis" with right-leaning Austrian and Italian populists. The very word *axis*—the name of the Nazi-Fascist alliance in World War II—was a jarring note from an old playbook.

*Since 2015, the number of refugees entering the country has dropped dramatically to well below two hundred thousand a year. But Germany still has one of the highest numbers of refugees of any country worldwide, according to the United Nations High Commissioner for Refugees (UNHCR); only Turkey, Pakistan, Uganda, and Sudan have more. Germany is the only Western industrialized nation on that UN list of nations that have welcomed refugees.

Angela Merkel was exhausted from putting out fires. But, displaying her remarkable resilience once again, she survived to compete in the election not by lashing out at Seehofer but by following her usual strategy with overconfident bullies: by talking. At noon, on July 2, 2017, after negotiating all night, Seehofer and the chancellor emerged from the CDU's Berlin headquarters, smiling wanly. The precise details of their horse-trading remain confidential. What is known, however, is that Merkel relented on a few peripheral issues while not yielding on what the Bavarian most wanted: a cap on the number of refugees to be granted asylum in the future. Merkel's core policy going into the election remained intact.

Standing next to the impressively tall Seehofer, the five-foot-four chancellor was asked by a reporter about what still separated the two recent foes. "Almost a foot," she deadpanned. Then, taking another page from her classic playbook, she shortly thereafter appointed Seehofer minister of the interior for her fourth term. The conversion of the Bavarian populist seemed complete when, two years later, Seehofer publicly called her "an outstanding person" whom he was "proud" to work with, and gushed, "There is no one in Europe as trusted as Angela Merkel."

But the AfD would not be so easily tamed. A few months into her first term, thirty-nine-year-old Alice Weidel approached the Bundestag lectern. Wearing her signature well-tailored jacket, crisp white shirt, and pearls, she furrowed her brow and chopped the air as she breathlessly spat out a list of "crimes" purportedly committed by Merkel's government and its predecessors: accepting bribes, spending the taxpayers' money "like crazy," terrible corruption. During her rant, Weidel offered not a single proposal and suggested no bills or laws for the Bundestag to consider. Once finished, she grimly gathered her papers at the lectern and returned to her seat. Only her cochair, Gauland, rose to offer his congratulations. The rest of the legislative body was silent.

Merkel followed Weidel to the lectern. "The beautiful thing about a liberal democracy is that everyone has the right to talk about what they believe is important for the country," she said with a bright smile, as the chamber erupted in relieved laughter and applause. The chancellor then quickly moved to address issues that actually mattered to her country: she proposed a summit to combat housing shortages, create new day care centers, improve care for the elderly, and expand digital access in rural areas. On this final topic, she went off script, speaking with authority as she outlined Germany's need to catch up with global competitors from Silicon Valley to Shenzhen, China. She closed her twenty-minute speech with the issue to which she now nearly always returned: her fear that the liberal order is under threat. Reminding the Bundestag that, after World War II, Germany received eleven million refugees—primarily from the Soviet-occupied East—she insisted, "We are a nation of refugees." She also took the opportunity to remind her colleagues in parliament of their shared values, saying, "Those who believe that nations can succeed on their own—nationalism in its purest form—[oppose] those who believe that finding common solutions is the way."

Applause interrupted her final sentence. Weidel's bitter diatribe had driven home Merkel's warning more forcefully than the chancellor's calm words. The AfD may have made its way into the German federal government, but it had also isolated itself there. Germany is a mature democracy that, more than any European country, has assimilated the high cost of accommodating racists and is simply not ready to welcome extremists into the highest reaches of its government. On that, even Merkel's more conservative critics in the CDU agreed.

Nevertheless, the anger that catapulted the AfD into the Bundestag remained a slow-burning fuse in German life—specifically in the East. In August 2018 the fuse was lit in Chemnitz—formerly Karl-Marx-Stadt—a Saxon town that claimed the dubious distinction of having the country's highest rate of hate crimes against foreigners. The alleged killing of a carpenter of Cuban descent by an asylum-seeking Middle Eastern man provided the AfD and local neo-Nazis with a convenient excuse to riot. Beneath a forty-ton statue of Karl Marx, eight thousand demonstrators turned their pent-up rage against their chancellor. Local police were caught unprepared, but the AfD was ready.

"When the state can't protect its citizens anymore, the citizens take to the street and protect themselves," tweeted a local AfD lawmaker. The sight of marchers sporting Nazi paraphernalia—at least one flashed the Hitler salute—shocked much of the country. For two days, the fascists had the run of Chemnitz's streets, chasing dark-skinned residents and attacking a kosher restaurant.

"Hate has no place in this country. There is no excuse or justification for attacking people who look different," Merkel decried from Berlin, while Alexander Gauland praised the mob as "concerned citizens" and insisted that "Hatred is not a crime." But that was all the chancellor said—again seeming not to want to draw any more attention to the horrible events.

Three months later, Merkel finally arrived in Chemnitz. It was much too late, and she had put it off too long. This, too, is characteristic of the sometimes overly cautious, confrontation-averse Angela Merkel. "I know my face is polarizing," she told an unsmiling audience of 120 inside a defunct locomotive factory. Outside, a much larger crowd shouted, "Merkel must go!" But the chancellor continued speaking softly, sounding more like a therapist than a politician. "You are being told lies. Don't let those who spread hate dictate to you," she implored her audience.

Why, one man asked plaintively, do so many of us feel like losers?

"Some of you aren't seeing your grandchildren grow up because your children have moved away," the chancellor answered empathetically. "Things were lost. But we've achieved so much!" In saying "we," she identified herself with these East Germans. She was there to comfort, not to chide.

Without defensiveness or any attempt to justify her policies, for two tense hours, Merkel answered sometimes hostile questions. Hers was a different tone than the one struck by the youthful and somewhat condescending Angela, who sneered at those of her fellow East Germans less nimble at adapting than herself. Age, the passage of time, and her own brushes with near failure had sanded down some of that arrogance. Then, too, these were her fellow citizens who might still be within reach of reason and compassion. They were not demonstrators spitting invectives at their chancellor. Perhaps she could yet persuade them to release some of their hostility. Humbled by the recent elections, she deployed her humanity—rather than her usual command of facts—to try to lure them back.

Gradually, the mood in the hall shifted. Her repeated use of *we* drained some aggression from the angriest in the audience. Toward the end of the session, a man in the back called out, "Thank you, Chancellor, for the overall good situation in the country." Taken aback, Merkel was momentarily at a loss for words. "Well, I don't think many of you came here today to hear Angela Merkel praised," she said finally, looking both surprised and pleased nonetheless. It was a small good sign. But outside, the larger crowd continued to shout "*Hau ab, Hau ab*" ("Scram, get out of here!"), drowning out Merkel's voice.

Merkel never wavered in her determination to retire according to her own schedule. Not even the abhorrent images of neo-Nazis running freely in the streets of Chemnitz diverted her from her goal of leaving politics before she was driven to do so. Quite the reverse. "We saw each other during Oktoberfest, at the Berlin Opera, shortly after the Chemnitz riots," said Paul Krüger, her old friend and colleague from her days in Kohl's Cabinet. He and I met in the restaurant of a hotel in the former East, in Potsdam, where he had recently stepped down as mayor. The décor was predominantly brown, a color once favored in the East and much loathed by Angela Merkel.

"She never seems stressed out, but she seemed especially relaxed that day," Krüger recalled. "She asked how I was doing, and I answered that I hesitated to say I was doing well." Then he told her: "I feel very sorry for you, Angela, because I see how much trouble these idiots are giving you, every single day." Kruger continued to describe to me his perplexing encounter with the chancellor.

"As we were chatting, other people approached her, so we said our good-byes. Then, suddenly, she started running after me. 'I wanted you to know,' she said, 'that I'm doing well too. In fact, I feel great!' I wondered what that was all about, her rushing after me like that. A few days later, I found out."

On December 7, 2018, Merkel returned to Hamburg, her birthplace, to say her farewells to the Christian Democratic Union she had led for eighteen years. Worn out by bitter party politics, she was calling it quits as the party's leader—though, of course, she remained Germany's chancellor. She would still be the CDU's unofficial and, by now, historic leader, and still guide its policy and pick its brightest leaders. But henceforth, her power would be based on her undeniable stature, not party position. Others could tend to party business—she would be above politics. Angela Merkel wanted to spend her last three years in office focusing on her real passion: global affairs.

From the stage of the cavernous Congress Center, she faced more than a thousand CDU members—no longer overwhelmingly male—many of whom had never known another party chair. There was a valedictory mood in the hall. Helmut Kohl's *Mädchen,* who had revived the Christian Democratic Union at its lowest point—in 2000, during the kickback scandal—was saying good-bye. She began her speech with self-deprecating humor: "My first party slogan in 2000 was 'To the Point.' For many, that took getting used to! Where was Germany in this slogan? Where was the future? Where was something about our values, our security? Nowhere. Only 'To the Point.' Typical Merkel: dry as a bone."

The audience laughed at the shared memory of the chancellor's awkward debut. Then, returning to her East German beginnings, something she'd started doing more and more in recent years, Merkel went off script, recalling the exhilaration of those early days after the wall came down. "For us, those were incredible times of great curiosity, awaiting new things, 'Go into the open,' I wrote in a friend's book. What a prospect! Freedom in a new era. . . . Our future was solely in our own hands," she said with obvious nostalgia for those early days, electric with promise.

Reflecting on her style as chancellor, she acknowledged, "I asked a lot of you. I resisted attacking opponents—and chose the scalpel or silence—not the sword. I know I tested your nerves." It wasn't exactly an apology, but something close; an admission that perhaps she might have delivered the Far Right a more devastating blow. At the same time, those gathered in front of her understood that was simply not in the nature of the woman they had come to respect for her sometimes idiosyncratic—and even exasperating—ways. But when she closed her speech, it was in a tone that was no longer that of a politician, but one that made clear she had no regrets for taking the higher ground. She sounded like the pastor's daughter. "I was not born chancellor or party chair," she said. "I always intended to conduct my politics with dignity and to leave in dignity. Time is limited for us all."

On their feet now, for a full ten minutes, the delegates applauded their chair. Many of them brandished signs that read, "Thanks, Boss!" Men and women alike brushed away tears. Merkel's eyes shone; she blinked fast, as she always does when she is moved.

Merkel desperately wanted to leave politics to her chosen successor, Annegret Kramp-Karrenbauer, a centrist fifty-seven-year-old politician from Saarland, so that she could spend her last three years as chancellor focusing on pressing issues such as strengthening the EU and addressing climate change. But it was not to be. At least, not yet.

•　　•　　•

Angela Merkel was forced back into domestic politics by events near Weimar, a city in the historically freighted province of Thuringia, where the
Nazis first won power before moving on to win nationally in 1933. The
past is never really past in Germany. On occasion, the chancellor arrived
late to appointments because unexploded Russian bombs, relics of the Second World War, had been found near the chancellery, snarling traffic. But
nowhere in Germany does the past loom larger than in Weimar—its very
name an echo.

In February 1919, three months after the end of World War I, deputies
from all over Germany gathered in Weimar, the capital of German high *Kultur*, the spiritual home of Goethe, Schiller, the Dutch philosopher known
as Erasmus, and composer Franz Liszt, to try to dig out from under the
physical and moral rubble. They assembled in a charming Baroque court
theater to lay the foundation for a new German republic: the Weimar Republic. A Jewish lawyer and liberal politician named Hugo Preuss drafted
a new constitution. In elections that followed, centrist parties won overwhelming popular support, while conservatives eked out a mere 10 percent
of the vote. Fourteen years later, Nazis were setting fire to fifty thousand
books written by Jews, as Joseph Goebbels, the Nazi propaganda chief, announced the end of the "age of Jewish intellectualism." All it took was a
global depression and a cunning demagogue to light the fire that engulfed
the Weimar Republic, ending Germany's first experiment with democracy.

The parallels between 1933 and 2020 were alarming, as a similar scenario now threatened the Federal Republic.

In February 2020 Merkel was shocked to learn that the Christian Democratic Union, under new leader Kramp-Karrenbauer, had joined forces
with the AfD to elect Thomas Kemmerich, a member of the liberal Free
Democratic Party, minister president of Thuringia. AKK, as she is known,
thus broke Merkel's prohibition on cooperating with the extreme Right by
siding with the AfD to elect a state leader in the small eastern state—an

instance of German politics at its most obscure. (The absurdly complex German parliamentary system necessitates coalitions among its various parties to achieve majorities, as was the case here; for a period, the FDP had been part of Merkel's ruling coalition.) This alliance between the CDU and the AfD to elect a member of the liberal FDP was a bridge too far for the chancellor. It was also the end of the very brief term of Merkel's hand-picked successor. Annegret Kramp-Karrenbauer resigned the following day for not preventing this near fiasco.

Merkel wasted no time in reacting to the Faustian bargain her own party had briefly struck. Interrupting a state visit to South Africa, she noted grimly, "It is a bad day for German democracy," and called for Kemmerich's election to be annulled. Given her stature and authority, it was, and new elections were called.* But the cost of this reckless transaction was high, leaving Merkel without a successor as party chair. A crisis was averted, but narrowly. The AfD is not going away. But Angela Merkel soon will.

*If this strikes the reader as illegal, it was not. Kemmerich's election with AfD support violated a convention among all mainstream German parties to refuse any cooperation with the Far Right group. On March 4, 2020, Bodo Ramelow of the Linke (Left) Party was elected minister president—the very same position he'd held from 2014 until just a month before.

French president Emmanuel Macron and Merkel share a moment of closeness in Compiègne, in northern France, as they mark the one hundredth anniversary of the end of World War I. Their relationship was not always this harmonious, but the pair worked hard to get along. They knew they had to stand united against the growing threat of authoritarianism and populism from both Moscow and Washington.

17

A PARTNER AT LAST?

A man who is nothing but a "moral man" would be a fool.
— Hans Morgenthau, German American political scientist of
the twentieth century, "Six Principles of Political Realism"

In May 2017 a thirty-nine-year-old progressive economist named Emmanuel Macron upended French politics, reversed a populist tide, and became France's youngest head of state since Napoléon Bonaparte. Angela Merkel knew and respected Macron from his days as economics minister in the Cabinet of the previous president, François Hollande. She celebrated his thumping of nationalist Marine Le Pen, the Far Right candidate supported by both Trump and Putin. "He carries the hopes of millions of French people and of many Germans," the chancellor said. Foremost among them: Angela Merkel.

Merkel never claimed leadership of the West; it had been thrust upon her, and she accepted it reluctantly. But two months into her final term as chancellor, she was no longer alone on the world stage, holding back the tide against authoritarianism. At last, there was a capable leader of another major European power who supported her vision for the Continent. Though they both shared the still ephemeral dream of a United States of Europe, the impatient, impulsive Macron wanted it *now*. Merkel, slow to move and playing a longer game, preferred to proceed with far greater caution. Furthermore, although Trump's demagogy repulsed her, she was still more deeply attached to the transatlantic alliance than the new French leader was. Soon Macron's and Merkel's differences in style and temperament would assert themselves.

Nations, like people, often learn more from failure than from triumph, and Merkel and Macron are both exquisitely products of their national narratives. Merkel hails from a culture that, since its humiliating defeat in World War II, does not celebrate military victories and mostly flies its country's flag to celebrate soccer championships. Some of Berlin's most visited landmarks memorialize the catastrophic failures of the Third Reich; Auschwitz is Germany's symbol of World War II. This is a nation aspiring to humility and to do better than it has in the past, and Merkel's approach to leadership is similarly humble. Even the gray-uniformed, stodgy Bundeswehr, Germany's national army, tries hard to pass little noticed.

Being inconspicuous, Angela Merkel's goal since her days as the brightest student in class, is far from the aim of France's splendidly uniformed Garde Republicaine, or Republican Guard, with its gleaming brass helmets, braided jackets, and red trousers tucked into shiny boots. France is the only Western democracy that still holds military parades. On Bastille Day in July 2017, the new president of the United States, Donald Trump, was so dazzled by the sight of the majestic guards on horseback, followed by an ostentatious display of the country's latest military hardware on Paris's grand Champs-Élysées, that he sought to orchestrate a similar military spectacle in Washington, DC—something that America frowns upon almost as much as Germany does.

To imagine tanks rumbling down Berlin's Kurfurstendamm is to imagine the apocalypse. For France, the enduring symbol of WWII is *La*

Resistance. "*We* liberated France," Charles de Gaulle insisted, in his fanciful version of events.* While the Napoleonic Wars of 1803 through 1815 left misery and bloodshed in their wake, the Paris Metro today whizzes past stops named for its greatest battles, among them: Austerlitz, Solferino (fought under Napoleon III) . . . Macron's first act as president was to ride up the Champs-Élysées in a camouflage military jeep and light a flame in honor of France's war dead at the Arc de Triomphe. For Merkel, the drama of war belongs on the stage of the Bayreuth Wagner Festival, not in politics.

Macron's first trip as president, in 2017, was to Berlin, to meet with Angela Merkel. The image of the two of them, Europe's longest-serving democratic leader alongside its newest and youngest, had the air of a ritual blessing. But the plain-spoken, middle-aged scientist-turned-politician, then in her thirteenth year as chancellor, and the dashing, slightly built Macron, fresh from delivering a body blow to French politics, were not an obvious fit. "A little magic dwells in each beginning," a smiling Merkel said, quoting the German writer Hermann Hesse, as she welcomed Macron to the chancellery. Never one to get carried away by rhetoric, she added quickly, "The magic lasts only when there are results." (English was their common language, something new in the centuries-old Franco-German relationship, which heretofore had generally relied on translators between heads of state.) The remark didn't stop the French president from beaming with pride at sharing the world stage with this historic figure. At the same time, Macron seemed perfectly at ease in his interactions with Angela Merkel, twenty-four years his senior—exactly the same age as his wife, Brigitte Macron.

*In 1995, following the American-led negotiations to end the savage war in Bosnia, Europe's bloodiest since World War II, French president Jacques Chirac insisted that the peace treaty be signed at the Élysée Palace in Paris—despite the fact that it had been hammered out behind the barbed wire fences of Wright-Patterson Air Force Base in Dayton, Ohio. Fragile glory was still glory.

The pair shared the goal of a strong Europe able to resist incursions by Vladimir Putin, an increasingly assertive China, and a threatening Donald Trump. After a string of weak leaders, Merkel was relieved that she now had a brilliant and ambitious partner in this fight, happy that Macron gave France back its pride after the ailing Chirac, the impetuous Sarkozy, and the ineffectual Hollande. But that didn't mean she'd simply be Macron's copilot. "Pace yourself," Merkel counselled Macron, which was not the advice the exuberant new president was seeking.

Captive of no political party save the one of his own creation, La Republique en Marche! (an exclamation point would never feature in any political party with which Merkel was affiliated), Macron was eager for disruption, spelling out his program for reform in a book immodestly titled *Revolution.** We cannot allow the extremists on the Left and the Right to be the only disruptors, he told Merkel. "You and I, Angela, we have to disrupt!" He warned his counterpart that if he failed, Germany might have to deal with Marine Le Pen, the head of France's Far Right National Front.

Macron had come to power with the heady ambition of enhancing what he called European sovereignty. In a ninety-minute speech delivered in the Sorbonne's historic Grand Amphitheater, Macron set off more rhetorical fireworks than the world had heard from Merkel during her entire career, as he proposed a tightly integrated eurozone, with a single banking system, a common European bond, and a common migration regime. Europe lacked all of those institutions, as had been made devastatingly clear by both the financial and the refugee crises, revealing the EU's absence of a common policy in either realm. (The Covid-19 pandemic that ambushed the world

---

*Macron's choice of slogan for his 2022 reelection campaign, "Nous, Francais" (translated roughly as "We the French"), was not one that the antinationalist Merkel would ever approve—and more or less sums up the gulf between them.

in 2020 would reveal a similar weakness in its public health infrastructure.) "European sovereignty requires constructing, and it's up to us to do it!" he exhorted his audience, all the while looking to Merkel for support. While the French-German partnership has always been the cornerstone of the European Union—they were the most populous and largest Continental nations, after all—an undertow of rivalry and exasperation between the two has been just as much a fact of European life for centuries. It is only in the twenty-first century that they no longer resolve those differences on the battlefield.

Charles de Gaulle, the Resistance war hero and president from 1958 until 1969, likened the relationship to that of a horse and carriage, "with Germany being the horse, and France the coachman," which was not exactly how Angela Merkel regarded the dynamic between the two countries. One time Sarkozy, turning on the charm, said to Merkel, "Angela, we are made to get along. We are the head and legs of the European Union." The chancellor shot back acidly, "No, Nicolas, you are the head and legs. I am the bank."

In truth, Merkel was in no position to answer Macron's challenge to disrupt Europe. For starters, the French constitution provides the president greater powers than is granted in any other Western democracy. Germany's chancellor rules by persuasion and consensus under a powerful party structure and a diffuse federalist system. Although the chancellor appoints the Cabinet, she chooses from the major parties, not just her own. Macron had just smashed France's political parties, virtually creating his own. With Merkel's obsession regarding austerity and thrift, and with a population that strongly endorsed those qualities, she hesitated to endorse a single banking system that Germany—the economic powerhouse of Europe—might have to prop up.

European self-sufficiency was Macron's goal. But his plan for a standing European army—so that the Continent would be less dependent on NATO for its defense—was an especially hard sell for the antimilitary Merkel. For her, despite Trump's outrageous behavior, that was taking things too far, too fast. She remained an Atlanticist.

Merkel also noted what sorts of changes Macron did *not* propose. France accepted Germany as an economic powerhouse, but not as a political equal. If France and Germany were to share an EU budget and an integrated banking system, why not a shared European seat on the UN Security Council? France would not hear of that; the UN's founders had decided in 1945 that the so-called permanent representatives on the Security Council would be France, China, Russia, the United Kingdom, and the United States—not a precise reflection of the world's most powerful states seven decades later, but enormously significant to France. The view in Merkel's chancellery was that France cared more for the symbols of power than it did European unity.

Perhaps the problem was also that the pair's timing was off. The battle-weary chancellor was in her political twilight; Macron was just starting out, and though she liked him when he was Hollande's minister of finance, she felt he grew arrogant once he became president. ("I know he's smart, but why does he have to show off all the time?" she commented to aides.) Observing Macron scolding a Parisian youth who addressed him as "Manu," one Merkel aide noted that, during the war, Londoners had often called out, "Hello, Winnie!" to prime minister Winston Churchill without getting a lecture from their hero. Macron's ambitions were naked—an unappealing quality to Merkel, who shields hers like priceless jewels.

Then, too, she may well have felt a twinge of all-too-human envy at the meteoric ascent of such a youthful and inspiring new spokesman for Europe. While editorials presaged her waning leadership, they hailed Macron's energy and passion. "The real France is back!" crowed the president of the European Commission, Jean-Claude Juncker. While she was tied up for six frustrating months trying to form a new coalition government, glowing headlines hailed Macron as the new global maestro. "He's conducting international politics, and I'm stuck here," Merkel grumbled from Berlin.*

With a skeptical eye, she observed her new political partner's attempted courtship of Trump, whom he dazzled with Gallic pomp with a dinner at the Eiffel Tower, and that splendid Bastille Day military parade on the Champs-Élysées. Appealing to Trump's personal vanity, Merkel felt, produced at best short-term gains. She predicted that Macron's seduction campaign of this hollow narcissist would ultimately prove useless. And indeed, by November 11, 2018, as Macron welcomed Angela Merkel to Paris to commemorate the centennial of the end of World War I, he had abandoned his attempt to charm the volatile Trump—an exercise in futility, as Merkel surely predicted.

Macron and Merkel showed genuine warmth on that day, touching foreheads when they met in Compiègne, outside Paris, and holding hands in the historic train car where Germany had initially signed the armistice ending World War I. Twenty-two years later, in 1940, the mighty Nazi Wehrmacht steamrolled across France in just seven weeks. Adolf Hitler forced France's Marshall Philippe Pétain to accept his humiliating diktat in that same dining car. For the next four-plus years, France had to submit to brutal German occupation under the collaborationist Vichy regime. Now, as the two heads of state, Merkel and Macron, reclaimed Compiègne in the name of European unity, the scene was a reminder of the speed with which the wheels of history turn.

---

*It was the energy and charisma he projected that garnered glowing headlines. Macron was mostly preoccupied trying to reform France's stagnant economy and tax code, as well as attempting to bring to heel the populist Yellow Vest movement of nationwide protests against his fuel tax. Still, Merkel could only envy the much freer rein of the semi-imperial French presidency.

The following day, like mourners at a funeral, eighty heads of state, shielded by black umbrellas against a downpour, marched shoulder to shoulder up the Champs-Élysées to the Arc de Triomphe. Trump was absent from this solemn procession. Arriving late, he sat sulking, phone in his twitchy palm (though he momentarily perked up when Vladimir Putin, who arrived even later, grabbed his hand). Forced to listen to Macron's history lesson, Trump looked like he would rather have been almost anywhere else. "The old demons are returning," Macron noted darkly. "Nationalism is a betrayal of patriotism. It says, Our interest first; who cares about the others?" he said, in a pointed rebuke of the sullen American in the front row.

A few days later, more than a year following his Sorbonne speech, Angela Merkel finally answered Macron's plea for her support in constructing a "sovereign Europe." Looking buoyant and wearing a blue jacket to match the EU banner, she entered the European parliament in Strasbourg. Waving and smiling to the 705 members representing twenty-seven states, she mounted the podium of what she called "the greatest parliament in the world" and surprised many. The chancellor who despises war said the time had come for "a real, true European army," endorsing one of Macron's core ideas.

The two countries agreed to a new joint program to coordinate and integrate their defense and security tasks, and to collaborate in developing a new generation of European fighter jets. This program would be outside the EU and NATO and would share intelligence and operational capabilities among its members. (Twenty-one other European nations would join, though details remained to be finalized.) Faced with an increasingly hostile and unpredictable world, Germany overcame some of its aversion toward armed missions abroad. Trump's bullying and preference for authoritarians, alongside Putin's naked aggression, can be credited with Merkel's support of Macron's initiative.

But Macron kept racing ahead of her with his attempt to "disrupt" the

European status quo. When he was awarded the prestigious Charlemagne Prize in May 2018, he pointedly beseeched Merkel, sitting in the front row of the Coronation room of Aix-la-Chapelle (Aachen in German) town hall, "Germany cannot have a perpetual fetish about budget and trade surpluses, because they come at the expense of others. Wake up! Let's not be divided, let's not show fear, and let's not wait!" he said, blindsiding his "partner" by the force of his rhetoric and its direct summons to action. Reviving Europe was her goal too, but, typically, she needed to think his proposals through—and, unlike Macron, she had to consult with her government.

A month later, at a meeting in her rustic, official retreat, an hour from Berlin, Merkel accepted Macron's plan for a banking union to prevent future financial crises in Europe—another partial endorsement of his grander scheme for a sovereign Europe.

Relations between Macron and Merkel remained rocky. Once again displaying his flair for drama, the French president surprised world leaders gathered at a summit at the French seaside resort of Biarritz the following summer with an unannounced guest: Iran's foreign minister, Mohammad Javad Zarif. He hoped to broker a deal between Iran and Trump, who had opted out of the 2015 agreement reached under the Obama administration banning Iran's nuclear weapons production. "It's fine if it leads to something," was Merkel's skeptical reaction to Macron's initiative. It did not. Macron had not laid the groundwork for such a diplomatic breakthrough with the meticulous care that the German chancellor might have. The Iranian wasn't the week's only unexpected guest. Merkel was annoyed when Macron invited Putin to a private dinner at his summer residence several days later in hopes of bringing Russia back into the European family.

During the Biarritz summit, as Macron played the suave and unpredictable host, Merkel seized the chance for a small taste of freedom. Tourists sunbathing on the Biarritz beach were startled by the sight of a familiar figure in such an unfamiliar context: chancellor Merkel, in white sneakers and casual white pants, skirting the rim of the rushing tide, while her dark-suited security guards formed a rough V around her—doing their futile best to pass unnoticed. Leading the group was her ever-present spokesman, Steffen Seibert, in shirt sleeves and bare feet, his pants rolled up as he carried his dress shoes. Only Merkel, it seemed, had come prepared for a beach walk.

It seemed symbolic, a sign that, with two years left in her term, the chancellor was beginning to step away. However frustrating it may have been to see the man she'd hoped could be a full partner in creating a more united Europe wining and dining Europe's belligerent foe, she wasn't going to make a fuss. Macron was another in a long line of peacocks with whom she had done business. Besides, Macron—unlike Putin, Trump, Erdogan, and the others—shared her values: faith in democracy, the rule of law, and pluralism. Better to enjoy a walk along the beach; drama had never been her way.

She wasn't offstage yet.

The contained friction between Merkel and Macron exploded in public later that year, when, without giving her advance notice, Macron lashed out at NATO in a high-profile interview in the weekly newspaper the *Economist*. The French president argued that Europe had to acknowledge "the brain death of NATO," given the unreliability of the United States. Merkel found Macron's comments "unhelpful." To question NATO was to weaken the Western democratic order, in her view.

Shortly following Macron's provocative comments, he was in Berlin to mark the thirtieth anniversary of the fall of the Berlin Wall. During a small dinner at the official Bellevue Palace, the two leaders finally aired their differences. Those present, however, claimed their tone was friendly and laced with good humor throughout. "There is an element of mutual respect between them, but they are so different," observed Thomas Bagger, chief foreign policy advisor to the German president. "They have had to go the extra mile to make the relationship work."

"I understand you," Merkel told Macron. "You like to break things, and I have to mop up after you." She also chided her French counterpart for breaking EU ranks in his solo overtures to Russia and his veto of North Macedonia's ascension to the EU, which she viewed as a concession to Moscow. Much as she appreciated Macron's desire for a stronger Europe, she let him know that going out on a limb alone to get there would only weaken the Continent as a whole.

The most emotional part of their two-hour dinner, however, had nothing to do with Trump or with Putin or with any other swirling crisis. It was a celebration of the transformative event of Angela Merkel's life: the fall of the wall. Present at the dinner were three former East German dissidents who had been at the barricades during those historic days. The three spoke of their "Bastille Day," but for them, it wasn't November 9, the day the wall fell, but rather a month earlier, when seventy thousand East Germans marched in Leipzig, facing the very real prospect of violence. They were prepared for the Stasi to fire on them, just as the Chinese military had at Tiananmen Square that June. But fear, as Werner Schultz, one of the dissidents, said, had "jumped to the other side": the Stasi were now afraid of the people. These three East Germans felt that *they*—not Reagan, Bush, Gorbachev, or Kohl—liberated themselves. National pride was not a uniquely French quality after all.

Macron listened with rapt attention as Merkel recalled her own experiences of that night: rushing from the sauna, towel under her arm, to the newly opened crossing on Bornholmer Strasse to begin her new life. A dinner that had begun with a spirited airing of grievances between allies ended with the two finding common ground. Recounting the historic reunification of Germany in 1989,* Merkel and Macron parted with a renewed sense of Europe's common history and shared fate.

Even as Merkel and Macron were dining in Berlin, a virus was already spreading in China that would soon bring the pair together once more—and prove that Merkel had found the partner she sought in Macron. Others, however, were losing faith in her.

At the end of 2019, as Merkel marked the close of her fourteenth year as chancellor, the British newspaper the *Guardian* published a damning take on her career. "Angela Merkel Must Go," the distinguished Oxford-based historian Timothy Garton Ash wrote in an anguished tone, arguing that, with Merkel at the helm, Germany "is the slow beating heart of a well-fed businessman resting on his office couch after an ample lunch." He admitted that Merkel's passionate commitment to a balanced budget made Germany's economy among the healthiest democracies. But Garton Ash faulted her excessive caution and her failure to embrace Macron's attempt to "revolutionize" Europe and give it "Napoleonic ambitions."

"I would respectfully suggest," he concluded "that keeping Merkel in office is not in the best interest of either Germany or Europe. . . . It's time for a change."

Change did indeed arrive in 2020. But Merkel's presence in office turned out to be not only in the best interest of Germany and Europe but also of the rest of the world.

---

*The official date of German reunification is October 3, 1990, but this conversation was about the dramatic events surrounding the fall of the wall in 1989.

Angela Merkel addressed the nation on March 18, 2020, on what was for her an unusual platform: television. Her tone, which combined compassion and authority in equal measure was unprecedented. She led Germany with unmatched calm and poise through the early, traumatic months of the Covid-19 pandemic.

18

TOWARD THE END

It seems ridiculous, but the only way to fight the plague is with decency.
—Albert Camus, French philosopher and writer (1913–1960)

Events, dear boy, events.
—Harold Macmillan, British prime minister from 1957 to
1963, when asked what would determine his legacy

Angela Merkel spent her final two years in office securing policies that would live on after she stepped down. But, unlike most others who reach the pinnacle of power, she also tried to connect with people to whom she had given short shrift earlier in her career.

With time, Merkel has allowed herself to feel something gentler for the closed world of her youth and for those who "did not share in my good fortune": those East Germans who feel unacknowledged and underappreciated for their post-unification struggles. "It isn't just people on the Right who feel this way," she told audiences in the former East Germany in 2019. "Others feel it too; they just aren't as vocal. I know that there are villages dying because children and grandchildren have moved away." More frequently now, she used the phrase "*we* East Germans"—a new expression of solidarity

Having spent much of her political career eliding the subject of her origins, now she sometimes sounded almost nostalgic recalling that long-ago life behind the fearsome wall, when her mother and father were still alive, and she was the studious Parson's daughter. The German word *Sehnsucht*, which encompasses nostalgia, longing, and other indefinable emotions that come with recalling the distant past, best describes this.

For Merkel, East Germany increasingly became about the sights, sounds, and smells of childhood. Asked what comes to mind when she recalls her youth, she replied, "Pines, and hay, and the smell of potatoes in the potato steamer. We had friends and families with whom we celebrated birthdays and Christmases; with whom we shared our grief. The fact that we couldn't travel to America didn't define every day."

Asked to name her favorite film once, the chancellor chose the 1972 East German dark comedy *The Legend of Paul and Paula*. It is a revealing choice, surely not based on the movie's artistic merits, but on the time and place it evokes for Angela Merkel. The film offers a sentimental look at the most human aspects of life in the East: young love under strained circumstances. The kitchens are tiny and shared with neighbors, the paint is peeling, and the cars are boxy Trabis, as the wheezing Trabants were affectionately called. Everybody is uniformly poor. Seated next to her husband at the film's 2013 revival, the chancellor's face seemed to light up with pure pleasure that only images of *Heimat* (there is no English word for this deep sense of the familiar) can stir. Suddenly she was no longer chancellor of the Federal Republic of Germany but eighteen years old again—her age when she first saw the film—en route to study physics at Leipzig University.

Nevertheless, until the very end, a subset of East Germans remained unbending in their harsh judgement of the chancellor from the East. Direct confrontation of foes is, of course, not Merkel's style. Yet there were times when she could not avoid encounters with those who made no attempt to mask their bitter resentment of her. While attending a town hall in her own electoral district in the town of Stralsund in 2019, a portly, fair-haired man sitting in the front row raised his hand and identified himself as "Thomas Naulin, *AfD* member," before lashing out at Merkel. "You have led us into a dictatorship. . . . Basic rights have been severely curtailed, freedom of the press does not exist . . . [Communist] East Germany would be green with envy if they saw this." He concluded his rant by saying, "As an AfD member, I don't have the right to freedom of expression."

"First of all," Merkel replied in a dead calm tone, "you are sitting here, in the first row, and are not in any danger because of the question you asked." Those in the audience old enough to recall that Naulin's provocative remarks would have landed a citizen of the German Democratic Republic in jail tittered nervously. "Nor do I feel that the AfD are inhibited from telling me and my colleagues what they think in the Bundestag," she continued.

"As to who represents the people, who is a patriot, there are different opinions. You believe it's you. I believe I am just as much a part of the people. . . . As to whether I believe that I have divided the country with my policies: I don't believe that any country is alone in the world. . . . I will always say that [my refugee policy] was the right thing to do. . . . We can't merely protect our own wealth. We can't just think of ourselves," she told the hushed audience. "We are part of the world."

It was an astonishing—even moving—performance. Yet Merkel's patient, thoughtful, noncombative search for common humanity often seemed a plea from another era. Hers may have been a lone voice, but she would continue to exercise it during the time left to her.

Increasingly, too, during her last years in office, Merkel called out the absence of women in high places—mostly with well-aimed barbs. In October 2018, in the Baltic seaport of Kiel, at the Global Forum for Young Leaders, Merkel surveyed the all-male lineup of Germany's putative future and noted dryly, "Pretty manly." Then, turning serious, she commented, "Fifty percent of the people are missing. And let me tell you: women enrich life. Not only in private, but in politics, too. You don't know what you are missing!" The audience erupted in awkward laughter, and the group of young men being honored appeared slightly less cocky—perhaps even a shade less *manly*.

Merkel had not forgotten the condescension with which her own ambitions had been treated by Germany's political elite, as when one minister told her, "You know, girl, if I didn't think you were so nice, I wouldn't vote for this nonsense," in reference to an equal rights law she had championed as minister for women and youth. By the end of her tenure as chancellor, she had quietly transformed a thoroughly patriarchal culture into one that was more woman friendly. Speaking at a November 2018 celebration of a hundred years of women's suffrage in Germany, she said, "Today nobody laughs anymore when a young girl says she wants to become a minister or even chancellor one day. Some people," she added, pausing for comic effect, "even wonder if *a man* would be fit for that job." Smiling at her own cheekiness, Merkel let the waves of laughter wash over her.

Sitting on stage at the University of Pretoria in South Africa in February 2020, one arm draped casually on the backrest, she answered students' questions with the self-assurance of a feminist with nothing left to prove: "Be self-confident. Don't let others take the bread out of your mouth. Dare to disagree. Don't let them humiliate you"—all advice the ambitious young Angela had to figure out for herself.

Her most powerful weapon in fighting for women remained her own example. She demonstrated that a woman could lead without the usual theatrics of the powerful. In the Bundestag, with the absolute confidence born of a mastery of facts, she routinely rebuffed attacks and answered questions with the calm air of a chess computer. For example, when a member of the Social Democratic Party was unable to finish her question regarding strengthening nursing home staff in the allotted sixty seconds, and her microphone was turned off, the chancellor jumped in coolly. "To come to your rescue: I think I can guess where you were heading with this." Merkel proceeded to lecture the MPs on the arcane rules governing German nursing homes, "leaving them," in the words of one observer, "woozy with the abundance of information." And she frequently urges, "Girls, go into science!" Hers is a style that makes the aggressive, blustering male leader look dated.

Yet Merkel is rarely credited with being an advocate for women. And it's true she has never used the chancellor's bully pulpit to deliver a full speech on the need to empower the half of the population that is still radically underrepresented in political life. As with her approach to many controversial subjects, Merkel is an incrementalist who works for change obliquely. For example, she entrusted the most traditionally "masculine" portfolio, the Defense Ministry, to a mother of seven, Ursula von der Leyen, paving her way to assume the European Commission presidency. She prefers to lead by example.

At the end of 2019, Merkel repaid a historic debt. She had been to Nazi concentration camps in Buchenwald, Dachau, and Sachsenhausen. She had laid a wreath at Yad Vashem in Jerusalem. She had not, however, been to the bleakest of Europe's monuments to man's capacity for evil: Auschwitz, the largest of the Nazi killing camps, located in Poland. On this winter day, the chancellor walked slowly down the gravel path leading to the wrought iron gates emblazoned with the cruel lie *"Arbeit Macht Frei"* ("Work Makes You Free"), in solemn silence. During a previous era, this might have been an obligatory display of goodwill. But in December 2019, with anti-Semitism and racism stoked by populists from Heidenau, Saxony, to Charlottesville, Virginia—and with the AfD in the Bundestag and Trump in the White House—her words, delivered in front of a wall of family portraits of victims, were like a tocsin:

"These days it is necessary to say this clearly: We must confront those who stir up prejudice and incite hatred against people of different faiths and origins. Auschwitz was a *German* death camp, run by *Germans*. We Germans owe it to the victims, and to ourselves, to keep alive the memory of the crimes committed, to identify the perpetrators, and to commemorate the victims. . . . This is not open to negotiation. It is an integral part and will forever be an integral part of our identity."

With unflinching precision, Merkel catalogued the crimes that Germans had committed there "against people who had a name, a history, a dignity, a story. . . . [It] is beyond human comprehension. . . . And yet it happened. Therefore, it can happen again," she said, quoting Auschwitz survivor Primo Levi.

In her final year, Merkel rebuffed questions of "legacy." "I'm too busy to ponder such things," was the dismissive answer I received when I asked a close aide what Merkel hoped would be her legacy. Impatient with self-examination—and explanations in general—that was typical of the chancellor. Nevertheless, in her low-key way, she was working to safeguard her legacy of a Germany more tolerant of outsiders and more understanding toward a swath of its own Eastern population. She reminded Germans of the need to wrestle with their country's past in perpetuity.

She also had more plans for Germany's future. In her New Year's Eve speech of December 31, 2019, Angela Merkel promised she would finally become the "Climate Chancellor." "Global warming is real, and it is threatening," she told Germans, more forcefully than is her style. "We have to do everything humanly possible to overcome this challenge. At sixty-five, I am at an age at which I personally will no longer experience all the consequences of climate change that will occur if politicians do not act." She planned to act.

At the same time, Merkel was overseeing an initiative, under Eva

Christiansen's leadership, to improve digital access in the East and rural parts of Germany. Since Merkel does not believe that talking alone changes minds, she hoped that disgruntled *Ossis* could be brought closer to the rest of the country if they saw concrete improvements in their daily lives.

The last time I was in the chancellery, in early February 2020, Angela Merkel was researching quantum computing, an exponentially faster computing system that, some predict, will become the next stage of computing. The chancellor had also just finished reading a long paper on Clearview AI, an American tech company that provides facial recognition software used by private companies, law enforcement agencies, universities, and individuals. Artificial intelligence was looming large, especially as it was rapidly being developed and implemented in China, threatening Germany's famed automobile industry with self-driven electric cars. But it wasn't just cars: AI was about to revolutionize medical care and the way wars are fought, and to dominate information technology. China, Merkel knew, was taking the necessary next steps to become the world leader in artificial intelligence committing billions of dollars into research and development. With its centrally planned economy, Beijing could move much faster than a cumbersome democracy such as Germany.

Merkel wanted to fully understand the rapidly expanding digital revolution in all its aspects: not only its promise, but also its potential dangers for society—particularly regarding the use of facial recognition technology. With her relish for the new, her scientific training, and her confidence in dealing with data, she mastered technical terrain faster than most politicians could. The Chinese were galloping ahead, and Merkel was determined that Germany—and Europe—not lose their innovative edge, though she feared it was happening already.

This was February 2020, just weeks before the chancellery—and much of the world—went dark, and the chancellor became a Covid-19 crisis manager. Events, as ever, forced her to shift her priorities.

• • •

On March 19, 2020, she faced what she referred to her as the country's "greatest crisis since World War II." Angela Merkel, a politician not known for her communication skills, delivered a transformative message to her people in a national televised address. She was shown against the potent visual backdrop of the Reichstag and flanked by the German and European Union flags—a platform she had used only in her annual New Year's Eve addresses—and so the German people paid attention. Her tone, blending empathy and force in equal measure, was not one they had ever heard from their leader. The speech Merkel delivered that day changed the course of a deadly virus in her country and, given its relentless spread, beyond Germany's borders as well.

"*Es is ernst*," Merkel said with unaccustomed intensity. "This is serious." She repeated the admonition like a tolling bell: "Please take it seriously." And the German people trusted her because, in fifteen years, she had never lied to them. She may have bored them and often failed to explain her decisions adequately, but she rarely embellished facts and certainly didn't make them up. Accumulated trust now saved lives.

Her emotions contained but unmistakable, Merkel appealed to Germans' best instincts. "We are a community in which every life and every person counts. . . . These are not abstract numbers or statistics. They are a father or a grandfather; a mother or a grandmother. They are people," she said, her simple, declarative sentences far more calming in this crisis than soaring rhetoric. She spoke not as politician but as a friend to friends, a parent to children, one human to another. Her words were clearly her own. While two of her closest advisors, Beate Baumann and Steffen Seibert, had written the first draft, the chancellor stayed up rewriting late into the night. When she delivered the address, she did so in a single take, without a slipup, her message powerful because it was heartfelt.

Everything in her improbable life—from her childhood seeped in the

Lutheran ethos of service, to her decades as a scientist-turned-politician—
seemed to have prepared Merkel for this final crisis. Ever mindful of Germany's dark history, she promised the German people transparency. "We
are a democracy. We do not live by constraint, but by shared knowledge and
participation," she said, before announcing:

"We are shutting down. Stop socializing. Work from home. You can't
go to school or to bars or to football games." She reminded her population
that she knew something about confinement. "For someone like me, for
whom freedom of travel and movement was a hard-won right, such restrictions can only be justified as an absolute necessity. In a democracy, they
should never be decided lightly, and only temporarily—but at the moment,
they are indispensable to save lives," she emphasized.

Calmly, but gravely, her fingertips forming their familiar triangle on the
desk in front of her, Merkel addressed the nation as if they were her family.
"The hardest part will be that we will miss human encounters," she warned.
"But keeping our distance from others is a sign of caring. . . . How high the
number of victims will be, how many loved ones we lose, is largely in our
hands." She closed with a plea: "Please take good care of yourself and take
care of your loved ones. . . . We have to find ways to show affection and
friendship. Skype, phone, email, and maybe write letters again. The mail is
getting delivered!" Science and empathy delivered in equal measure.

A few days after her speech, Merkel was seen pushing a shopping cart
in her local Berlin market. The press photos captured only two bottles of
wine and a few rolls of toilet paper in the chancellor's cart. No one could
accuse her of staging this perfect example of one of her key messages to the
nation: "Do not hoard!" As most Germans were aware, the chancellor had
done her own shopping throughout her tenure. She did not need to reinvent herself to suit the current crisis.

While many leaders lingered in denial, Angela Merkel led with calm
competence. From Washington to Moscow, and within Germany itself,

the myriad voices that had attacked her were now silent, waging their own battles for political, or even literal, survival. In a time where high anxiety, bravado, and magical thinking spread confusion and, ultimately, death, Merkel's support at home soared to a historic 80 percent.

When lives—not politics or ambition—were at stake, she revealed her truest self. As the coronavirus spread and shifted direction daily, tracking the virus required a scientist's respect for precision and facts. Reading up on the history of the Spanish flu—which killed roughly fifty million people around the globe after World War I—Merkel had a sense of what was coming. "It helps that the chancellor can handle numbers," said Dr. Christian Drosten, director of the Institute of Virology at Berlin's Charité University Hospital, who helped identify the SARS virus in 2003. But a background in science alone does not translate into statesmanship. A German chancellor's power to regulate domestic affairs is limited, based primarily on consent and consensus. It was Merkel's power of persuasion and careful martialing of projections that convinced Germany's sixteen sometimes reluctant states, which control school closings and stay-at-home orders, to lock down quickly.

During the refugee crisis, she had learned to her peril that at a time of national crisis, she has to be *present* and visibly in charge. Such regular communication was particularly urgent given the presence of another virus: social media, blindingly fast at spreading conspiracy theories and misinformation. "I ask you not to believe rumors, but only official communications," the chancellor urged the German people. "Everything I am telling you comes from the experts." She appeared always as part of a team, flanked by her health minister, Jens Spahn, and other relevant officials, eager to share credit with those around her. Never a voice from on high, during the pandemic she stayed on the ground without ever losing her authority.

As balmy spring weather beckoned to a population tired of weeks of confinement, she assured her countrymen that she had a precise formula for their liberation—and for a future lockdown, which she saw as inevitable. "If the transmission number were to go up to 1.2" per infected person, she explained, "hospitals could reach a crisis point in July. If it were to go up to 1.3, the crisis would come sooner, in June." Unlike facilities in many parts of the developed world, German hospitals never reached the crisis point. From the outset, fifty thousand people were tested each day, allowing officials to effectively trace the movements of those who were infected. Because of this, Germany suffered only one-third the death count seen in France. After learning that one of her own doctors had tested positive for Covid, the chancellor set a national example by going into full quarantine for two weeks herself.

"My life has changed. It now consists largely of phone calls and video conferences," she said, speaking to the nation from quarantine. Not even a global pandemic, however, could persuade the fiercely private chancellor to allow the world a peek into her home. Cameras never revealed the books lining her shelves or her taste in art and furniture. Merkel ran the country with her voice, chairing Cabinet meetings and phone conferences with heads of state from her small Berlin apartment—one that no head of state or even loyal staffer had ever visited.

Once derided for pressing the ideal of the frugal "Swabian housewife," who sweeps her front porch on her fellow European Union members, Merkel's fifteen years of insisting on a tight budget now paid off. Germany went into the health crisis with a surplus, and when its chancellor called for a lockdown, payments to families, tax cuts, and business loans amounted to four times that of the United States' rescue package, without the need to take on debt. *Kurzarbeit* (short-term work), a hundred-year-old state system that pays companies to keep workers on their payroll through crises, was quickly scaled up. As a result, Germany expected only a 6 percent drop in GDP, compared to France's loss of 10 percent to 13 percent.[*]

During the early weeks of the crisis, Merkel, despite being a champion of European solidarity, put her population first. As the virus moved north from Italy, Germany closed its borders. In a continent where people and goods have been smoothly crossing borders for decades, it was a shock to see barriers spring up—but the chancellor felt that, as she was asking a great deal of her constituents, her first responsibility was to support Germany. For this, she later apologized. "Our first reflexes were national, which was wrong," she told the Bundestag. "A global pandemic requires joint, international action, and mutual support." Once her own nation seemed under a degree of control, Merkel began to think globally.

With a surge of popular support at her back, the chancellor could spend her personal capital to make Europe safe not just from the virus but also against other, future threats. Unlike during the euro crisis, her response to Covid's continentwide human and economic toll would be swift and dramatic. The scourge of the pandemic enabled her to make a final, bold move.

In the age of social distancing, Merkel and Macron could no longer touch foreheads in solidarity, but Europe's two powerhouses nonetheless came together to give the suffering continent a much-needed boost. A split-screen teleconference on May 18, 2020, showed Macron, beaming and suntanned from chairing his Cabinet in the Élysée gardens, and a smiling Merkel jointly announce a historic €500 billion recovery fund. Once this grant had the support of the France and Germany, the other countries were

---

[*]In fact, at the end of 2020, the German economy shrank by only 5 percent—among Europe's smallest declines. By comparison, France and Italy each experienced a 9 percent drop, while the United Kingdom suffered its worst decline in three hundred years, at 11.3 percent.

more or less compelled to support it, although hammering out the details would not be easy.

This was not a loan that the neediest European nations would have to repay, but an outright grant—a first for the EU. "Germany and France are fighting together for the European idea," the chancellor said. Far more than a mere budgetary decision, this was the fulfilment of Merkel's and Macron's vision of a strong and united Europe that cares for and protects its poorest members; those hit hardest by the pandemic. Such an infusion of funds represented a near revolutionary policy change for Merkel and for fiscally conservative Germany—no more "Queen of Austerity." With this grant, she overcame her own and her countrymen's obsession with thrift and fear of hyperinflation.

"What we've accomplished here is sensational," enthused Macron. In understated Merkel-speak, the chancellor said, "We've patched things up, so to speak, between Germany and France." This time the French president was closer to the truth. Granting the European Union unprecedented fiscal muscle was hailed a Hamiltonian moment by some—a reference to the 1790 agreement between Alexander Hamilton and Thomas Jefferson that federalized the debts of the different American states. After years of debate in Brussels, an actual United States of Europe seemed on the cusp of reality.

Merkel surprised even her closest allies with this dramatic turn, underscoring the intensely private and secretive nature of her decision-making. Macron, who had waged a campaign for her to endorse such a move for three years, was informed only a short while before their joint video conference. Thus Merkel revealed once again that she is not wedded to ideology or dogma, in politics or in economics; that she learns from her own mistakes; and that she is open to new ideas regardless of their source—as long as they work.

"In hard times, you have to stick up for an idea," she explained. The idea was rapid and compassionate relief for the hardest hit and preventing

Europe from fracturing. With the usual cold blasts blowing from Putin's Russia, an increasingly xenophobic and aggressive China, and Covid continuing to spread suffering, disregarding all borders, "the nation state alone has no future," she declared.

Merkel thus seized a global health crisis to forge new solidarity among European nations. The image of Merkel and Macron, flanked by the blue-and-gold European Union banner as they pledged to rescue the most vulnerable nations of the Continent, sent a powerful message to nationalists and populists from Washington to Moscow. In addition, it muted the chancellor's home-grown critics: not only the AfD, but also conservative members of her own Christian Democratic Union who had never reconciled to her nudging the party too far to the center. Angela Merkel's competence in fighting the crisis, and her decency and statesmanship in its aftermath, temporarily silenced the AfD's empty bluster, as well as the conservatives' grumbling. The AfD, in particular, foundered, its support dipping to below 10 percent at times. A party fueled by rage found little political traction in indignation against a virus. It became the anti-lockdown party, which only lost the AfD its more moderate followers.

Merkel spent her sixty-sixth birthday in the futuristic glass-and-steel headquarters of the European Council in Brussels, performing what was likely to be one of her final and most important feats of negotiation. The twenty-six other heads of state who had gathered around the vast round table on July 17 waited until she had entered the vast hall before they began the practical business of saving Europe. They needed to bridge the seemingly unbridgeable divide between Europe's wealthy North, less advantaged South, democratic West, and authoritarian-tending East.*

---

*Merkel's and Macron's recovery plan proposed that the European Commission borrow money and spend it on grants to help needier countries. Offering grants rather

Upon the chancellor's arrival, the leaders of Europe burst into spontaneous applause in her honor—and perhaps in sheer pleasure at being together
for the first time since Covid had shut down in-person diplomacy that February. A jaunty Merkel, visibly exhilarated to be back in the fray, was the only
one who wore the medically prescribed N-95 mask; the others wore custom-
ized masks emblazoned with their national insignias. As one who leaves few
things to chance, her choice in protective equipment signalled that she took
the pandemic extremely seriously as well as the fact that she was there not
merely as the leader of Germany but also as the leader of all Europe.

Given that 2021 was to be the chancellor's final year, there was an unspoken sense of history being made in that vast chamber. Merkel was in no
mood for nostalgia, however. Her body language was all determined business. The outbreak of Covid-19 presented the most serious threat Europe
had faced since the Second World War, she told them. In *Mutti* mode, she
chided the Bulgarian prime minister for not keeping his nose covered. As a
stark reminder of the extraordinary times, the meeting room was scrubbed
down every few hours, and a doctor remained on standby just outside the
door. No more than two heads of state were allowed in the elevator at a time.

After months of frustrating video conferences with heads of state talking past one another, searching for Mute buttons, and enduring dropped
connections, Merkel was back in command. For the next five days, in a total
of ninety hours of negotiations—talks were interrupted only by quick snack
breaks for the Brussels specialty of *pommes frites* (double-fried French
fries) and working meals—the chancellor gave the world a master class
on statecraft. No loquacious speeches, no ad hominem attacks, no one-
upmanship, just the exhausting work of finding common ground for the

---

than loans was hard to swallow for some northern countries, with their healthier
economies and more conservative fiscal policies. Persuading them was Merkel's and
Macron's challenge.

common good—the kind of intense human interaction that cannot be accomplished by grandstanding or over a virtual connection.

Merkel's brand of diplomacy has always depended on face-to-face contact: the careful reading of unspoken cues, body language, silences, and the spontaneous give-and-take that can be done only in person. She allowed everyone in the socially distanced gathering to have his or her say—even when Hungary's Viktor Orban picked up the demagogue's bullhorn. "Why do you hate me and Hungary so much?" he asked the group, as if he *were* Hungary. Too much was at stake for the others to be diverted by such play.

After a day of heated exchanges and no clear consensus in sight, at two in the morning on July 18, the group broke out the champagne to celebrate the chancellor's birthday. The president of Portugal presented Merkel with the Portuguese Nobel Laureate José Saramago's novel *Blindness*, whose heroine saves those afflicted with a viral "white blindness," leading them to safety—a poignantly expressive gift. Macron's birthday gift for Merkel was a case of her favorite white Burgundy.

The talks grew intense the following day. "We aren't here because we want to be invited to each other's birthday parties. We are here because we do business for our own countries," said the Dutch prime minister, Mark Rutte. He urged that grants be tied to member states' adherence to the rule of law. The EU is about certain values, not just trade, Rutte reminded leaders like Orban. In response, the Hungarian strongman snapped (bafflingly), "You are behaving like the Communists."

Hour by hour, Merkel, supported by her junior partner, Macron, brought the fractious nations closer together. She persuaded the so-called frugals—the Netherlands, Austria, Sweden, Denmark, and Finland—that "an extraordinary situation demands extraordinary effort," including the unprecedented opening of their countries' treasuries to a no-strings rescue of Italy, Spain, Greece, and other EU nations severely impacted by the pandemic. Frequently consulting her beloved charts and figures, Merkel reminded them of the immediate stakes: a deeper recession, high unemployment, ever wider gaps between the rich and poor, and social unrest on a continent where such situations have never ended well. She did not need to remind her fellow heads of states that Europe—beset by local populists who feed off rage at "Brussels," not to mention Xi Jinping's naked ambitions, Putin's campaign to keep the Continent permanently at odds and divided, and the United States on an election's knife edge—could not risk abandoning any of its member states to the pandemic or to the demagogues. As they haggled into the early morning hours for a second day, worldwide deaths from the pandemic passed six hundred thousand.

Tempers frayed by the end of the second long day. Macron, riled by the Austrian chancellor Sebastian Kurz, who walked out of their working dinner to take a phone call, slapped the great table and thundered, "You see, Kurz doesn't care. He doesn't listen to the others. . . . He handles his press and *basta*. Enough." Kurz quietly sat down and did not get up again. If Merkel, the sixty-six-year-old leader of the West, had the stamina to keep talking through four nights, then surely the thirty-three-year-old Austrian chancellor could stick it out.

At three o'clock on Saturday morning, Merkel and Macron met in the bar of the Hilton Brussels Grand Palace, a vintage 1970s hotel where they both were staying, for a glass of white wine. The talks had reached an impasse. The "frugals" were unbending. The prosperous and fiscally conservative (and stubborn, in Merkel's view) Dutch held fast to their position of no grants without conditions, until the lack of progress and exhaustion evaporated the celebratory mood of the day before. Macron told his staff to prepare the presidential plane for a last-minute takeoff.

Merkel, more accustomed to the roller coaster-ride of high-stakes negotiations, held fast. Ultimately, Europe's heavyweights, she and Macron, presented a united front that gradually wore down the holdouts. The two most populous states of the EU proved unbeatable when they worked together. None around that table wanted to undermine the union at this moment of crisis or jeopardize their own reputations by abandoning the talks—especially as most of them stood to gain from the rescue package. The heads of state *had* to come to an agreement; the pandemic was a crucible from which none could easily walk away.

"Deal!" tweeted the Council president, Charles Michel, at five thirty in the morning on July 21. Macron's tweet was more elegant: "A historic day for Europe." Typically, the woman largely responsible for the breakthrough understated the achievement. "We've acted responsibly in agreeing to these compromises." Only her eyes, weary but crinkled with sheer relief, gave away that behind her mask, Angela Merkel was smiling.

Beyond the $859 billion spending plan to rescue Europe's most Covid-ravaged countries was something even more powerful. For once, the much-derided European Union was acting as a whole, not as a collection of selfish nations, each looking for its own cut. When they agreed to nearly $400 billion in outright grants (with another $360 billion more in loans), no strings attached, the wealthy northern nations resisted burying the poorer countries in debt—as Merkel and Germany had done during the 2008 euro crisis. The money would come from the *collective*—from bonds sold on behalf of the EU—to which Germany would contribute the lion's share. France and Germany did not specify whether some new taxes or higher national contributions based on the size of their economies would be necessary. Merkel said the €500 billion should be paid back over "a long time" and that her country would shoulder almost a third of the funds.*

---

*The details regarding the distribution of the funds as well as new revenue sources for the EU budget were left to the European parliament to approve and the European Council to work out. If passed, they will tap a highly liquid bond market to pay for the rescue fund, with financing spread over seven years, in line with the EU budget framework.

"We must act in a European way so that we get out of the crisis well and strengthened," the chancellor told reporters. In doing so, the EU established a precedent and a structure for future crises, taking an enormous step toward achieving a union that was less bureaucratic and more *human*.

Angela Merkel spent her remaining time in office asserting Europe's need to "take its fate into its own hands." For Merkel, Europe had to stand for something more than common markets and borderless travel. "Europe is not neutral; Europe is part of the political *West*," she insisted. In a stroke of good fortune, the chancellor assumed the six-months-long rotating presidency of the European Union's executive body in July 2020. She used this opportunity to focus not on Europe alone but in relation to another of her pressing concerns.

"China is one of the key players of this century," she announced at the outset of her term, and proclaimed that China would be a priority during her six months at Europe's helm. Given Merkel's personal history—and having made more trips to China than any other head of state—she was less surprised than many other leaders by Beijing's suppression of information regarding the early Covid outbreak in the city of Wuhan. Control of information and the denial of bad news is the way of one-party authoritarian states, as she well knew. Nevertheless, Beijing's bare-knuckled crackdown on Hong Kong and its detention of a million Uighur Muslims in "reeducation camps" shocked her and presented the chancellor with her final dilemma—one without a clear solution.

China is not on the road to democratization—that much was plain. When Angela Merkel began her annual trips there in 2005, Marxist-Leninist ideology enforced by the only legal party, the Communists, was secondary to accommodation with the West on politics, economics, and even issues of national security. Merkel had experienced a similar hopeful experiment with a more humane socialism during the 1968 Prague Spring.

That attempt at "socialism with a human face" was crushed by Soviet, East German, and other Warsaw Pact tanks and armies—a heartbreak for the youthful Angela.

The chancellor had hoped China would continue on the path of reform and moderation it began after the death of Mao Tse-tung 1976. In 2012, however, Xi Jinping, the new Communist Party chairman, made clear that his priority was absolute power for the party and for himself. While the world was diverted by Covid, Xi only hardened his authoritarian grip. His confidence, assertiveness, and ambitions are global, and his means of achieving them seemed almost unlimited, with China on track to surpass the United States as the world's largest economy within the present decade.

This (along with the virus that still surged, and a disorganized EU vaccine rollout) challenged Angela Merkel's final months. For the chancellor, given its immense reach, China must be engaged. But how? She deemed bombastic statements counterproductive. As far as Merkel is concerned, public attacks only strengthen the hands of Chinese nationalists. Hers was a hardheaded yet nuanced approach. China, not the United States, is now the European Union's top trade partner. Quite simply, Germany needed more favorable trade terms with the Asian titan. Nor could there be real progress on climate change—or preparing for the next pandemic—without China at the table. That is the new reality, and Angela Merkel is above all a realist. Unlike most strongmen on the world stage, she is not trapped by the need to look tough. She is after results, no matter how modest.

During the last days of a year whose passing the world cheered, Angela Merkel achieved her final diplomatic triumph: a historic agreement between Beijing and the twenty-seven states of the European Union. In her second to last day in the rotating European Union presidency, she persuaded the fractious member states to agree to a deal that would open Chinese markets—leveling the playing field for trade between the two, at least to some degree—and even attempt to tackle the always thorny issue of high-tech security.

Though the EU has not released the full body of the complex set of trade, financial, climate, and human rights agreements—a decade in the making—its main achievements are clear. China agreed to lift significant trade and banking barriers, as well as ease burdensome requirements for joint ventures between the EU and Beijing. The deal also promised progress on climate change and an unprecedented commitment to involve civil society, reform its use of forced labor, as well as other concessions on human rights. Of course, any agreement is only as good as its implementation, and Angela Merkel will no longer be in power to hold Beijing to its promises. But the chancellor saw China as an unavoidable global force—the last expanding Communist power on the planet—and December 2020 was her last chance to turn her many years of building trust with the Chinese leadership into a concrete legacy.

Knowing how carefully Merkel calibrates advantage versus disadvantage, one can see why she seized that particular moment to push for a deal, despite signals from the incoming Biden administration that she hold off until "the West"—if that were still a viable category, after Trump and after Brexit—could present a united front. She calculated shrewdly that China, too, was eager for an agreement before the United States fully rejoined the alliance Trump had spent four years abusing. A newly united West would present a tougher adversary for Beijing, so Xi might be willing to make concessions now, before that happened. So, once again, she took advantage of an opening to move policy. Merkel's stature with the Chinese leadership, as well as with her fellow EU heads of state—combined with her dogged determination—got the deal done.

Angela Merkel achieved her final diplomatic coup without the benefit of the intense, human-to-human interaction she prefers in high-stakes diplomacy: no pulling up of chairs to overwhelm the recalcitrant with her command of facts, no hunching over charts and maps. Her final piece of diplomacy was carried out in the manner of the world in lockdown: via flickering images on giant screens.

Some of her fellow EU leaders complained that Merkel had pushed too forcefully for a deal that was technocratic and practical—as if Xi were a leader "we can do business with," as British prime minister Margaret Thatcher said once of Mikhail Gorbachev—regardless of his autocratic rule. The deal was too much about German interests, some EU members complained, since Germany is one of China's top five trading partners, and its automobile and industrial sectors were avid for easier Chinese market access.* But Angela Merkel wanted an agreement, and the others found it impossible to deny her this cap on her long career. With her grounding in science, and with the emergence of new coronavirus variants threatening to prolong the pandemic, Merkel saw beyond ideology to the need for rivals to collaborate on borderless issues such as health and climate. Admittedly, this was an agreement based not on values but on European self-interest— and it was by no means risk free. Deepening Europe's economic ties to China might make the EU more vulnerable to pressure from a nation that promotes certain policies Angela Merkel abhors. This was the chancellor practicing Realpolitik, Henry Kissinger would likely applaud. By Merkel's lights, however, an imperfect agreement, where both sides gain as well as give up something,† was always better than none.

---

*In 2020 Germany exported nearly €100 billion worth of goods to China, half of all EU exports to that country. And Germany bought even more from China than it exported there, making China its biggest overall trading partner—the driver of Germany's export growth. The EU-China trade deal will facilitate that growth and balance the existing trade imbalance.
†Even without the full text of the agreement published, it is clear China ceded a level of market control in opening up sectors to European trade and joint ventures.

When the deal was done, she said in her dry style, "We must have no illusions: China is a competitor . . . but a level playing field must prevail." The playing field would be somewhat more level now. It was welcome news for European business interests, but it also solidified China's global influence and reach. Merkel, at her most pragmatic, dealt with the world as she found it, not as she had once hoped it would become. *

Merkel had another motive in pushing for this agreement with China during her final days as president of the European Council. She was sending Washington a signal: Europe can act unilaterally in its own interest. When the freshly inaugurated President Biden proclaimed, "Politics does not have to be a raging fire," one could almost hear Angela Merkel exhale, "Amen." Alliances are founded on trust, however, and that trust has been frayed. For four years, Europe weathered multiple crises without Washington's help, and it will not suddenly resume its subordinate position in the transatlantic alliance. As unseen threats arose, threatening its most sacred trust, America was not vigilant. For Angela Merkel, this was the bitter legacy of the unruly and dangerous tenure of Donald Trump. She, one of the most pro-American of European leaders, was, in effect, declaring the end of US hegemony. *Pax Americana,* the international order forged by Washington in the wake of the Second World War, was history.

---

*But Merkel's engagement effort toward Beijing was badly undermined by China's increasingly harsh rhetoric and policies. As of the summer of 2021, the European Parliament, the body meant to finalize the trade and investment treaty the chancellor negotiated, put the agreement on hold.

Epilogue

The important work of moving the world forward does not wait to be done by perfect men.

—George Eliot (pen name of English novelist
Mary Ann Evans) (1819–1880)

With her final year dominated by the pandemic that surged and waned with the seasons, Merkel had little time to ponder her future life as a private citizen. Like most people, she missed her pre-Covid life. Videoconferences never filled the void for this politician who enjoys matching wits against others face-to-face. Her trips were mostly to Brussels for EU conferences, but, Merkel admitted, "It's not as much fun when even the restaurants are closed." She found relaxation in her daily walks, accompanied mostly by masked and socially distanced aides. The promise of a vaccine broke Berlin's wintry gloom. For Merkel, the fact that BioNTech, a small German firm founded by Turkish immigrants, was among the first to gain approval for marketing its vaccine, was a source of particular pride.

Covid's second wave during the winter of 2020 struck Germany hard, however, with the more contagious British mutation preventing efforts to finally bring the pandemic under control. The EU's vaccine rollout revealed the institution's inexperience with such a massive continentwide undertaking. As the virus took the form of new variants, Germans now paid the price for a government that was constructed to diffuse authority—and thus to slow down decision-making—even in a national emergency. The population, exhausted by curfews and quarantines, no longer approached Covid-19 as foe to be vanquished. Merkel, too, wearied of this invisible enemy. With the maddeningly slow vaccination rollout, her continued calls for the nation's patience lost their potency. The shock value of her blend of passionate intensity and humanity early in the pandemic was not something she could repeat a year later.

Still, Angela Merkel's remarkable global stature, enhanced by the astonishing fact that not a breath of scandal marred her sixteen years as chancellor, meant that the chancellor avoided the sad fate of most politicians: even in her final months she was not a *lame duck*. Seen as above politics, she had become both symbol and reflection of her country,

However much she protested that she had no time to ponder the future or her legacy, in her quiet moments, Angela Merkel surely must have wondered what it would feel like when there would be no place she had to be, no global crisis to solve, no dictator to bring to heel, no security or media shadowing her every move—a time when she might book a flight to one of those places she dreams of visiting.

After sixteen years at the helm of Europe's most powerful country, Merkel had become an almost perfect political machine: running, executing, and managing her party, her country, and what remains of the West. The fact that her role never became her identity will ease Angela Merkel's transition. Unlike most politicians, she seemed emotionally self-sufficient: she never hungered for the public's affection in the manner of a Bill Clinton or her own predecessors, Gerhard Schröder and Helmut Kohl. The most powerful woman in modern history is perfectly at ease being herself. She will not miss the narcotic of power, having never deeply inhaled its fumes.

She will not be undone now that the world's attention has shifted to her successor and to a new cast of players on the world stage.

She once referred to "my damned duty" as chancellor—a Lutheran formulation from the pastor's daughter. She more than fulfilled her "damned duty": she left behind a Europe—though still reeling from the pandemic and despite Britain's departure—more united than ever. In leaving the chancellery, Angela Merkel's greatest reward is her sense of duty done. Her father moved to the East because he felt he was needed there as pastor. Though she chose a different path, his daughter, too, chose to serve.

The world will not see a different persona emerge now that Merkel is no longer chancellor. Curious, open to new ideas, avid to understand how things work and what motivates people—these are qualities that predate her sixteen years in office. Late in her tenure, during an official dinner in Bellevue Palace, Merkel spoke not of all the problems bearing down on her—not of Xi or Putin or the American elections that preoccupied much of the world—but of her days as a postgraduate student in Prague. She reminisced about her fondness for the great Czech poet Jan Skácel, (who contrasted Communist repression with the free syntax of the Czech language) a man who—she reminded those present—Milan Kundera, another acclaimed writer from that country, said made learning the Czech language worthwhile. Merkel's passionate interest in the world beyond politics never abated. And though she does not believe that the arc of the moral universe bends toward justice, age and power have not made her either a cynic or a pessimist. "I belong to the optimists," she has said. "For me, the image of Sisyphus, the man who keeps rolling the rock up the mountain, isn't hopeless at all." All this augurs well for the next chapter of her improbable journey.

Nor was she moving from a palace into modest quarters: she never left her rent-controlled apartment in central Berlin. Her description of a perfect day sounds perfectly ordinary: "I will sleep long, have a relaxed breakfast.

Then I'll go out for some fresh air, chat with my husband or with friends. I might go to the theater, to the opera, or listen to a concert. If I'm rested, I might read a good book. And I would cook dinner. I like cooking!" These are the dreams of a person who had not been truly free for the last sixteen years. Though no longer young, Merkel is spry enough to enjoy the simplest of pleasures: country rambles, leisurely meals with (nonpolitical) friends, and music and books instead of charts, polls, and position papers. These pleasures will not replace the satisfaction of outsmarting a foe with her legendary stamina and command of facts. But, never one to ruminate over *feelings*, she will observe her own reaction to this new life with a scientist's curiosity. In the short term, she is likely to spend time near her childhood home in the province of Brandenburg, where she first learned to love nature and which she still regards as her *Heimat,* or spiritual home. She'll travel, too. Among her stated dreams is to fly over the Andes Mountains— an idealized destination; a metaphor for freedom. If she finds she misses her place among the powerful, she will not lack for options to rejoin them in some capacity. But this much we know of Angela Merkel: she will not be rushed. If she returns to public life, it will be on her own terms.

She who does not relish retrospection will now have time to reflect on her legacy. For Germany's self-image—and how the rest of the world regards the former Third Reich—Angela Merkel's refugee policy has been transformational. Nothing short of astonishing is that the country responsible for the Holocaust is now regarded as the world's moral center. And though the integration of a million refugees has been incremental, by the time Merkel left the chancellery, it was clear that their arrival had not overwhelmed the country of eighty-two million. Neither the German welfare system nor its schools—nor even its state budget—suffered seriously. Nor, for the most part, has the refugees' Islamic faith hindered their integration. Still, she cannot avoid acknowledging the high cost of her boldest act as chancellor. The AfD is the child of the Merkel era.

In many ways, the world is a much rougher place than the one she inherited as chancellor in 2005—through little fault of her own. As taboos keep falling, and political norms keep shifting, it is unclear how long Angela Merkel's politics of reason and moderation will endure. For now, in her homeland, at least, her legacy seems secure. On January 16, 2021, the CDU picked Armin Laschet as her successor as party chair. Laschet, prime minister of North Rhine–Westphalia, Germany's most populous state, was a fierce defender of Merkel's refugee policy, as well as an unapologetic advocate for a strong and united Europe.

Still, one wonders, now that Merkel is no longer at the table of world leaders, will her successors stay up all night in search of a sliver of common ground?

Having recently entered those iron gates that cruelly promise *"Arbeit Macht Frei,"* Merkel is conscious that human weakness always plays at the margins of civilization. In her final years, she was reminded daily of how vulnerable democracy is and how short people's memories are. Though the land to which she has always looked for inspiration and support—the United States—has rejoined Merkel's multilateral world, it did so battered and exposed.

Her final act during the Trump administration was synchronizing the EU's reaction to Joe Biden's victory: a single note from the group of allies, signalling to Trump that his effort to divide the West had failed. She knew, however, that the danger had not passed. Although she outlasted Trump, Vladimir Putin—in power since 2000—was still in the Kremlin, freely and openly brutal. And she was shattered by the sight of a mob incited by an American president storming the US Capitol on January 6, 2021. The fittingly violent end of the Trump years provoked a rare emotion from Angela Merkel: "I'm angry," she said, "and sad." Even more disturbing for her was that the Big Lie of a stolen election survived Trump. She recognizes the power of Big Lies. It was the Big Lie that Germany was "stabbed in the back" by Communists and Jews after World War I that helped to catapult Hitler to the Reichstag. Trump's tumultuous exit only confirmed Angela Merkel's deepest conviction: democracy is fragile and, if treated carelessly, can slip away. Trump may have been defeated; Trumpism survives.

Once, at an event at the chancellery for volunteers who had helped with refugee resettlement, I asked Angela Merkel what was the single quality that sustained her during her long political life. "Endurance!" she answered, flashing a smile that lifts her lined features, including her very blue eyes. She's a marathoner, not a sprinter, and defied our ever-diminishing attention spans by *enduring* for sixteen years as chancellor. Angela Merkel more than endured, however. Her resilience—her singular ability to spring back after personal or political losses—has powered her extraordinary journey. Though she strives for humility, she is well aware that she is an example for the next generation, as it searches for role models in a landscape largely devoid of them.

Insofar as it is possible for the most powerful woman in the world to remain herself, she has. She is still the serious girl in the back of the class, observing and speaking only when she had something to say. She leaves no Merkel Doctrine. "We are all part of the world," as she quietly reminded an enraged AfD member, is as close as we will get to a worldview from this woman of few words. She knows that no country—not Germany, China, or the United States—can survive long behind a wall. That is her childhood's most enduring lesson and Angela Merkel's legacy.

Merkel, whose goal was always to retire before she became a "political wreck," can be justly proud of having left at the very height of her powers rather than being driven from office, as all of her predecessors have. In the dignity of her leave-taking, she provided a final example to those politicians who mistake the office for themselves and refuse to let go. Merkel showed them how democracy is meant to work.

She also left a more personal legacy. Perhaps the most striking image to emerge from Europe's financial rescue of 2020 was that of Angela Merkel and Ursula von der Leyen, president of the European Commission, side by side in Brussels, at the EU's capital. In September 2020 a Pew Research Center survey found Angela Merkel to be the world's most trusted leader, regardless of gender. This, then, may be her vaunting accolade: putting beyond all doubt the capacities of a woman in charge. A great deal of what she was able to achieve was not done *in spite* of her being a woman but *because* she was one. Again and again, she was able to park her ego in pursuit of her desired outcome. Negotiating is an arduous, patience-trying process—unsuitable work for those seeking immediate attention and credit. Most politicians desperately seek both, and most, it must be said, are male. Attention and credit were the least of the rewards Angela Merkel sought. Outcome was her singular goal. Though a handful of other women are doing impressive jobs leading their countries, their numbers are, sadly, still too few for us to draw definitive conclusions regarding their superior fitness for highest office based on their more-controlled egos. Based on Angela Merkel's example, however, it is hard not to jump to that conclusion.

Others, women and men, will follow. None, however, will repeat her singular odyssey. Aware of how remarkable her journey has been—from the hamlet of Templin inside Soviet-controlled East Germany, to the center of the global stage—Merkel can have few regrets of roads she has not taken. As the most inner directed of politicians, whose highest standard of behavior is her own, she left with a sense of having done her best, without compromising her values. When asked once what she wanted history books to say about her, she answered, "She tried." In an age of dead-certain demagogues, the humility and decency of Angela Merkel's chosen epitaph speaks for itself.

Acknowledgments

Writing the life story of a subject so little interested in having her story told has been, to say the least, challenging. The absence of a paper trail—no journals or private correspondence or even staff memos have been available from one of recent history's most private public figures—only enhanced the challenge. Nevertheless, Angela Merkel allowed me to observe her at work during the past four years and has not prevented me from speaking with some of her closest friends and aides. Knowing how scrupulously she guards her privacy, I am grateful for the degree of freedom she allowed me, and for the generosity of her aides' and friends in submitting to hours of questions from me over the last four years. I have done my utmost to repay their kindness and their faith in me with a serious and balanced biography of Angela Merkel. Though often frustrating, piercing the enigma of this unique figure has been a powerful—and even life-altering—experience for me, for which I am grateful.

I wish to particularly thank Eva Christiansen, Volker Schlöndorff, Thomas Bagger, Wolfgang Ischinger, and Christoph Heusgen for their many hours of always enlightening conversation over the past years. Volker's friendship and memories of his interactions with Angela Merkel vastly enrich this account. I thank him from the bottom of my heart. Long before I started this work, the distinguished German American historian Fritz Stern and my late husband, Richard Holbrooke (whom Fritz accompanied to Bonn when Richard was ambassador), helped to bring both Angela Merkel and postwar Germany to vivid life, and deepened my understanding of this land's multilayered history. Sadly, neither Fritz nor Richard are alive to read this, but I hope they would approve of the result. The American Academy in Berlin—my late husband's proud legacy —was my refuge on and off during my research. I thank Gahl Burt and Berit Ebert for their always warm welcome and their friendship. I can never sufficiently thank Travis Penner, who took time from his duties at the academy to accompany me on travels through Germany and was my indispensable translator and researcher. I also thank Almut Schoenfeld, who helped me navigate Germany's complex politics and shared her immense knowledge of Berlin during the early stages of my research. I also thank the Rockefeller Foundation for granting me a fellowship to their sublime Bellagio Center on Lake Como where I wrote my first draft. Back in New York, Ramya Jayanthi, eternally unflappable, kept me and my research more or less together. I am fortunate to have had her steady and intelligent presence. Geoffrey Schandler and Ida Rothchild made wonderful suggestions in the structure of my early drafts, and I thank them for their thoughtful input. My friends and much-admired fellow scribes Richard Bernstein and Anne Nelson gave unselfishly of their time and made many improvements on the manuscript. I thank my indispensable friend Joel Motley, among my first and most discerning readers, for his many contributions and support throughout the lock down. My friend, the Danish American writer Morten Hoi Jensen also made smart contributions to the final draft. Crary Pullen lived up to her reputation as a remarkable photo researcher; the book was enriched by the wonderful images that she found.

I began this work with my editor of the past four books, the legendary Alice Mayhew. Although Alice left us suddenly just as Covid surged, her presence and her years of wise counsel and boundless enthusiasm did not leave me—or this book. I am grateful for the brilliant team of Priscilla Painton and Megan Hogan at Simon & Schuster for making this new child theirs and for their many suggestions, too. To have achieved such a seamless transition during lockdown has been remarkable.

As always, Amanda Urban was my friend, spur, and guide throughout. I cannot imagine my writing life without her in my corner.

Nor can I conceive of life without my essential tribe: my offspring Lizzie and Chris, as well as Corrine and Ilona, my siblings Julia and Andrew, nephews and nieces Mathieu, Sabine, Lucien, Leonard, Orson, Nicolas, Lili, and Joaquim. Dispersed in Paris, Brussels, New York, Fort Worth, Texas, and Inverness, California, we overcame long distances this past hard year with Zoom calls, FaceTime, and borderless love.

Among the many people to whom I am indebted for making this project interesting and often even enjoyable is this partial list of the people I interviewed—many in multiple sessions. I cannot thank them enough for their patience and for their matchless insights:

Alexis Papahelas, Almut Möller, Andreas Apelt, Anna Sauerbrey, Antony Blinken, Ben Rhodes, Bernd Ulrich, Lady Catherine Ashton, Charles Kupchan, Charlotte Knobloch, Christian Demuth, Christoph Heusgen, Dr. Christoph Meyer, Constanze Stelzenmüller, David Gill, Daniel Baer, Derek Chollet, Derek Scally, Dekel Peretz, Ellen Ueberschär, Ambassador John Emerson, Ambassador Emily Haber, Erika Benn, Eva Christiansen, Evelyn Farkas, Fiona Hill, Frank Mieszkalski, Fritz Stern, Gary Smith, Georg Diez, Griff Witte, Henrik Enderlein, Henry Kissinger, Richard Haass, Henry "Hank" Paulson, Herlinde Koelbl, Secretary of State Hillary Rodham Clinton, Jacques Rupnik, Jacqueline Boysen, Jacqueline Ross, James Davis, Joerg Hackerschmidt, Joseph Stiglitz, former president Joachim Gauck, former foreign minister Joschka Fischer, Joshua Yaffa, Karl-Theodor von Guttenberg, Karen Donfried, Karin Pritzel, Kevin

Rudd, Kerstin Kohlenberg, George Diez, George Packer, Lars Zimmermann, Lawrence Bacow, former president Lothar de Maizière, Marcus Walker, Manuela Villing, Roger Cohen, Daniel Benjamin, Joshua Hammer, Matthew Pottinger, Melanie Annan, Michael Birnbaum, Michael Naumann, Michael Schindhelm, Nicolaus Fest, Paul Krüger, Peter Jungen, Peter Schneider, Philip Murphy, Rachel Donadio, Reiner Epplemann, Reinhard Günzel, Reinhold Haberlandt, René Pfister, Robin Alexander, Steffen Seibert, Shai Levy, Josef Joffe, Shimon Stein, Sigmount A. Königsberg, Stefan Kornelius, Stephen Greenblatt, Thomas Bagger, Thorsten Benner, Thomas de Maizière, Timothy Snyder, Stefan von Holtzbrinck, Peter Wittig, Tim Wirth, Timothy Garton Ash, Ulrike Demmer, Ulrich Schöneich, Ulrich Wilhelm, Victoria Nuland, Volker Berghahn, Volker Schlöndorff, Werner Patzelt, William Drozdiak, Yascha Mounk.

Notes

In writing this book, I was fortunate to be able to draw on interviews conducted by German writers and journalists before Angela Merkel virtually ceased giving nonpolicy-related statements after she became chancellor in 2005. Those sometimes remarkably probing and thoughtful exchanges, which I have translated from the original German, proved indispensable in capturing Merkel's life and times in her own words. Though I have not changed their meaning, for the sake of clarity, I have made alterations in the translations. Hence, at times I cite the source of a given passage without the specific page number, which may no longer correspond.

I thank these fellow historians of an exceedingly private public figure for capturing the chancellor through her own words and in her native language: Herlinde Koelbl (*Spuren der Macht: Die Verwandlung des Menschen durch das Amt*), Gerd Langguth (*Angela Merkel*), Angela Merkel (*Daran glaube ich: Christliche Standpunkte*, edited by Volker Resing), Angela Merkel with Hugo Müller-Vogg (*Mein Weg: Ein Gespräch*), Andreas Rinke (*Das Merkel Lexikon: Die Kanzlerin von A–Z*); Evelyn Roll (*Die Kanzlerin: Angela Merkels Weg Zur Macht*), and Moritz von Uslar (*100 Fragen an*).

Herlinde Koelbl, *Spuren der Macht: Die Verwandlung des Menschen durch das Amt—Eine Langzeitstudie*, 1st ed. (Munich, Ger.: Knesebeck Verlag, 1999).

Gerd Langguth, *Angela Merkel Aufstieg zu Macht*, 3rd ed. (Munich, Ger.: Deutscher Taschenbuch Verlag, 2005).

Angela Merkel: *Daran glaube ich: Christliche Standpunkte* (*I Believe in That: Christian Viewpoints*), updated and expanded ed., ed. Volker Resing (Leipzig, Ger.: St. Benno Verlag, 2017).

Angela Merkel with Hugo Müller-Vogg, *Mein Weg: Ein Gespräch* mit Hugo Müller-Vogg, 1st ed. (Hamburg, Ger.: Hoffmann und Campe Verlag, 2005).

Andreas Rinke, *Das Merkel Lexikon: Die Kanzlerin von A-Z (The Chancellor from A–Z)*, 1st ed. (Springe, Ger.: zu Klampen Verlag, 2016).

Evelyn Roll, *Die Kanzlerin: Angela Merkels Weg Zur Macht (The Chancellor: Angela Merkel's Path to Power)*, 4th ed. (Berlin, Ger.: Ullstein Buchverlag GmB, 2013).

Moritz von Uslar, *100 Fragen an . . . (100 Questions To . . .*), 3rd ed. (Cologne, Ger.: Verlag Kiepnheuer & Witsch, 2004).

SPEECHES AND OFFICIAL DOCUMENTS

Bundestag: Official Bundestag documents can be found here: https://www.bundestag .de/dokumente.

Chancellery: Speeches, interviews, other documents relating to the chancellor can be found on the chancellery website here: https://www.bundeskanzlerin.de/bkin-de /aktuelles/.

Munich Security Conference: There are different pages for each MSC year): https:// securityconference.org/en/msc-2020/speeches/.

PROLOGUE: THE PASTOR'S DAUGHTER

This chapter is based on the author's interviews with Eva Christiansen, Volker Schlöndorff, Joachim Gauck, Ben Rhodes, Governor Philip Murphy, David Gill, Bernd Ulrich, Herlinde Koelbl, Michael Naumann, and Melanie Amman.

Throughout the book, I do not provide dates for my interviews, as they were generally followed up with subsequent queries and further interviews.

xi   *"Thanks for the suggestion"*: Alexander Osang, "Chancellor Merkel—Woman in Amber," *Der Spiegel*, August 31, 2017; "Angela Merkel—Over but Not Out," *Süddeutsche Zeitung*, December 1, 2018.

xii   *"While Merkel is standing"*: Nico Friedt, "She Knows Something That You Don't Know," *Die Zeit*, March 2, 2018.

xiii   *"a bit more poetry"*: Lara Marlowe, "As Merkel Tires, Macron Emerges," *Irish Times*, September 28, 2017.

xiii   *"I think things through"*: Herlinde Koelbl, interviewed by the author.

xv   *"Asserting authority"*: Koelbl, *Spuren der Macht*.

xv   Hubris, *Merkel's behavior suggests*: Alexander Osang, "The German Queen," *Der Spiegel*, May 11, 2009.

xv   *"Myself, as often as possible"*: Koelbl, interview by author; see also Koelbl, *Spuren der Macht*.

xv   *"to see the Rocky Mountains"*: Merkel, interviewed by Melanie Amann and Florian Gathmann, *Der Spiegel*, November 5, 2019.

CHAPTER 1: AGAINST THE TIDE
This chapter is based on the author's interviews with Michael Naumann, Ulrich Schöneich, Andreas Apelt, Reiner Epplemann, Lothar de Maizière, Michael Schindhelm, Jacqueline Boysen, Eva Christiansen, Erika Benn, and Volker Schlöndorff.

For background on the Kasners' experiences in Hamburg and their decision to go to Brandenburg, see Ralf Georg Reuth and Günther Lachmann, *Das Erste Leben der Angela M.*, 4th. ed. (Piper, Munich 2013).

1 *"I would have travelled anywhere"*: *Der Spiegel*, January 26, 2016; Reiner Epplemann, clergyman, and Ellen Ueberschär, of the German Protestant Foundation and head of the Heinrich Boll Foundation, interviewed by the author.

1 *Horst had warned*: "Visit to the Pastor from Templin," *Berliner Zeitung*, June 2, 2005.

5 *"We came as Christians"*: Roger Cohen, "From East to West," *New York Times*, June 1, 2001.

5 *"My father had to milk"*: Merkel, interviewed by Herlinde Koelbl, see *Spuren Der Macht*.

6 *Despite the privileges*: George Packer, "The Astonishing Rise of Angela Merkel," *New Yorker*, December 1, 2014.

7 *"I remember a gardener"*: Angela Merkel: *Daran glaube ich: Christliche Standpunkte* (*I Believe in That: Christian Viewpoints*), updated and expanded ed., ed. Volker Resing (Leipzig, Ger.: St. Benno Verlag, 2017).

8 *"I was seven"*: Merkel, interviewed by Koelbl.

9 *"Russian is a beautiful"*: Gerd Langguth, *Angela Merkel* (Munich, Ger.: Deutscher Taschenbuch Verlag, 2005). See also Koelbl and Müller-Vogg, interviews.

9 *Marie Curie*: Volker Riesing, Daran Glaube Ich.

10 *"I believe that this world"*: Angela Merkel's speech to Protestant Christian Convention, 1995; Ueberschär, interview.

10 *Merkel's faith*: Angela Merkel, "What It Means to Be a Christian and a Politician" (speech, Templin Congregation of Pastor Ralf Gunther Schein, Templin, Ger., 2014).

11 *"Malachi sees the violence"*: Angela Merkel, speech re her faith, see *Deutscher Evangelisher Kirchentag Dokumente*, 2005. Made available to the author by Ellen Uberschar.

11 *"Power per se"*: Angela Merkel with Hugo Müller-Vogg, *Mein Weg: Ein Gespräch mit Hugo Müller*, 1st ed. (Hamburg, Ger.: Hoffmann und Campe Verlag, 2005); Merkel, interviewed by Koelbl.

12 *When Merkel got home from school*: Merkel, interviewed by Koelbl.

14 *"There were people"*: in Merkel, *Daran glaube ich.*

17 *"I remember"*: Merkel, interviewed by Koelbl. For a description of Merkel's personal reaction to the crushing of the Prague Spring, see Evelyn Roll, "And It Was Summer," *Süddeutsche Zeitung Magazin,* September 2008.

18 *a youthful prank*: Ulrich Schöneich, Merkel's childhood friend, and Erika Benn, one of Merkel's schoolteachers, interviewed by the author; see also "Das Eiserne Mädchen," *Der Spiegel,* March 1, 2000.

CHAPTER 2: LEIPZIG—ON HER OWN

This chapter is based on the author's interviews with Merkel's fellow students and professors at the University of Leipzig, notably Frank Mieszkalski and Professor Reinhold Haberlandt, and with an early Merkel biographer, Jacqueline Boysen. See also Roll, *Merkel's Path to Power,* 428, regarding Merkel's " strong inner life."

21 *"I chose physics"*: Moritz von Uslar, *100 Fragen an . . . (100 Questions To . . .),* 3rd ed. (Cologne, Ger.: Verlag Kiepnheuer & Witsch, 2004).

22 *"I wanted to get away"*: Merkel with Müller-Vogg, *Mein Weg.*

25 *"I was always the girl"*: Rinke, *Das Merkel Lexikon.*

26 *"I noticed Angela"*: "One Day She Moved Out," *Focus,* no. 28, 2004.

CHAPTER 3: BERLIN

Much of this chapter is based on the author's interviews with author-filmmaker Michael Schindhelm.

29 *"My parents always told me"*: Stock, *Angela Merkel,* 9.

31 *"We married"*: Merkel, interviewed by Koelbl; Schindhelm, interview.

31 *"Angela packed up"*: Merkel with Müller-Vogg, *Mein Weg;* Gunnar Hink, "Mr. Merkel from Dresden," *Die Tageszeitung,* December 7, 2016.

31 *"Well, Angela"*: Schindhelm, interview; see also: Isaac Stanley-Becker and Luisa Beck, "The Pastor's Daughter," *Washington Post,* September 11, 2017.

32 *Unknown to Merkel*: Franziska Reich, "The Woman Who Came in from the Cold," *Stern,* May 5, 2005. Also: Schindhelm, interview, and see also Matthew Qvortrup, *Angela Merkel: Europe's Most Influential Leader* (New York: Overlook Ducksworth, 2016), 91.

35 *"There was not a single"*: Koelbl, Spuren Der Macht; Michael Schindhelm, author and filmmaker, interviewed by the author.

36 *"I had travelled alone"*: Wolfgang Stock, *Angela Merkel: Eine Politische Biographie* (Munich, Ger.: Olzog, 2000), 56.

37 Interview with Dr. Sauer in *Berliner Zeitung,* December 23, 2017.

CHAPTER 4: 1989

This chapter is based partly on the author's interviews with former German presidents Lothar de Maizière and Joachim Gauck, David Gill, Volker Schlöndorff, and Dr. Adreas Apelt.

See also Jana Hensel's excellent *After the Wall: Confessions from an East German Childhood and the Life That Came Next,* trans. Jefferson Chase (New York: Public Affairs, 2004).

40 *"I called my mother"*: Merkel, interviewed by Koelbl.

41 *"A few days after"*: Ibid.

41 *"What I disliked"*: Quentin Peel, "Angela Merkel—Woman of Power," *Financial Times,* December 14, 2012.

43 *"To me, he looked like"*: Ibid.

45 *"They were too ideological"*: Merkel with Müller-Vogg, *Mein Weg.*

45 *"I had been a good"*: Ibid.

46 *"Her response surprised me"*: Andreas Apelt, interviewed by author.

CHAPTER 5: THE APPRENTICE

This chapter draws on the author's interviews with Ambassadors Wolfgang Ischinger and Robert Kimmitt, former senator Timothy Wirth, former Secretaries of State Hillary Rodham Clinton and Henry Kissinger, former secretary of the Treasury Hank Paulson, Merkel's former defense minister, Karl-Theodor von Guttenberg; Bernd Ulrich, deputy editor of *Die Zeit;* and Herlinde Koelbl.

The author also knowledges gratefully the many hours of conversations with the eminent German American historian Fritz Stern, as well as with Richard Holbrooke.

50 *"When I made her the offer"*: Author's interview with Lothar de Maizière

53 *"Angela was amazed"*: Henry Kissinger, interviewed by the author.

54 *"Angela dressed"*: Lothar de Maizière, interview.

55 *"For a man, it's no problem"*: Merkel, interviewed by Koelbl.

55 *"Madame Chancellor, you look great!"*: Paul Lever, *Berlin Rules: Europe and the German Way* (London: I. B. Tauris, 2017), 23.

55 *there was a widespread*: Ambassador Wolfgang Ischinger, interviewed by the author.

57 *"I find it annoying"*: Merkel with Müller-Vogg, *Mein Weg.*

57 *Her first time*: Ambassador Robert Kimmitt, interviewed by the author.

57 *On that trip*: Ibid.

57 *a visit to a monastery*: Merkel, *Daran glaube ich.*

60 *sexist humor*: Merkel, interviewed by Brigitte Huber and Meike Dinklage, *Brigitte*, July 2, 2017.

61 *"I often feel physically"*: Merkel, interviewed by Koelbl, *Spuren der Macht*.

61 *"I am often in the firing line"*: Ibid.

62 *"It might have been"*: Ibid.

62 *"She asked me"*: Lever, *Berlin Rules*, 73.

63 *"Hers was a blend"*: Kimmitt, interview.

63 *"Well, Chancellor Kohl"*: Tim Wirth, interviewed by the author.

64 *"one of my greatest"*: Merkel, interviewed by Koelbl, *Spuren der Macht*.

64 *It is in small groups*: Hank Paulson, interviewed by the author.

65 *Lawrence Bacow*: Harvard University president Lawrence Bacow, interviewed by the author.

66 *"We got married"*: Merkel, interviewed by Koelbl, *Spuren der Macht*.

67 *"Why should I?"*: Roll, *Merkel's Path to Power*, 260.

68 *"First and foremost"*: Merkel, interviewed by Koelbl, *Spuren der Macht*.

68 *On April 10*: Osang, "Woman in Amber."

70 *In 2014, on her sixtieth birthday*: *Bild-Zeitung*, July 17, 2014.

CHAPTER 6: TO THE CHANCELLERY AT LAST

Interviews with the following provide background for this chapter: Henry Kissinger, Joschka Fischer, Christoph Heusgen, Thomas de Maizière, Thomas Bagger, Eva Christiansen, Bernd Ulrich, and Stefan Kornelius.

74 *in the weeks*: Kissinger, interview.

76 *"It's more important"*: Rinke, *Das Merkel Lexikon*, 282–86.

76 *"we all end up"*: *Bild-Zeitung*, July 2007.

76 *"Madame Chancellor"*: Judy Dempsey, writer, interviewed by the author.

82 *"There are no flatterers"*: Eva Christiansen, aide to Chancellor Merkel, interviewed by the author.

82 *"En route to the White House"*: Ischinger, interview.

83 *"You always have to be precise"*: Thomas de Maizière, interviewed by the author.

84 *Humor is Merkel's way*: Stefan Kornelius, journalist, interviewed by the author.

84 *"Once, she was telling us"*: René Pfister, journalist, interviewed by the author.

85 *"Why does she use such?"*: Joschka Fischer, former German foreign minister, journalist, interviewed by the author.

85 *a stern figure*: Fritz Stern, interviewed by the author.

86 *In the early spring of 2008*: Charlotte Knobloch, and Shimon Stein, Israeli ambassador to Germany, interviewed by the author.

89   *"I believe that a fundamental question"*: Christiansen, interview.

91   *Merkel understood*: Philip Oltermann, "The Paradox of Merkelism," *Prospect* online, last modified January 29, 2020, https://www.prospectmagazine.co.uk /politics/angela-merkel-profile-trump-germany-chancellor-prime-minister.

CHAPTER 7: HER FIRST AMERICAN PRESIDENT

This chapter relies on the author's interviews with Wolfgang Ischinger, Ulrich Wilhelm, Bernd Ulrich, and Ambassador Christoph Heusgen.

95   *"I've never looked like this"*: Udo Walz, hair stylist, interviewed by the author.

98   *The normally caustic*: *Economist*, February 9, 2006.

99   *"I like living here"*: Stefan Kornelius, *Angela Merkel: The Chancellor and Her World—The Authorized Biography* (London: Alma Books, 2013), 91; Rinke, *Das Merkel Lexikon*, 181. See also Langguth, *Angela Merkel*, regarding the chancellor's low key patriotism.

CHAPTER 8: DICTATORS

This chapter is informed by the author's interviews with Merkel's former defense minister, K. T. von Guttenberg; Thomas de Maizière; Ambassador Wolfgang Ischinger (president of the Munich Security Conference, where Putin delivered his anti-West diatribe in 2007); Merkel's spokesman Steffen Seibert; former spokesman Ulrich Wilhelm; Christoph Heusgen; Charles Kupchan; Fiona Hill; and Joshua Yaffa, Moscow correspondent for the *New Yorker*, and René Pfister, helped background the impact of the Putin-KGB relationship on the Russian leader's subsequent relations with Merkel. Trump White House aide Mathew Pottinger, and former Australian prime minister Kevin Rudd provided insights regarding Merkel's dealing with the increasingly authoritarian Xi Jinping.

See also Pfister, "Times of Turmoil," *Der Spiegel*, May 18, 2019; David von Drehle, "Putin's Virus," *Washington Post*, March 2, 2020.

102   *Stationed as a KGB officer*: *From the Horse's Mouth: Conversations with Putin*, 82, 83, 88, for a description of Putin's life and work in Dresden and his frantic attempt to destroy his files.

106   *"The main enemy was NATO"*: Ibid.

106   *"Why I Broke the Law"*: Kornelius, interview.

110   *"He always has this stony"*: Maxim Eristavi, interviewed by the author.

111   *"Our Lisa"*: Angela Stent, *Putin's World: Russia Against the West and with the Rest* (New York: Hachette, 2019), 104.

113 *"You have three choices"*: Andrew Higgins, "A Russian by Blood," *New York Times,* September 28, 2019.

113 *"Every time"*: Charles Kupchan, interviewed by the author.

114 *During her early years*: Ulrich Wilhelm and Christoph Heusgen, former German national security advisor, interviewed by the author.

116 *"We are celebrating"*: Pfister, interview.

117 *"I often speak with President Xi"*: Merkel, "Speech by Chancellor Merkel at the 55th Munich Security Conference on February 16, 2019, in Munich," Press and Information Office of the Federal Government online, accessed April 22, 2021, https://www.bundeskanzlerin.de/bkin-de/aktuelles/rede-von-bundeskanzlerin -merkel-zur-55-muenchner-sicherheitskonferenz-am-16-februar-2019-in -muenchen-1580936.

117 *"As was the case with Germany"*: Merkel, interviewed by Lionel Barber and Guy Chazan, *Financial Times,* January 15, 2020.

117 *"I believe that chips"*: Ibid.

CHAPTER 9: THE PRIVATE CHANCELLOR

The author's interviews with the following provided crucial material and background for this chapter: Eva Christiansen, Dr. Andreas Apelt, Ambassador Shimon Stein, Volker Schlöndorff, Christoph Heusgen, German ambassador to the United States Peter Wittig, Ambassador Harald Braun, Thomas Bagger, Renée Fleming, former Australian prime minister Kevin Rudd, Lady Catherine Ashton, Karen Donfried, Herlinde Koelbl, and Hillary Clinton,

121 *"I have tried"*: Merkel town hall meeting in Stralsund, August 13, 2019.

123 *"I would rather"*: Merkel, interviewed by Koelbl, in *Spuren der Macht.*

123 *"Sometimes all the talking"*: Ibid.

123 *While attending*: *Bild* online (https://www.rtl.de/cms/angela-merkel-verraet -privates-daheim-macht-ihr-mann-die-waesche-4660735.html.

124 *"I cannot imagine"*: Merkel, interviewed by Koelbl, in *Spuren der Macht.*

125 *During her early days*: Alexander Osang, "The German Queen," *Der Spiegel,* May 11, 2009.

125 *Years ago*: Ibid.

126 *Former British prime minister*: Martin Amis, *Inside Story: A Novel* (New York: Farrar, Straus and Giroux, 2020), 239.

129 *The pleasure she takes*: German ambassador Peter Wittig and Karen Donfried, interviewed by the author.

131 *"I would not be disappointed"*: *Haaretz* (Tel Aviv, Isr.), October 4, 2018; *Deutsche Welle,* October 4, 2018.

131   *After many hours with Merkel*: Kevin Rudd, former Australian prime minister, interviewed by the author.

132   *From across the Atlantic*: Hillary Clinton, interviewed by the author.

CHAPTER 10: LIMITED PARTNERS

The author's interviews with the following form the core of this chapter: in Washington: Antony Blinken; formerly in the Obama White House, Ben Rhodes, President Obama's advisor, as were Victoria Nuland, Charles Kupchan, Derek Chollet, and Ambassador John Emerson. In Berlin and New York: Christoph Heusgen, Thomas Bagger, and Stefan Kornelius, shared their experiences with the author. (Ambassador Heusgen has been Germany's ambassador to the UN since 2017.)

139   *Angela Merkel was slow*: Clinton, interview.

140   *"The idea that a person"*: Oltermann, "The Paradox of Merkelism."

141   *"Now do you see"*: Jane Kramer, "Letter from Europe," *New Yorker,* September 19, 2005.

142   *"Angela Merkel is exactly"*: Ben Rhodes, interviewed by the author.

142   *"Barack treasures you"*: Bernd Ulrich (who was present), interviewed by the author.

145   *"Christmas arrived early"*: Steven Lee Myers, *The New Tsar: The Rise and Reign of Vladimir Putin* (New York: Vintage Books, 2016), 439.

146   *"Rarely, if ever"*: Susan Rice, *Tough Love: My Story of the Things Worth Fighting For* (New York: Simon & Schuster, 2019), 360.

148   *When Obama arrived*: Christiansen and Heusgen, interviews.

149   *"I say this to you as"*: Rhodes, interview.

150   *"You're shitting me, right?"*: Rice, *Tough Love,* 362.

CHAPTER 11: EUROPE IS SPEAKING GERMAN NOW

Interview subjects for this chapter include Joseph Stiglitz, Liaquat Ahamed, Ben Rhodes, Stefan Kornelius, Bernd Ulrich, Catherine Ashton, Hank Paulson, Wolfgang Ischinger, Alexis Papahelas, editor of the Greek newspaper *Kathimerini,* Marcus Walker of *The Wall Street Journal,* and Gillian Tett of the *Financial Times.* (For a vivid description of the rolling financial crisis and Merkel's role in attempting to contain it, see J. Adam Tooze, *Crashed: How a Decade of Financial Crises Changed the World* (New York: Penguin Books, 2019).

155   *Merkel was enjoying*: Christiansen, interview.

155   *"The IKB is in trouble"*: Tooze, *Crashed,* 144.

156   *In Greece, Portugal, Spain, and Italy*: Paul Krugman, opinion, "Have

Zombies Eaten Bloomberg's and Buttigieg's Brains? Beware the Democrats of the Living Dead," *New York Times* online, February 17, 2020, https://www.nytimes.com/2020/02/17/opinion/bloomberg-buttigieg-economy.html?searchResultPosition=1; Rachel Denadio, "Official Warmth and Public Rage," *New York Times,* October 12, 2012.

159   *"You need to act"*: Rhodes, interview.

159   "Das ist nicht": Heusgen, interview; see also Barack Obama, *Promised Land,* (New York: Crown, 2020), 519–56.

160   *her chief European partner*: "Sarkozy Declare sa Flamme," *Vingt Minutes,* January 5, 2008, a free daily newspaper published by Schibsted and Ouest France Group.

161   *When the head of the Christian Democratic Union*: Kornelius and Ulrich, interviews.

162   *In 2015, in a decision*: Alexis Papahelas, interviewed by the author; see also Yanis Varoufakis, *Adults in the Room: My Battle with the European and American Deep Establishment* (New York: Farrar, Straus and Giroux, 2017), 331–50.

163   *"My dear people"*: Ulrich, interview.

CHAPTER 12: THE WAR IN UKRAINE—"GET ME ANGELA ON THE PHONE"
Interviewees for this chapter include Dan Baer, Victoria Nuland, Ben Rhodes, historians Timothy Snyder and Timothy Garton Ash, Evelyn Farkas, Emily Haber, Thomas Bagger, and Christoph Heusgen.

168   *"We feared the Russians"*: Evelyn Farkas, Obama Defense Department official, interviewed by the author.

170   *"Merkel had enormous"*: Victoria Nuland, Obama assistant secretary for European affairs, interviewed by the author.

171   *Seething quietly*: Ischinger, interview.

172   *"She would call Obama"*: Tony Blinken, Obama White House aide, interviewed by the author.

172   *"She drains the drama"*: Emily Haber, German ambassador to the United States, interviewed by the author.

172   *"she must be so pissed"*: Dan Baer, US ambassador to the Organization for Security and Co-operation in Europe (OSCE), interviewed by the author.

173   *"In people's hearts"*: Based on news reports.

174   *A month later*: Nuland, interview.

174   *"Merkel and Obama"*: Timothy Snyder, historian, interviewed by the author.

175   *Merkel was offended*: Heusgen, interview.

177   *President Obama, back in*: Derek Chollet, former US foreign policy advisor, interviewed by the author.

177 *"I think I know"*: Heusgen, interview.

178 *At times during their negotiations*: Patrick Donohue, journalist, interviewed by the author; see also Stent, *Putin's World,* 344.

178 *Reward for the long days*: Based on media reports.

179 *The chancellor, a firm believer*: Peter Jungen, investor and friend of the chancellor, interviewed by the author.

CHAPTER 13: THE SUMMER OF REEM

This chapter is based partly on interviews with Ambassador William Swing, former head of the UN's Office of Migration; spokesman for the chancellor, Steffen Seibert; former ambassadors Harald Braun (to the UN) and Robert Kimmitt (to Germany); Ellen Ueberschär; Henry Kissinger; Paul Krüger; Thomas Bagger; and Christoph Heusgen.

Unless otherwise indicated, Angela Merkel's quotes in this chapter are from three lengthy interviews the chancellor gave to broadcast journalist Anne Will of Germany's ARD broadcast network during the refugee crisis of 2015–16, available on YouTube: October 7, 2015, https://www.youtube.com/watch?v=cx3R-Cys50E, February 19, 2016, https://www.youtube.com/watch?v=9slKqESqOiU, and November 20, 2016, https://www.youtube.com/watch?v=lJwcfld8cWE

The description of the Merkel-Reem encounter is based on German television coverage of the event.

190 *"She should have tried"*: Kissinger, interview.

190 *"Lone decisions"*: Helmut Kohl, "Europe Before a Crucial Test," *Der Tagesspiegel,* April 17, 2016.

190 *"To shelter one refugee"*: George Packer, journalist, interviewed by the author.

190 *"At that moment"*: Ueberschär, interview.

190 *"I observed this"*: Paulson, interview.

191 *Nor did the chancellor*: Merkel, interviewed by Anne Will,ARD German Television broadcast available on YouTube February 29, 2016 https://www.youtube.com/watch?v=9slKqESqOiU.

191 *"Everybody pitched in"*: Seibert, interview.

192 *"If we can't put on a happy face"*: Merkel, *Bunte,* June 2, 2016; Merkel, "Speech by Chancellor Merkel on October 7, 2015, in Front of the European Parliament," Press and Information Office of the Federal Government online, accessed April 22, 2021, https://www.bundeskanzlerin.de/bkin-de/aktuelles/rede-von-bundeskanzlerin-merkel-am-7-oktober-2015-vor-dem-europaeischen-parlament-475792.

193 *Bad luck also played its part*: Thomas de Maizière, interview.

194 *" 'If we do that' "*: Christiansen, interview.

196 *In the small town of Heidenau*: Melanie Amman (eyewitness), interviewed by the author.

198 *Merkel also underestimated*: Patrick Kingsley, *The New Odyssey: The Story of Europe's Refugee Crisis* (Norwich, UK: Guardian Faber, 2016), 43; T. Hildebrandt and B. Ulrich, "In the Eye of the Storm," *Die Zeit*, September 20, 2015.

199 *"increased the cap"*: Rhodes, interview.

201 *The piazza between*: This section is based on various news reports of New Year's Eve 2016, as well as Amy Davidson, "Angela Merkel's Cologne Test," *New Yorker*, January 10, 2016.

203 *"If you believe that an aging"*: Ross Douthat, "Germany on the Brink," *New York Times*, January 9, 2016; Anna Sauerbrey, "Germany's Post Cologne Hysteria," *New York Times*, January 9, 2016.

CHAPTER 14: THE WORST OF TIMES
This chapter is based on the author's interviews with Ben Rhodes, Bernd Ulrich, Stefan Kornelius, James Davis, René Pfister, John Emerson, Thomas Bagger, Christoph Heusgen, and Eva Christiansen—many of them off the record.

205 *It is fascinating to note*: Michael Schindhelm, "Mocca Twice a Day with Angela," *Berliner Morgenpost*, March 8, 2000.

206 *"I would be happy"*: Stefan Wagstyl, editorial, *Financial Times*, January 26, 2016.

206 *Angela Merkel marked the centenary*: Volker Schlöndorff, film director, interviewed by the author.

210 *She chose the location*: Rhodes and Heusgen, interviews.

212 *The day following*: John Emerson, US ambassador to Germany, interviewed by the author.

CHAPTER 15: ENTER TRUMP
Background for this chapter regarding Washington in the age of Trump comes from interviews with Robert Kimmitt, Fiona Hill, Karen Donfried, Constanze Stelzenmüller, Derek Chollet, and Matthew Pottinger, while interviews with Wolfgang Ischinger, Kerstin Kohlenberg, Eva Christiansen, Thomas Bagger, Bernd Ulrich, René Pfister, Christoph Heusgen, and James W. Davis of Switzerland's University of St. Gallen describe the view from Berlin.

216 *To prepare*: Heusgen and Christiansen, interviews.

219 *"We feel like children"*: Ischinger, interview.

220 *Trump's preparation*: Philip Rucker and Carol Leonnig, *A Very Stable Genius* (New York: Bloomsbury, 2020), 165.

220 *"We reporters"*: Kerstin Kohlenberg, German journalist, interviewed by the author.

221 *Trump's habit*: Fiona Hill, interviewed by the author.

223 *"Despite what you have heard"*: Trump's tweets, here and throughout, are available in the public record.

223 *"Pay more to this guy?": Ischinger, interview.*

224 *"It is clear to me"*: Merkel, interviewed by Will, June 10, 2018.

224 *Asked what she liked*: Kornelius, *Angela Merkel*, 26.

226 *"Don't say I never gave you anything"*: Bergen, interview.

226 *"Are you as intelligent?"*: Haber, interview.

227 *"It's not pretty"*: Merkel, interviewed by Will, June 10, 2018.

228 *A poignant alarm*: Pfister, interview; see also Pfister, "Times of Turmoil," and "Apocalypse Merkel," Der Spiegel June 2, 2018.

229 *"Merkel increasingly noted the dangerous"*: Angela Merkel, "Speech by Chancellor Merkel at the 101st German Catholic Day on May 11, 2018, in Münster," Press and Information Office of the Federal Government online, accessed April 22, 2021, https://www.bundeskanzlerin.de/bkin-de/aktuelles/rede-von -bundeskanzlerin-merkel-beim-101-deutschen-katholikentag-am-11-mai -2018-in-muenster-1122406; Merkel, address at the 55th Munich Security Conference, February 16, 2019.

230 *Two months later*: Bacow, interview.

230 *"On that cloudless day"*: Ibid.; Stephen Greenblatt, professor at Harvard University, interviewed by the author.

233 *That summer*: Christiansen, interview.

234 *"I would simply say"*: Angela Merkel, "Summer Press Conference with the Federal Chancellor, July 19, 2019," Press and Information Office of the Federal Government online, accessed April 22, 2021, https://www.bundeskanzlerin.de /bkin-de/aktuelles/sommerpressekonferenz-1649640.

234 *"Our press association"*: Anna Sauerbrey, interviewed by the author.

CHAPTER 16: "SOMETHING HAS CHANGED IN OUR COUNTRY . . ."
This chapter is based on the author's interviews with AfD leaders in Berlin and Dresden and scholars, commentators, and practitioners of extremist politics in Germany (notably: Dr. Nicolaus Fest, Dr. Christian Demuth, Dr. Christoph Meyer, Karin Pritzel, Reinhard Günzel, Dr. Werner Patzelt) as well as with Joachim Gauck, Ambassador Shimon Stein, Michael Naumann, Bernd Ulrich, Thomas Bagger, Melanie Amman, Stefan Kornelius. In addition, I rely on reporting in both German and American media.

238 *"I'm not disappointed"*: Melanie Amann et al., "Merkel's Seed," *Der Spiegel,* September 26, 2017; and Klaus Brinkbaumer, "The Swing to the Right," editorial, *Der Spiegel,* September 26, 2017.

239 *"She reflects"*: Ambassador Shimon Stein, interviewed by the author regarding the impact of the AfD's strong showing

242 *"We need fearful people"*: Susan Neiman, *Learning from the Germans: Race and the Memory of Evil* (New York: Farrar, Straus and Giroux, 2019), 359.

242 *A visit to the AfD's*: Reinhard Günzel, local AfD leader, interviewed by the author.

244 *"In my childhood"*: Fischer, interview.

244 *"In the Old Testament"*: Lothar de Maizière, interview.000

244 *"That is ridiculous"*: Merkel, interviewed by Koelbl, *Spuren der Macht.*

244 *Merkel may have survived*: Kornelius, interview; Nico Fried, "And Suddenly There Is Unity," *Süddeutsche Zeitung,* October 9, 2017.

245 *"Eastern Man"*: Katrin Bennhold, "One Legacy of Merkel," *New York Times,* November 5, 2018.

249 *on July 2, 2017*: Based on news coverage of Merkel-Seehofer talks and Horst Seehofer, German minister of the interior, interviewed by Michael Stifler et al., *Augsburger Allgemeine,* July 7, 2019.

251 *"There is no excuse"*: Katrin Bennhold, "Chemnitz Protests" *New York Times,* August 30, 2018; "Angela Merkel Attacks the AfD," Deutsche Welle, December 9, 2018, https://www.dw.com/en/angela-merkel-hits-out-at-afd-on-far-right-violence/a-45453193.

252 *a man in the back*: Merkel, interviewed by Jana Hensel, *Die Zeit,* January 24, 2019; Claus Christian Malzehn, "An Overdue Conversation Among East Germans," *Die Welt,* November 16, 2018.

252 *"We saw each other"*: Paul Krüger, German politician, interviewed by the author; Angela Merkel's Hamburg speech on December 7, 2018, is available on the official CDU website, at www.cdu.de.

CHAPTER 17: A PARTNER AT LAST?

For this chapter, the author's interview subjects include Thomas Bagger, Christoph Heusgen, Eva Christiansen, French political scientist Jacques Rupnick, journalist Christine Ockrent, former French foreign minister Bernard Kouchner, William Drozdiak, and Timothy Garton Ash.

264 *Then, too, she may well*: Marlowe, "As Merkel Tires."

265 *"He's conducting"*: Matthias Gebauer et al., "Germany's Incredible Shrinking Role," *Der Spiegel,* April 23, 2018.

265 *With a skeptical eye*: Lauren Collins, "The Bromance Myth of Trump and Macron," *New Yorker*, April 21, 2018.

268 *The contained friction*: Timothy Garton Ash, interviewed by the author; Leaders, "Assessing Emmanuel Macron's Apocalyptic Vision," *Economist*, November 9–15, 2019; "Germany Warns France Against Undermining NATO Security Alliance," Reuters online, last modified November 10, 2019, https://www.reuters.com/article/us-germany-nato/germany-warns-france-against-un dermining-nato-security-alliance-idUSKBN1XK08I.

268 *Shortly following*: Thomas Bagger, senior foreign policy advisor to the German president, interviewed by the author.

270 *At the end of 2019*: Ash, interview; see also Timothy Garton Ash, "Angela Merkel Must Go—for Germany's Sake, and for Europe's," *Guardian* (US) online, last modified November 22, 2019, https://www.theguardian.com/com mentisfree/2019/nov/22/time-to-go-angela-merkel-germanys-sake-europes.

CHAPTER 18: TOWARD THE END

The author interviewed Ambassadors Ischinger and Heusgen as well as Merkel advisor and confidant, Eva Christiansen, and German Presidential Advisor, Thomas Bagger for this chapter.

273 *With time, Merkel*: Merkel, town hall meeting in Stralsund, August 13, 2019, YouTube.

274 *"We had friends"*: Merkel, interviewed by Rinke, *Das Merkel Lexikon*, 181.

274 *Asked to name her favorite*: "Angela Merkel Suddenly Personal," *Berliner Morgenpost*, May 13, 2013; Melissa Eddy, "Merkel Offers a Peek," *New York Times*, May 17, 2013; *and see also Merkel*, interview by Rinke, *Das Merkel Lexikon*, 181.

275 *"Thomas Naulin"*: Angela Merkel, Saarland Townhall, August 13, 2019, https://www.ndr.de/fernsehen/sendyngen/zapp/Stralsund-Merkels-Antwort -auf-Rechtsaussen,kommunikationsstrategien100.html.

275 *In October 2018*: "Merkel: Over but Not Out.

275 *"Pretty manly"*: Pfister, interview.

276 *"You know, girl"*: Carl Dietr Spranger, "Weekend Long Read on Merkel," *Süddeutsche Zeitung*, April 5, 2020.

276 *In the Bundestag*: Pfister, interview.

277 *"Girls, go into science!"*: Ibid.

280 "Es is Ernst": The chancellor's March 19, 2020, Covid speech is available on the Bundestag website. See also: Christine Hoffmann, "The Merkel Bonus," *Der Spiegel* online, last modified December 16, 2020, https://www.bundesregierung

.de/breg-de/themen/coronavirus; Guy Chazan, "Angela Merkel Germany's Crisis Manager Is Back," *Financial Times,* March 27, 2020; Nico Fried and Mike Szymanski, "A Word of Warning," *Süddeutsche Zeitung* online, sued deutsche.de, last modified April 3, 2020; Laura Spinney, "Germany's Covid Expert," *Guardian* ( ), April 26, 2020; Philip Oltermann, "Angela Merkel Draws on Science Background in Covid-19 Explainer," *Guardian* (US) online, last modified April 16, 2020, https://www.theguardian.com/world/2020/apr/16/angela-merkel-draws-on-science-background-in-covid-19-explainer-lockdown-exit.

283 *"My life has changed"*: Holger Schmale, "Working from Home," *Berliner Zeitung,* April 1, 2020; Frank Jordans, "Merkel in Quarantine After Doctor Tests Positive for Virus," Associated Press online, last modified March 22, 2020, https://apnews.com/article/f71e89eacd7cc6f84b81991c03e82c31.

284 *In the age of social distancing*: Bagger, interview; Michael Birnbaum of the *Washington Post,* interviewed by the author; Victor Mallet, Guy Chazan, and Sam Fleming, "Merkel Makes a U Turn to Save Stricken Bloc," *Financial Times,* May 23, 2020; Peter Muller, "Merkel and Macron Find Strength for Europe," editorial, *Der Spiegel*, May 22, 2020.

288 *The talks grew intense*: Birnbaum, interview; Christine Ockrent, British journalist, interviewed by the author.

288 *Hour by hour*: Jean Pierre Stroobants and Virginie Malingre, "Bilaterales, Coups de Gueles et Portes qui Claques," *Le Monde,* July 20, 2020.

290 *Beyond the $859 billion*: Nikos Chrysoloras and John Ainger, "Why Europe's Pandemic Recovery Deal Is a Big Deal," *Washington Post,* July 21, 2020; Markus Becker, "Merkel's Triple Victory," *Der Spiegel* online, https://www.spiegel.de/international/europe/a-look-ahead-at-german-american-relations-after-trump-a-4c7ca237-fe2d-44d2-b2cb-9-aed83b8af28, November 19, 2020.

291 *For Merkel, Europe had to stand*: Angela Merkel, "Speech by Chancellor Merkel at the event "Foreign and Security Policy in the German EU Council Presidency" of the Konrad Adenauer Foundation on May 27, 2020," Press and Information Office of the Federal Government online, accessed April 22, 2021, https://www.bundeskanzlerin.de/bkin-de/aktuelles/rede-von-bundeskanzlerin-merkel-im-rahmen-der-veranstaltung-aussen-und-sicherheitspolitik-in-der-deutschen-eu-ratspraesidentschaft-der-konrad-adenauer-stiftung-am-27-mai-2020-1755884.

EPILOGUE

297   *With her final year*: "Citizen's Dialogue," *Die Zeit* online, last modified November 12, 2020; https://www.audible.com/pd/DIE-ZEIT-November-12-2020-Audiobook/B08292D7P8 ;

297   *"Merkel had little time"*: Merkel, interviewed by Barber and Chazan, January 16, 2020,   https://www.ft.com/content/00f9135c-3840-11ea-a6d3-9a26f8c3cba4. Except where indicted, quotes are from Merkel's speeches and are available on the Bundestag website

297   *"It's not as much fun"*: Christiansen, interview.

299   *The world will not see*: Bagger, interview.

299   *"I will sleep long"*: Merkel, town hall meeting in Saarland, August 13, 2019, https://www.ndr.de/fernsehen/sendungen/zap/Stralsund-Merkels-Antwort-auf-Rechtsaussen,kommunikationsstrategien100.html.

303   *"She tried"*: Ibid.

Bibliography

Aly, Götz. *Why the Germans? Why the Jews? Envy, Race Hatred, and the Prehistory of the Holocaust*. Translated by Jefferson S. Chase. New York: Picador, 2014.

Anonymous. *A Warning: A Senior Trump Administration Official*. New York: Twelve, 2019.

Applebaum, Anne. *Iron Curtain: The Crushing of Eastern Europe 1944–1956*. London: Allen Lane, 2012.

Ash, Timothy Garton. *In Europe's Name: Germany and the Divided Continent*. New York: Random House, 1993.

———. *The File: A Personal History*. Atlantic, 2009.

Belton, Catherine. *Putin's People: How the KGB Took Back Russia and Then Took On the West*. New York: Farrar, Straus and Giroux, 2020.

Boerner, Peter. *Goethe*. Translated by Nancy Boerner. London: Haus, 2005.

Bolton, John R. *The Room Where It Happened: A White House Memoir*. New York: Simon & Schuster, 2020.

Burns, William J. *Back Channel: A Memoir of American Diplomacy and the Case for Its Renewal*. New York: Random House, 2020.

Buruma, Ian. *The Wages of Guilt: Memories of War in Germany and Japan*. London: Atlantic Books, 1994.

———. *Year Zero: 1945 and the Aftermath of War*. New York: Penguin Press, 2013.

Crawford, Alan, and Tony Czuczka. *Angela Merkel: A Chancellorship Forged in Crisis*. Source: US Library of Congress, , 2013.

Dahrendorf, Ralf. *Society and Democracy in Germany*. W. W. Norton, 1967.

Dallek, Robert. *How Did We Get Here? From Theodore Roosevelt to Donald Trump*. New York: Harper, 2020.

Dawisha, Karen. *Putin's Kleptocracy: Who Owns Russia?* New York: Simon & Schuster, 2014.

Dendrinou, Viktoria, and Eleni Varvitsiote. *The Last Bluff: How Greece Came Face-to-Face with Financial Catastrophe & The Secret Plan for Its Euro Exit.* Athens: Papadopoulos, 2019.

Dobbs, Michael. *The Unwanted: America, Auschwitz, and a Village Caught in Between.* New York: Vintage Books, 2019.

Drozdiak, William. *Fractured Continent: Europe's Crises and the Fate of the West.* New York: W. W. Norton, 2017.

———. *The Last President of Europe: Emmanuel Macron's Race to Revive France and Save the World.* New York: PublicAffairs, 2020.

Erpenbeck, Jenny. *Go, Went, Gone.* Translated by Susan Bernofsky. New York: New Directions, 2015.

Faber, David. *Munich, 1938: Appeasement and World War II.* New York: Simon & Schuster, 2008.

Feldman, Lily Gardner. *Germany's Foreign Policy of Reconciliation: From Enmity to Amity.* Lanham, MD: Rowman & Littlefield, 2014.

Fisher, Marc. *After the Wall: Germany, the Germans, and the Burdens of History.* New York: Simon & Schuster, 1995.

Funder, Anna. *Stasiland: Stories from Behind the Berlin Wall.* New York: Harper Perennial, 2003.

Gessen, Masha. *The Man Without a Face: The Unlikely Rise of Vladimir Putin.* New York: Riverhead Books, 2014.

Goodwin, Doris Kearns. *Leadership in Turbulent Times.* New York: Simon & Schuster Paperbacks, 2018.

Green, Stephen. *Reluctant Meister: How Germany's Past Is Shaping Its European Future.* London: Haus, 2016.

Gunther, John. *Behind the Curtain.* New York: Harper and Brothers, 1949.

Harris, Robert. *Munich.* London: Arrow Books, 2017.

Harrison, Hope M. *Driving the Soviets up the Wall: Soviet-East German Relations, 1953–1961.* Princeton, NJ: Princeton University Press, 2003.

Herf, Jeffrey. *Divided Memory: The Nazi Past in the Two Germanys.* Cambridge, MA: Harvard University Press, 1997.

Hill, Fiona, and Clifford G. Gaddy. *Mr. Putin: Operative in the Kremlin.* Washington, DC: Brookings Institution Press, 2013.

Holler, Wolfgang, and Kristin Knebel. *The Goethe Residence.* Weimar, Ger.: Klassik Stiftung Weimar, 2016.

Isikoff, Michael, and David Corn. *Russian Roulette: The Inside Story of Putin's War on America and the Election of Donald Trump.* New York: Twelve, 2018.

Judt, Tony. *A Grand Illusion? An Essay on Europe*. New York: New York University Press, 2011.

———. *Postwar: A History of Europe Since 1945*. New York: Penguin Books, 2005.

Kagan, Robert. *The Jungle Grows Back: America and Our Imperiled World*. New York: Vintage Books, 2018.

Kershaw, Ian. *Roller-Coaster: Europe, 1950–2017*. New York: Penguin Books, 2019.

Kessler, Harry. *Berlin in Lights: The Diaries of Count Harry Kessler, 1918–1937*. New York: Grove Press, 1971.

Kingsley, Patrick. *The New Odyssey: The Story of Europe's Refugee Crisis*. Norwich, UK: Guardian Faber, 2016.

Klemperer, Victor. *I Will Bear Witness: A Diary of the Nazi Years*. New York: Random House, 1999.

Kornelius, Stefan. *Angela Merkel: The Chancellor and Her World—The Authorized Biography*. London: Alma Books, 2013.

Kramer, Jane. *The Politics of Memory: Looking for Germany in the New Germany*. New York: Random House, 1996.

Krastev, Ivan, and Stephen Holmes. *The Light That Failed, A Reckoning*. New York: Penguin Books, 2019.

Le Carré, John. *A Small Town In Germany*. New York: Pocket Books, 1968.

Lever, Paul. *Berlin Rules: Europe and the German Way*. London: I. B. Tauris, 2017.

Loeckx, Renilde. *Cold War Triangle: How Scientists in East and West Tamed HIV*. Leuven, Belg.: Lipsius Leuven, 2017.

MacDonogh, Giles. *On Germany*. London: Hurst, 2018.

MacGregor, Neil. *Germany: Memories of a Nation*. New York: Vintage Books, 2014.

Machiavelli, Niccolo. *The Prince*. Translated by Tim Parks. New York: Penguin Books, 2009.

MacLean, Rory. *Berlin: Portrait of a City Through the Centuries*. New York: St. Martin's Press, 2014.

Medvedev, Sergei. *The Return of the Russian Leviathan*. Translated by Stephen Dalziel. Medford, MA: Polity, 2020.

Middelaar, Luuk van. *Alarums & Excursions: Improvising Politics on the European Stage*. Translated by Liz Waters. Newcastle upon Tyne, UK: Agenda, 2019.

Moore, Charles. *Margaret Thatcher: The Authorized Biography—At Her Zenith: In London, Washington and Moscow*. New York: Alfred A. Knopf, 2016.

———. *Margaret Thatcher: The Authorized Biography—From Grantham to the Falklands*. New York: Vintage Books, 2013.

Mounk, Yascha. *Stranger in My Own Country: A Jewish Family in Modern Germany*. New York: Farrar, Straus and Giroux, 2014.

Mushaben, Joyce Marie. *Becoming Madam Chancellor: Angela Merkel and the Berlin Republic*. Cambridge: Cambridge University Press, 2017.

Myers, Steven Lee. *The New Tsar: The Rise and Reign of Vladimir Putin*. New York: Simon & Schuster, 2015.

Neiman, Susan. *Learning from the Germans: Race and the Memory of Evil*. New York: Farrar, Straus and Giroux, 2019.

Obama, Barack, *A Promised Land*. New York: Cown, 2020.

Pond, Elizabeth. *Beyond The wall: Germany's Road to Unification*. Washington, DC: Brookings Institution, 1993.

Powell, Jonathan. *The New Machiavelli: How to Wield Power in the Modern World*. New York: Vintage Books, 2011.

Power, Samantha. *The Education of An Idealist*. New York: Dey Street Books, 2019.

Qvortrup, Matthew. *Angela Merkel: Europe's Most Influential Leader*. New York: Overlook Duckworth, 2017.

Renterghem, Marion Van. *Angela Merkel: L'ovni Politique*. Paris: Les AreÃÄnes, 2017.

Rhodes, Benjamin. *The World as It Is: A Memoir of the Obama White House*. New York: Random House, 2018.

Rice, Susan. *Tough Love: My Story of the Things Worth Fighting For*. New York: Simon & Schuster, 2019.

Rosenberg, Tina. *The Haunted Land: Facing Europe's Ghosts After Communism*. New York: Vintage Books, 1996.

Roth, Philip. *American Pastoral*. New York: Vintage International, 1998.

Rucker, Philip, and Carol Leonnig. *A Very Stable Genius: Donald J. Trump's Testing of America*. New York: Bloomsbury, 2020.

Schneider, Peter. *Berlin Now: The City After the Wall*. New York: Farrar, Straus and Giroux, 2014.

———. *The wall Jumper: A Novel*. Translated by Leigh Hafrey. New York: Pantheon Books, 1983.

Service, Robert. *Kremlin Winter: Russia and the Second Coming of Vladimir Putin*. London: Picador, 2020.

Smith, Hannah Lucinda. *ErdogÃÜan Rising: The Battle for the Soul of Turkey*. London: William Collins, 2019.

Snyder, Timothy. *Bloodlands: Europe Between Hitler and Stalin*. New York: Basic Books, 2012.

———. *The Road to Unfreedom: Russia, Europe, America*. New York: Vintage Books, 2019.

Stengel, Richard. *Information Wars: How We Lost the Global Battle Against Disinformation & What We Can Do About It*. New York: Atlantic Monthly Press, 2019.

Stent, Angela. *Putin's World: Russia Against the West and with the Rest*. New York: Hachette, 2019.

Stern, Fritz. *The Politics of Cultural Despair: A Study in the Rise of the Germanic Ideology*. Berkeley: University of California Press, 1961.

Taubman, William. *Gorbachev: His Life and Times*. New York: W. W. Norton, 2017.

Taylor, Frederick. *Dresden, Tuesday, February 13, 1945*. New York: HarperCollins, 2004.

Tellkamp, Uwe. *The Tower: Tales from a Lost Country*. New York: Penguin Books, 2016.

The Condé Nast Traveler Book of Unforgettable Journeys: Great Writers on Great Places. Edited and with an introduction by Klara Glowczewska. New York: Penguin Books, 2012.

Throp, Claire. *Angela Merkel*. Chicago: Raintree, 2014.

Tooze, J. Adam. *Crashed: How a Decade of Financial Crises Changed the World*. New York: Penguin Books, 2019.

Traverso, Enzo. *The New Faces of Fascism: Populism and the Far Right*. Translated by David Broder. Brooklyn, NY: Verso, 2019.

Varoufakis, Yanis. *Adults in the Room: My Battle with the European and American Deep Establishment*. New York: Farrar, Straus and Giroux, 2018.

Vickers, Marques. *Vladimir Putin and Dresden, Germany: The Genesis of Myth Making*. Herron Island, WA: Marquis, 2016.

Vonnegut, Kurt. *Slaughterhouse-Five*. New York: Random House, 1969.

Watson, Peter. *The German Genius: Europe's Third Renaissance, the Second Scientific Revolution, and the Twentieth Century*. New York: Harper Perennial, 2011.

Wyden, Peter. *Wall: The Inside Story of Divided Berlin*. New York: Simon & Schuster, 1989.

Yaffa, Joshua. *Between Two Fires: Truth, Ambition, and Compromise in Putin's Russia*. New York: Tim Duggan Books, 2020.

Image Credits

INTERIOR

1. Marcus C. Hurek/Picture Alliance/dpa
2. Interfoto/Alamy
3. Courtesy of Michael Schindhelm
4. Gerard Maile/AFP/Getty Images
5. Thomas Omo/Photothek/Getty Images
6. Jens Buettner/dpa/Alamy
7. Guido Bergmann/BPA/Picture-Alliance/dpa
8. Wolfgang Rattay/Reuters/Alamy
9. Marcus Fuehrer/dpa Picture-Alliance/Alamy
10. Michael Kappeler/AFP/Getty Images
11. Evangelos Bougiotis/EPA/Shutterstock
12. Courtesy Daniel Baer/Twitter
13. YouTube
14. Odd Anderson/AFP/Getty Images
15. Jesco Denzel/Bundesregierung/Getty Images
16. Andreas Arnold/dpa/AFP/Getty Images
17. Philippe Wojazer/AFP via Getty Images
18. Armando Babani/EPA/EFE/Shutterstock

INSERT

1. Jörg Gläscher/Laif/Redux
2. Bogumil Jeziorski/AFP via Getty Images
3. API/Gamma-Rapho

4. Ebner/Ullstein Bild
5. API/Gamma-Rapho
6. Dmitry Astakhov/ITAR-TASS/AP/Shutterstock
7. Rainer Jensen/dpa/Zuma Press
8. Chip Somodevilla/Getty Images
9. Pete Souza/Barack Obama Presidential Library
10. Bernd Von Jutrczenka/dpa/Alamy
11. Mark Stewart/Camera Press/Redux
12. Sean Gallup/Getty Images
13. Courtesy of Jason Williams
14. SplashNews

Index

Page numbers in *italics* refer to illustrations.